Word 2016

FOR DUMMIES®

A Wiley Brand

by Dan Gookin

FOR DUMMIES®
A Wiley Brand

Word 2016 For Dummies®

Published by: **John Wiley & Sons, Inc.,** 111 River Street, Hoboken, NJ 07030-5774, www.wiley.com

Copyright © 2016 by John Wiley & Sons, Inc., Hoboken, New Jersey

Published simultaneously in Canada

For general information on our other products and services, please contact our Customer Care Department within the U.S. at 877-762-2974, outside the U.S. at 317-572-3993, or fax 317-572-4002. For technical support, please visit www.wiley.com/techsupport.

Wiley publishes in a variety of print and electronic formats and by print-on-demand. Some material included with standard print versions of this book may not be included in e-books or in print-on-demand. If this book refers to media such as a CD or DVD that is not included in the version you purchased, you may download this material at http://booksupport.wiley.com. For more information about Wiley products, visit www.wiley.com.

Library of Congress Control Number: 2015949749

ISBN 978-1-119-07689-6 (pbk); ISBN 978-1-119-07695-7 (ebk); ISBN 978-1-119-07685-8 (ebk)

Manufactured in the United States of America

10 9 8 7 6 5 4 3 2 1

Table of Contents

Introduction

The only thing standing between you and your writing is your word processor. Yeah, I know: It's supposed to be helpful. Well, it tries. Computers can do only so much. But you, as a smart person, are capable of so much more. I'm guessing that's why you opened this book.

Welcome to *Word 2016 For Dummies,* which removes the pain from using Microsoft's latest, greatest, most confusing word-processing software ever! This book is your friendly, informative, and entertaining guide to the routine of processing words that is Word 2016.

Be warned: I'm not out to make you love Word. This book won't make you enjoy the program. Use it, yes. Tolerate it, of course. The only promise I'm offering is to ease the pain that most people feel from using Microsoft Word. Along the way, I kick Word in the butt, and I hope you enjoy reading about it.

About This Book

I don't intend for you to read this book from cover to cover. It's not a novel, and if it were, it would be a political space opera with an antihero and a princess fighting elected officials who are in cahoots with a galactic urban renewal development corporation. The ending would be extremely satisfying.

This book is a reference. Each chapter covers a specific topic or task you can accomplish by using Word 2016. Within each chapter, you find self-contained sections, each of which describes how to perform a specific task or get something done. Sample topics you encounter in this book include

- ✔ Moving a block
- ✔ Checking your spelling
- ✔ Saving your stuff!
- ✔ Text-formatting techniques
- ✔ Working with tables in Word
- ✔ Plopping down a picture
- ✔ Mail merge, ho!

I give you no keys to memorize, no secret codes, no tricks, no presentations to sleep through, and no wall charts. Instead, each section explains a topic as though it's the first thing you read in this book. Nothing is assumed, and everything is cross-referenced. Technical terms and topics, when they come up, are neatly shoved to the side, where you can easily avoid reading them. The idea here isn't for you to master anything. This book's philosophy is to help you look it up, figure it out, and get back to work.

How to Use This Book

You hold in your hands an active book. The topics between this book's yellow-and-black covers are all geared toward getting things done in Word 2016. All you need to do is find the topic that interests you and then read.

Word uses the mouse and keyboard to get things done, but mostly the keyboard.

I use the word *click* to describe the action of clicking the mouse's main (left) button.

This is a keyboard shortcut: Ctrl+P. Press and hold down the Ctrl (Control) key and type the letter *P,* just as you would press Shift+P to create a capital *P.*

Sometimes, you must press more than two keys at the same time, such as Ctrl+Shift+T. Press Ctrl and Shift together and then press the T key. Release all three keys.

Commands in Word 2016 exist as *command buttons* on the Ribbon interface. I may refer to the tab, the command group, and then the button itself to help you locate that command button.

Menu commands are listed like this: Table⇨Insert Table. This direction tells you to click the Table command button and then choose the Insert Table item from the menu that appears.

 Some of Word's key commands are kept on the File screen. To access that screen, click the File tab on the Ribbon. To return to your document, click the Back button, found in the upper-left corner of the File screen and shown in the margin. Or you can press the Esc key.

When I describe a message or something else you see onscreen, it looks like this:

```
Why should I bother to love Evelyn when robots will
eventually destroy the human race?
```

If you need further help in operating your computer, I can recommend my book *PCs For Dummies,* 13th Edition (Wiley). It contains lots of useful information to supplement what you find in this book.

Foolish Assumptions

Although this book was written with the beginner in mind, I still make a few assumptions. Foremost, I assume that you're a human being, though you might also be an alien from another planet. If so, welcome to Earth. When you conquer our planet, please do Idaho last. Thanks.

Another foolish assumption I make is that you use Windows as the computer's operating system. It could be Windows 7, Windows 8, or Windows 10. Windows 9 is not covered in this book. Differences between Windows versions are trivial as far as Word is considered, but do keep in mind that this book isn't about Windows.

Your word processor is Microsoft Word 2016. It is *not* Microsoft Works. It is not an earlier version of Word. It is not WordPerfect. It is not a version of Word that runs on a Macintosh.

Throughout this book, I use the term *Word* to refer to the Microsoft Word program. The program may also be called Word 2016 or even Microsoft Office Word 2016. It's all Word as far as this book is concerned. Word 2016 is part of the Microsoft Office 2016 suite of programs. This book doesn't cover any other part of Microsoft Office, though I mention Excel and Outlook wherever they encroach on Word's turf.

What's Not Here

Word is one heck of a program. Covering the entire thing would fill a book several thousand pages long. (I kid you not.) My approach in this book is to cover as much basic word processing as possible. For that reason, some advanced features got pushed off the table of contents.

I give you some information about macros, though it's super slim. Covering macros without a technical description is difficult. If the publisher ever lets me increase this book's size to more than 408 pages, I'd be happy to add a macro chapter; the publisher's address is in this book's front matter, in case you want to lobby on my behalf.

Some of Word's more esoteric features are touched on lightly here. For example, I could spend about 70 pages detailing what can be done with graphics in Word, but I limit myself to only a dozen pages.

Finally, this book doesn't cover using Word to make a blog post or create a web page or how to use Word as your email program. Word does these things, but I consider this a word-processing book rather than a Word-does-everything book.

Icons Used in This Book

This icon flags useful, helpful tips or shortcuts.

This icon marks a friendly reminder to do something.

This icon marks a friendly reminder *not* to do something.

This icon alerts you to overly nerdy information and technical discussions of the topic at hand. The information is optional reading, but it may enhance your reputation at cocktail parties if you repeat it.

Where to Go from Here

Start reading! Observe the table of contents and find something that interests you. Or look up your puzzle in the index.

Read! Write! Let your brilliance shine!

My email address is dgookin@wambooli.com. Yes, that's my real address. I reply to all email I receive, and you'll get a quick reply if you keep your question short and specific to this book or to Word itself. Although I enjoy saying "Hi," I cannot answer technical support questions or help you troubleshoot your computer. Thanks for understanding.

You can also visit my web page for more information or as a diversion: www.wambooli.com. This book's specific support page can be found at www.wambooli.com/help/word. I place errata and updates on that page, as well as write frequent blog posts with Word information, tips, and tricks.

The publisher also maintains a support page, complete with updates and such. You can visit their site here: www.dummies.com/go/word2016fdupdates. This book's online cheat sheet can be located here: www.dummies.com/cheatsheet/word2016. And the web extras mentioned in each chapter's introduction are hidden on this page: www.dummies.com/extras/word2016.

Enjoy this book. And enjoy Word. Or at least tolerate it.

Part I
Your Introduction to Word

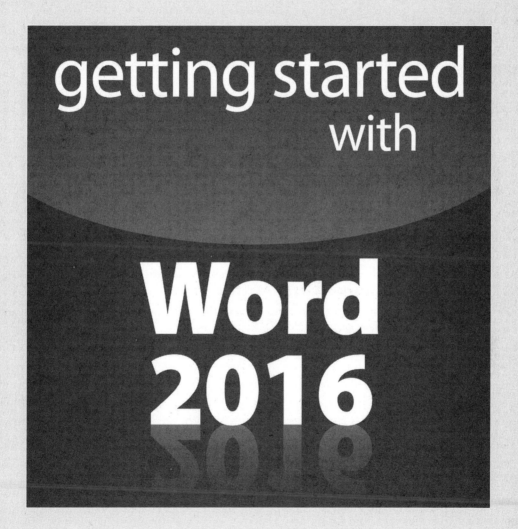

In this part . . .

- ✔ Learn how to start Word 2016 and decipher the Word screen.

- ✔ Familiarize yourself with how to quit and minimize Word 2016.

- ✔ Get to know the PC keyboard and the touchscreen.

- ✔ Learn how to read the status bar and discover secret symbols representing special characters in your text.

Chapter 1

Hello, Word!

· ·

· ·

*L*ife would be easier if you used a pencil to write text. You could grab a copy of *Pencils For Dummies* and be on your way. That book is far thinner than this one and has more illustrations, which some people find enriching. Your ambitions are most likely higher, which is why you've chosen, or had the choice thrust upon you, to use Microsoft Word as your text composition tool. That's a good decision, but Word remains a far, far more complex tool for composing text than a wooden cylinder filled with graphite.

Start Your Word Day

As computer software, Microsoft Word dwells in the realm of Windows. To get work done in Word, you must contend with the multitudinous ways available in Windows to run the Word program. These methods can vary from the obvious to the obnoxiously cryptic, so instead I present you with the three most common ways to start your Word day.

> ✔ Before you can use Word, your computer must be on and ready to work. So turn on your PC, laptop, or tablet if it's not already on and toasty. Log into Windows.

> ✔ Do not attempt to make toast in your computer.

✔ Ensure that you sport a proper posture as you write. Your wrists should be even with your elbows. Your head should tilt down only slightly, although it's best to look straight ahead. Keep your shoulders back and relaxed. Have a minion gently massage your feet.

Starting Word the traditional way

Propriety demands that I show the traditional, boring way to start Word. Let me be quick:

1. **Press the Windows key on the keyboard.**

   The Windows key is adorned with the Windows logo icon, which I won't illustrate here because it's changed over the years. The key is nestled between the Ctrl and Alt keys to the left of the spacebar. A duplicate is found on the right side of the spacebar. Use either key.

2. **Look for Microsoft Word on the Start menu.**

   The item might be titled Word or Word 2016 or something similar.

   If you don't find Word right away in Windows 10, click the All Apps button to hunt it down. In Windows 7, click the All Programs button.

   Sometimes Word is found on a Microsoft Office or Office 2016 submenu.

3. **Click the Word icon or button to start the program.**

Watch in amazement as the program unfurls on the screen.

Starting Word the best way

The *best* way to start Word, and the way I do it every day, is to click the Word icon on the taskbar. Word starts simply and quickly.

The issue, of course, is how to get the Word icon on the taskbar. Follow these steps:

1. **Find the Word icon on the Start button's All Programs menu.**

   See the preceding section, Steps 1 and 2.

2. **Right-click the Word icon.**

3. **Choose the command Pin to Taskbar.**

The Word icon is *pinned* (permanently added) to the taskbar.

Starting Word in Windows 8 (for the few who still use Windows 8)

One of the reasons Windows 8 was so aggressively unpopular was that it eschewed the traditional Start button menu for a tile-based Start screen. If you're still burdened with Windows 8, or you run Windows 10 in Tablet mode, start Word by pressing the Windows key on the keyboard and then clicking the Word 2016 tile on the Start screen.

You can stick the Word icon to the taskbar, as described in this chapter: Click the Word tile on the Start screen and then choose the command Pin to Taskbar. (The Pin to Taskbar command is at the bottom of the screen.)

Opening a document to start Word

You use the Word program to create *documents,* which are stored on your computer in much the same way as people pile junk into boxes and store them in their garages. To start Word, open a document. Follow these steps:

1. **Locate the document icon.**

   Use your Windows kung fu to open the proper folders and hunt down a Word document icon, similar to what's shown in the margin.

2. **Double-click the icon.**

   This step is a standard Word operation: Double-click an icon to open a program. In this case, opening a Word document starts Word.

The document is opened and presented on the screen, ready for whatever.

- ✔ You use Word to create documents. They're saved to storage on your computer or in the cloud. Details are offered in Chapter 8.

- ✔ The document name is assigned when it's originally saved. Use the name to determine the document's contents — providing that it was properly named when first saved.

- ✔ Document icons are managed by Windows. If you need to find a lost document, rename it, or organize your documents into a folder, you use Windows, not Word.

Behold the Word Program

Like all programs in Windows, Word offers its visage in a program window. It's the place where you get your word-processing work done.

Working the Word Start screen

After starting Word, the first thing you may see is something called the Word Start screen, as shown in Figure 1-1. It's friendlier than that ominous empty page that's intimidated writers since the dawn of paper. (The blank page comes later.)

You can use the Start screen to open a previously opened document, start a new document based on a template, or start with a blank document.

Show Word's templates   Show your own templates

Choose a previous document   Start a new blank document

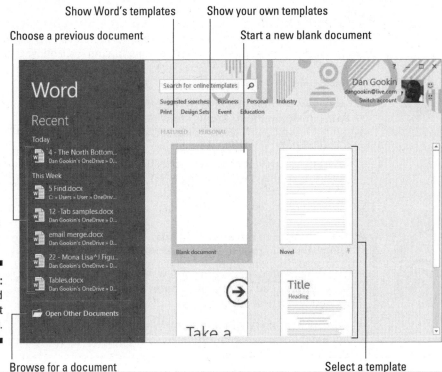

Figure 1-1:
The Word
Start
screen.

Browse for a document   Select a template

Previously opened documents are listed on the left side of the window, as illustrated in Figure 1-1. Word's templates are found under the heading Featured. Templates you've created appear under the Personal link. Click a template thumbnail to create a new document based on that template.

To start on a blank document, click the Blank Document template. Then you see the ominous empty page, which I wrote about earlier.

Once you've made your choice, Word is ready for you to start writing. Word is also equally content if you just stare at the screen and await inspiration.

- ✔ The Word Start screen doesn't appear if you start Word by opening a document. See the earlier section, "Opening a document to start Word."

- ✔ You can also disable the Start screen so that Word starts with a blank document. See Chapter 33.

- ✔ The Word Start screen appears only when you first start Word. It does not appear if you start a new document while the Word program window is already open.

Examining Word's main screen

Writing is scary enough when you first see the blank page. With a computer, that level of terror just isn't good enough. Therefore, Word festoons its program window with all kinds of controls. I recommend that you refer to Figure 1-2 to get an idea of some basic terms. Ignore them at your peril.

The details of how all the gizmos and whatnot in the Word window work are covered throughout this book. They give you more control over your document, although the basic task of typing text is pretty straightforward. See Chapter 2 to get started.

- ✔ To get the most from Word's window, adjust the window size: Use the mouse to drag the window's edges outwards. You can also click the window's Maximize button (refer to Figure 1-2) to have the window fill the screen.

- ✔ The largest portion of Word's screen is used to compose text. It's blank and white, just like a fresh sheet of paper. If you choose to use a template to start a new document, this area may contain some preset text.

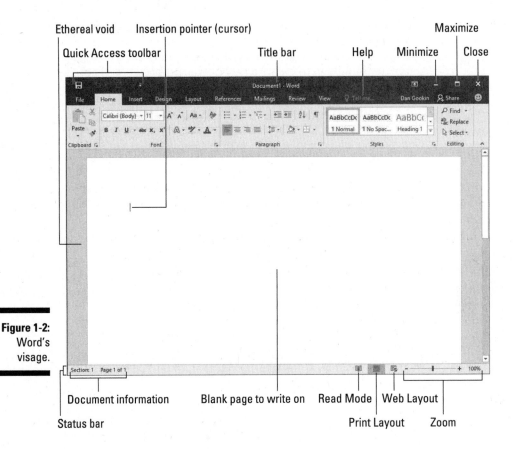

Ethereal void   Insertion pointer (cursor)

Quick Access toolbar   Title bar   Help   Minimize   Close

Maximize

Figure 1-2:
Word's
visage.

Document information   Blank page to write on   Read Mode | Web Layout

Status bar   Print Layout   Zoom

Working the Ribbon

An important part of Word's interface is the Ribbon. It's where a majority of Word's commands dwell and where settings are made. These items appear as buttons, input boxes, and menus.

The Ribbon is divided into tabs, as shown in Figure 1-3. Each tab holds separate groups. Within the groups, you find the command buttons that carry out various word-processing duties.

To use the Ribbon, first click a tab. Then locate the command you need by scanning the group names, and then hunting down the button. Click the button to activate the command or to display a menu from which you can choose a command.

Current tab

File tab   Other tabs   Command button   Ribbon Display Options menu

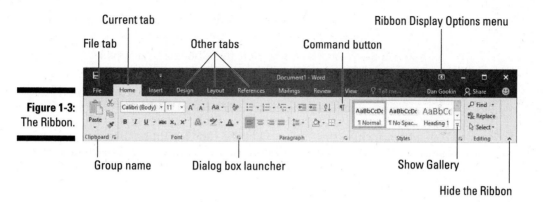

Figure 1-3:
The Ribbon.

Group name   Dialog box launcher   Show Gallery

Hide the Ribbon

- ✔ Some items on the Ribbon let you input text or values, or make other settings.

- ✔ Galleries on the Ribbon display a smattering of tiles. To see them all, click the Show Gallery button in the lower-right corner of the gallery, as illustrated in Figure 1-3.

- ✔ Use the dialog box launcher icon in the lower-right corner of a group to open a dialog box relevant to the group's function. Not every group features a dialog box launcher.

- ✔ The amazingly frustrating thing about the Ribbon is that it can change. Some tabs may appear and disappear, depending on what you're doing in Word.

- ✔ To ensure that you always see all the command buttons, adjust the program's window as wide as is practical.

- ✔ Clicking the File tab replaces the contents of the Word window with a screen full of commands and other information. To return to the Word window, click the Back button (shown in the margin) or press the Esc key.

Showing and hiding the Ribbon

The good news is that you can hide the Ribbon if it bothers you. That way you see more document and less junk. The bad news is that you might accidentally hide the Ribbon when you don't want to.

To control the Ribbon, use the Ribbon Display Options menu, located in the upper-right part of the Word window and illustrated in Figure 1-3. Choose an item to determine how to display the Ribbon. Your choices are

Auto-Hide Ribbon: The most annoying choice, the Ribbon appears only when you hover the insertion pointer near the top of the document.

Show Tabs: With this choice, only the Ribbon's tabs appear. Click a tab to summon the rest of the Ribbon.

Show Tabs and Commands: This option shows the entire Ribbon — tabs and commands — as illustrated in Figures 1-2 and 1-3.

To temporarily hide the Ribbon, click the Hide the Ribbon button, labeled in Figure 1-3. To bring back the Ribbon, click a tab and then at the spot where the Hide the Ribbon button appears. Click the pushpin icon to make the Ribbon stick.

I recommend that you keep the Ribbon visible as you discover the wonders of Word.

Changing the document view

Just to keep you on your toes, Word offers multiple ways to view your document. The blank area where you write, which should be full of text by now, can be altered to present information in a different way. Why would you want to do that? You don't! But it helps to know the different ways so that you can change them back.

The standard way to view a document is called Print Layout view. It's the view shown in this book and it's how Word normally starts. A virtual page appears on the screen, with four sides and text in the middle. What you see on the screen is pretty much what you'll see in the final results, whether printed or published as an electronic document.

The other views are

Read Mode: Use this view to read a document like an eBook. The Ribbon and pretty much the rest of Word is hidden while in Read mode.

Web Layout: This view presents your document as a web page. It's available should you undertake the dreadful possibility of using Word as a web page editor.

Outline: This mode helps you organize your thoughts, as covered in Chapter 25.

Draft: The Draft view presents only basic text, not all the formatting and fancy features such as graphics.

To switch between Read Mode, Print Layout, and Web Layout views, click one of the View buttons, found in the lower-right corner of the Word program window (refer to Figure 1-2).

To get to Outline and Draft views, as well as to see all View modes in one location, click the Views tab and choose a command button from the Views group.

Making text larger or smaller

When the information in Word's window just isn't big enough, don't enlarge the font! Instead, whip out the equivalent of a digital magnifying glass, the Zoom command. It helps you enlarge or reduce your document, making it easier to see or giving you the Big Picture look.

Several methods are available to zoom text in Word. The most obvious is to use the Zoom control found in the lower-right corner of the Word window on the status bar. Adjust the slider right or left to make the text larger or smaller, respectively.

To make the text appear on screen as close to actual size as possible, click the 100% button on the status bar.

- ✔ Zooming doesn't affect how a document prints — only how it looks on the screen.

- ✔ For more specific zoom control, click the View tab and use the commands found in the Zoom group.

- ✔ If the mouse has a wheel button, you can zoom by pressing the Ctrl key on your keyboard and rolling the wheel up or down. Rolling up zooms in; rolling down zooms out.

Cajoling Word to help you

Like most Windows programs, a Help system is available in Word. You can summon it by pressing the F1 key, which displays the Word Help window. There you can type a topic, a command name, or even a question in the box to search for help.

The F1 key also works any time you're deep in the bowels of Word and doing something specific. The Help information that's displayed tends to be specific to whatever you're doing in Word. Little buttons that look like question marks also summon Word Help.

In the age of Google, Word also offers a Tell Me help box on the Ribbon, as illustrated in Figure 1-2. Type a topic or question in the box and press the Enter key to see a quick list of commands or suggestions, or to obtain online help.

End Your Word-Processing Day

It's the pinnacle of etiquette to know when and how to excuse oneself. For example, the phrase "Well, I must be off," works a lot better than growling, "Something more interesting must be happening anywhere else" — especially at Thanksgiving. The good news for Word is that's completely acceptable to quit the program without hurting its feelings.

Quitting Word

When you've finished word processing and you don't expect to return to it anytime soon, you quit the Word program. Click the X button in the upper-right corner of the Word program window (refer to Figure 1-2).

The catch? You have to close each and every Word document window that's open before you can proclaim that you've completely quit Word.

The other catch? Word won't quit during that shameful circumstance when you have unsaved documents. If so, you're prompted to save the document, as shown in Figure 1-4. My advice is to click the Save button to save your work; refer to Chapter 8 for specifics on saving documents.

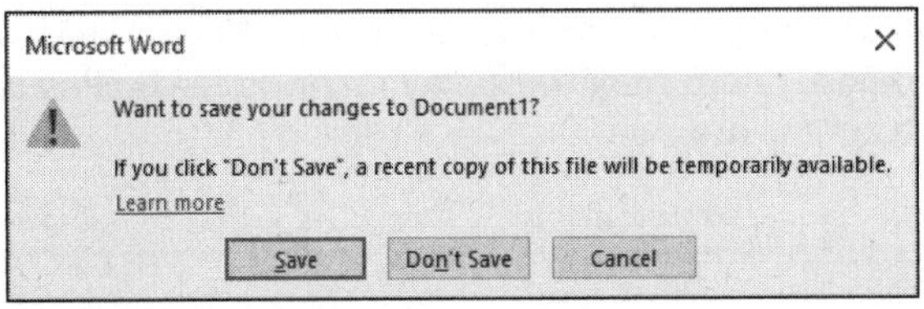

Figure 1-4: Better click that Save button!

> Microsoft Word ✕
>
> ⚠ Want to save your changes to Document1?
>
> If you click "Don't Save", a recent copy of this file will be temporarily available.
> Learn more
>
> [Save] [Don't Save] [Cancel]

If you click the Don't Save button, your work isn't saved and Word quits. If you click the Cancel button, Word doesn't quit and you can continue working.

- ✔ You don't have to quit Word just to start editing another document. Refer to the next couple of sections for helpful, timesaving information.

- ✔ After quitting Word, you can continue to use Windows by starting any other program, such as Spider Solitaire or perhaps something more relaxing, like *Call of Duty*.

Closing a document without quitting Word

You don't always have to quit Word. For example, if you're merely stopping work on one document to work on another, quitting Word is a waste of time. Instead, you can *close* the document.

To close a document in Word and not quit, follow these steps:

1. Click the File tab.

The File screen appears. Commands line the left side of the screen, as shown in Figure 1-5.

Commands

Return to document

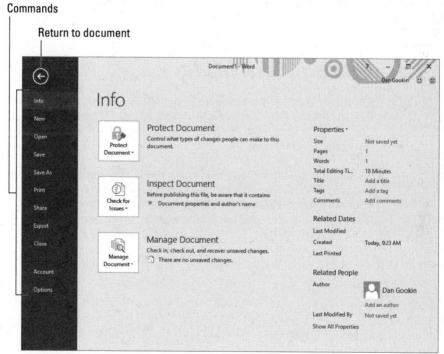

Figure 1-5:
The File tab
screen.

2. Choose the Close command.

3. Save the document, if you're prompted to do so.

The shame! Always save before closing. Tsk-tsk.

After it's closed, you return to the main Word window, although a document isn't shown and many of the command buttons are dimmed (unavailable). At this point, you can start working on a new document or open a document you previously saved.

Bottom line: There's no point in quitting Word when all you want to do is start editing a new document.

- There's no urgency to close a document. I keep mine open all day, even when I go off to do something un-work related like play a game or see who's being obnoxious on Facebook. To return to your document at any time, click its button on the Windows taskbar.

- The keyboard shortcut for the Close command is Ctrl+W. This command may seem weird, but it's used to close documents in many programs.

- To swiftly start a new, blank document in Word, press Ctrl+N.

Setting Word aside

Don't quit Word if you know that you will use it again soon. In fact, I've been known to keep Word open and running on my computer for *weeks* at a time. The secret is to use the Minimize button, found in the upper-right corner of the screen (refer to Figure 1-2).

Clicking the Minimize button shrinks the Word window to a button on the taskbar. With the Word window out of the way, you can do other things with your computer. Then when you're ready to word-process again, click the Word button on the taskbar to restore the Word window to the screen.

Chapter 2

The Typing Chapter

*W*ord processing is about using a keyboard. It's typing. That's the way computers were used for years, long before the mouse and all the fancy graphics became popular. Yep — ask a grizzled old-timer and you'll hear tales of ugly text screens and keyboard commands that would tie your fingers in knots. Though things today aren't that bad, I highly recommend that you bone up on your keyboard skills to get the most from your word-processing duties.

Input Devices Galore

When you process words, you're typing: clickity-clack-clack. You use your fingers and one thumb to manipulate the computer keyboard. It's an important part of getting text on a page, but also important is the mouse. No, you don't type with the mouse, but you'll do some pointing and clicking in additional to clickity-clack-clacking.

Using the PC keyboard

I'm sure you can easily recognize a computer keyboard, but do you know the official terms that refer to its various keys?

Relax: No one does.

Rather than look at all 100+ keys as a marauding hoard, consider how the keys are clustered into groups, as illustrated in Figure 2-1. To best use Word and understand how the keyboard is referenced in this book, it helps to know the general keyboard areas illustrated in the figure.

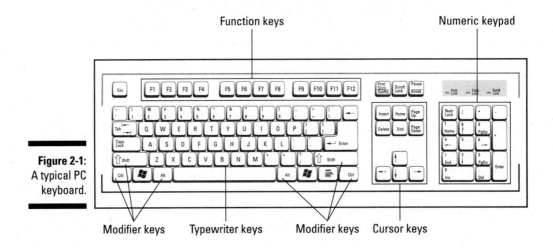

Figure 2-1:
A typical PC
keyboard.

Of all the keys, a few play important roles in the word-processing task. They are

> **Enter:** Marked with the word *Enter* and sometimes a cryptic, bent-arrow thing, this key is used to end a paragraph of text. See the later section, "Pressing the Enter key."

> **Spacebar:** The only key with no symbol, it inserts a space between words and sentences. Yes, just one space. See the later section, "Whacking the spacebar."

> **Tab:** This key inserts the tab character, which shoves the next text you type over to the next tab stop. Using this key properly is an art form. Chapter 12 is dedicated to its use.

> **Backspace and Delete:** Use these keys to back up and erase text. Yes, erasing text isn't a job always left to the editor. Read more about these keys in Chapter 4.

Every character key you press on the keyboard produces a character on the screen, on the blank part where you write. Typing those character keys over and over is how you write text on a word processor.

> ✔ A laptop keyboard's layout is different from the desktop keyboard layout shown in Figure 2-1. Primarily, laptop keyboards lack a numeric keypad. The cursor keys are clustered tight around the typewriter keys in unusual and creative patterns. The function keys might be accessed by pressing special key combinations.

- Keys on the numeric keypad can be number keys or cursor keys. The split personality is evident on each key cap, which displays two symbols. When the Num Lock key's lamp is on, the keys generate numbers. When the lamp is off, the keys serve as duplicate cursor keys.

- Cursor keys control the cursor, which is officially known as the *insertion pointer* in Microsoft Word. The cursor keys include the four arrow keys (up, down, left, right), and also the keys Home, End, PgUp (or Page Up), PgDn (or Page Down), Insert, and Delete.

- Ctrl is pronounced "control." It's the control key.

- The Delete key may also be labeled Del on the keyboard.

- The modifier keys, Shift, Ctrl, and Alt, work in combination with other keys.

Understanding the mouse pointer

Though word processing is a keyboard thing, you will eventually lift your hand from the keyboard to fondle the computer mouse. The mouse is used to choose commands, move around the document, and select text. Specific information on these tasks is found throughout this book. For now, it helps to understand how the mouse pointer changes its look as you work in Word:

 For editing text, the mouse pointer becomes the I-beam.

 For choosing items, the standard 11 o'clock mouse pointer is used.

 For selecting lines of text, a 1 o'clock mouse pointer is used.

The mouse pointer may change its appearance when *click-and-type* mode is active: Teensy lines appear to the left, right, and below the I-beam mouse pointer. Refer to Chapter 32 for information on click-and-type.

 When you point the mouse at a command button or any icon on the Word screen, you see a pop-up information bubble. The text in the bubble describes the command and perhaps offers information on how the command is used.

Keyboard Dos and Don'ts

You don't need to know how to type to use a word processor. And if you don't know how to type, see the nearby sidebar, "Do I need to learn to type?," although I can tell you that the answer is "Yes." It also helps to know a few typing dos and don'ts that are particular to word processing.

"Do I need to learn to type?"

No one needs to learn to type to use a word processor, but you do yourself a favor when you learn. My advice is to get a computer program that teaches you to type. I can recommend the *Mavis Beacon Teaches Typing* program, even though I don't get any money from her and none of her children resemble me. I just like the name Mavis, I suppose.

Knowing how to type makes the word-processing chore a wee bit more enjoyable.

Following the insertion pointer

Text you compose in Word appears at the *insertion pointer*'s location. The insertion pointer looks like a flashing vertical bar:

|

Characters appear *before* the insertion pointer, one at a time. After a character appears, the insertion pointer hops to the right, making room for more text.

- ✔ The insertion pointer moves as you type, but its location can be set to any location in the document. Chapter 3 covers moving the insertion pointer around in more detail.

- ✔ Some documentation refers to the insertion pointer as a cursor. The mouse pointer might also be referred to as a cursor. For clarity, this book refers to the insertion pointer and mouse pointer without ever using the term *cursor.*

Whacking the spacebar

Pressing the spacebar inserts a *space character* into the text. Spaces are important between words and sentences. Withoutthemreadingwouldbedifficult.

The most important thing to remember about the spacebar is that you need to whack it only once when word processing. Only *one* space needs to appear between words and after punctuation. That's it!

- ✔ I'm serious! Back in the dark ages, typing instructors directed students to use two spaces between sentences. That extra space was necessary for readability because typewriters used monospaced characters. On a computer, however, the extra space does nothing and potentially leads to formatting woes down the road.

✔ Anytime you feel like using two or more spaces in a document, what you need is a tab. Tabs are best for indenting text as well as for lining up text in columns. See Chapter 12 for details.

Backing up and erasing

When you make a typo or another type of typing error, press the Backspace key on the keyboard. The Backspace key moves the insertion pointer back one character and erases that character. The Delete key also erases text, though it gobbles up characters to the *right* of the insertion pointer.

See Chapter 4 for more information on deleting text.

Pressing the Enter key

In word processing, you press the Enter key only when you reach the end of a paragraph. Do not press the Enter key at the end of a line.

When your text gets precariously close to the right margin, Word automatically wraps the last word on the line down to the next line. This *word wrap* feature eliminates the need to press Enter at the end of a line.

✔ Don't use the Enter key to double-space your text. Double-spacing is a paragraph format in Word. See Chapter 11 for more information.

✔ Don't press the Enter key twice to add extra space between your paragraphs. That extra space is added automatically, provided it's part of the paragraph format, also covered in Chapter 11.

✔ If you want to indent a paragraph, press the Tab key after pressing Enter. As with other word-processing rules and regulations, paragraphs can be indented automatically, provided that format is applied, as covered in (you guessed it) Chapter 11.

Stuff That Happens While You Type

As you madly compose your text, fingers energetically jabbing the buttons on the keyboard, you may notice a few things happening on the screen. You might see spots. You might see lines and boxes. You may even see lightning! All are side effects of typing in Word. They're normal, and they're presented to help you.

Watching the status bar

The reason it's the *status* bar is that it shows you the status of your document, updating information as you type. A collection of information appears starting at the left end of the status bar and marching right, as shown in Figure 2-2.

Figure 2-2:
Stuff that
lurks on the
status bar.

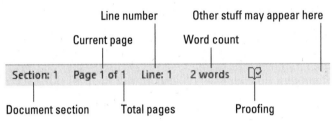

The status bar information is updated as your document changes. Use the information to see, for example, which page and line you're editing, the word count, and so on.

The info tidbits on the status bar are customizable. Chapter 29 explains how to control what information appears on the status bar.

Observing page breaks

As your document gains length, Word shows you where one page ends and another page begins. This visual assistance helps you keep elements on the same page, but also shows you how text flows between pages.

The visual clue for a new page is shown in Figure 2-3. In Print Layout view, the page break appears graphically. Text above the ethereal void is on one page, and text below the void is on the next page.

In Draft view, the page break appears as a line of dots from left to right across the document. And in other views, the page break may not show up at all. In that case, use the status bar to determine which page you're working on. For example, when the page-number indicator changes from 6 to 7, you've started a new page.

 ✔ You can change the gap between pages in Print Layout view. Point the mouse at the gap. When the mouse pointer changes, as shown in the margin, double-click to either close or open the gap.

> "Well," exclaimed Rabbit. "This is one of your messes I'm gladly not going to be a part of. Good day, Mr. Bear!"
>
> With that, Rabbit turned with his nose in the air, and walked stiffly in the other direction.
>
> "Oh, bother," said Pooh, still not knowing what to do with Piglet's mangled corpse.

Figure 2-3:
The page
break in
Print Layout
view.

✔ Don't force a page break by pressing the Enter key a gazillion times! Instead, see Chapter 13 for information on inserting page breaks in Word.

✔ The topic of page breaks brings up the concept of widows and orphans, which refer to a single line of text at the page's top or bottom, respectively. Word automatically moves such text to the next or previous page to prevent widows and orphans from happening.

Working collapsible headers

You may see a tiny triangle to the left of various headings in your documents, similar to what's shown in the margin. These triangles allow you to expand or collapse all text in the header's section. Click once to collapse the text; click again to expand it.

See Chapter 25 for a longer discussion of collapsible headers, as well as information on Word's outline mode.

Dealing with spots and clutter in the text

There's no cause for alarm if you see spots — or dots — amid the text you type, such as

```
This•can•be•very•annoying.¶
```

What you're seeing are *nonprinting characters*. Word uses various symbols to represent things you normally don't see: spaces, tabs, the Enter key, and more. These jots and tittles appear only when you've activated the Show/ Hide feature.

To use the Show Hide feature, follow these steps:

1. **Click the Home tab.**

2. **In the Paragraph group, click the Show/Hide command button.**

   The button features a paragraph symbol as its icon, shown in the margin.

To hide the symbols again, click the command button a second time.

- Why bother with showing the goobers? Sometimes, it's useful to check out what's up with formatting, find stray tabs visually, or locate missing paragraphs, for example.

- WordPerfect users: The Show/Hide command is as close as you can get to your beloved Reveal Codes command.

- The keyboard shortcut for the Show/Hide command is Ctrl+Shift+8. Use the 8 on the typewriter area of the keyboard, not the numeric keypad.

Understanding colorful underlines

When Word underlines your text without permission, it's drawing your attention to something amiss. These special underlines are not text formats. Here are a few of the underlines you may witness from time to time:

Red zigzag: Spelling errors in Word are underlined with red zigzags. See Chapter 7.

Blue zigzag: Grammatical and word-choice errors are flagged with a blue zigzag underline. Again, see Chapter 7.

Blue underlines: Word courteously highlights web page addresses by using blue underlined text in your document. You can Ctrl+click the blue underlined text to visit the web page.

Red lines: You may see red lines in the margin, underneath text, or through text. If so, it means that you're using Word's Track Changes feature. See Chapter 26.

Beyond these automatic underlines, you can apply the underline format to your text, choosing the type of underline and its color. See Chapter 10.

Part II
Your Basic Word

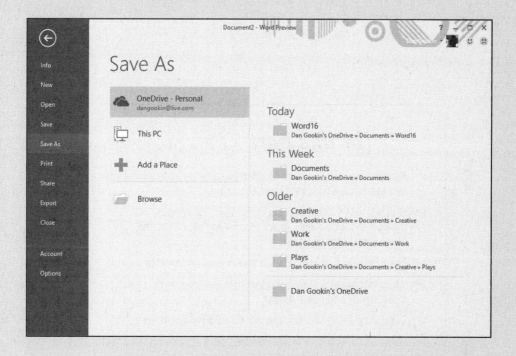

See how to use Word on a tablet or a touchscreen PC at
www.dummies.com/extras/word2016.

In this part . . .

- ✔ Discover how to use the scroll bars, move the insertion pointer, and get around with keyboard shortcuts.

- ✔ Find out how to delete characters, lines, sentences, paragraphs, and pages. You'll also be introduced to the lifesaving Undo command.

- ✔ Learn how to find and replace text in your documents.

- ✔ Work with blocks of text and see how you can mark, select, copy, move, and paste blocks.

- ✔ Customize the spell checker and AutoCorrect settings.

- ✔ Get familiar with how to preview and print your documents, both on paper and electronically.

Chapter 3

To and Fro in a Document

A computer screen is only so big. Your Word document can be much larger, perhaps requiring several monitors all stacked atop each other so that you could view it all at once. That somehow seems impractical. Therefore, Word offers techniques to let you hop, skip, and jump around your document, hither, thither, and yon.

Document Scrolling

It's ironic that the word *scroll* is used when referring to an electronic document. The scroll was the first form of portable recorded text, existing long before bound books. On a computer, scrolling is the process by which you view a little bit of a big document in a tiny window.

Working the vertical scroll bar

The document portion of the Word program window features a vertical scroll bar, illustrated in Figure 3-1. The scroll bar's operation is similar to the scroll bar in any Windows program. As a review, the figure illustrates the mouse's effect on parts of the scroll bar.

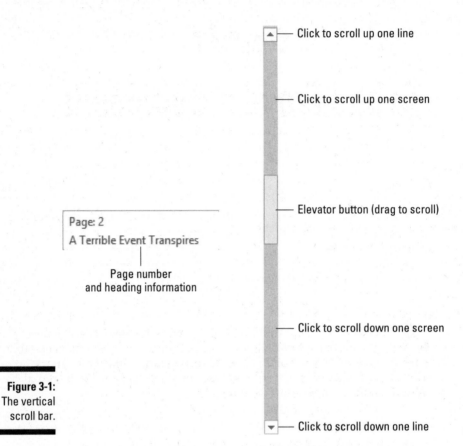

Click to scroll up one line

Click to scroll up one screen

Page: 2
A Terrible Event Transpires

Elevator button (drag to scroll)

Page number
and heading information

Click to scroll down one screen

Figure 3-1:
The vertical
scroll bar.

Click to scroll down one line

A key feature in the scroll bar is the elevator button (refer to Figure 3-1). Use the mouse to drag this button up or down to scroll the document. Its position in the scroll bar reflects the location of the text you see. For example, when the elevator button is at the top of the scroll bar, the window shows text at the start of the document.

- ✔ As you drag the elevator button up or down, you see a page number displayed, as shown in Figure 3-1. When a document is formatted with heading styles, you also see the heading title below the page number, as shown in the figure.

- ✔ The vertical scroll bar may disappear at times; move the mouse pointer over your text, and it shows up again.

- ✔ When the elevator button doesn't show up, or is dimmed, the whole document appears in the window. That means there's nothing to scroll.

- ✔ Because the elevator button's size reflects how much of the document appears in the window, the button grows smaller as your document grows longer.

✔ Using the scroll bar to scroll through your document doesn't move the insertion pointer. If you start typing, don't be surprised when Word jumps back to where the insertion pointer lurks.

Using the horizontal scroll bar

When your document is wider than can be displayed in the window, a horizontal scroll bar appears. It shows up at the bottom of the document part of the window, just above the status bar. Use the horizontal scroll bar to shift the page back and forth, left and right.

✔ Word automatically slides the document left and right as you type, but that action can be jarring. Instead, try to adjust the horizontal scroll bar to display as much of the text as possible. Or, if you can, make the document window wider.

✔ When the horizontal (left-to-right) shifting bugs you, consider using Word's Zoom tool to adjust the size of your document on the screen. See Chapter 1.

Scrolling with the mouse wheel

If your computer mouse sports a wheel button, you can use that button to scroll through your document. Roll the wheel to scroll up or down; the direction is set in Windows, so I can't for certain tell you whether rolling the wheel up scrolls your document up or down. Just try it to see how it works.

Some mice let you press the wheel button or tilt it from side to side. If so, press and hold down the wheel button and drag the mouse forward or back to slowly pan your document up or down. Tilt the wheel button from side to side to pan the document left and right.

Unlike using the scroll bars, when you use the mouse wheel to scroll the document, the insertion pointer stays on the page you're viewing. Use the Shift+F5 keyboard shortcut to return the insertion pointer to its previous spot. See the section, "Go Back to Where You Once Edited."

Move the Insertion Pointer

The beauty of a word processor is that you can edit any part of your document; you don't always have to work at "the end." The key to pulling off this trick is to know how to move the insertion pointer to the exact spot you want.

- ✔ Moving the insertion pointer is important! Scientific studies have shown that merely looking at the computer screen does no good.
- ✔ New text appears only at the insertion pointer. Text is deleted at the insertion pointer's location. Text is pasted at the insertion pointer. Formatting commands affect text where the insertion pointer lies blinking.

Commanding the insertion pointer

The easiest way to put the insertion pointer exactly where you want it is to click the mouse at that spot in your text. Point. Click. The insertion pointer moves.

Moving in small increments

For short hops, nothing beats using the keyboard's cursor keys to quickly move the insertion pointer around a document. The four arrow keys move the insertion pointer up, down, right, and left:

Press This Key	To Move the Insertion Pointer
↑	Up to the preceding line of text
↓	Down to the next line of text
→	Right to the next character
←	Left to the preceding character

Moving the cursor doesn't erase characters. See Chapter 4 for information on deleting stuff.

If you press and hold down the Ctrl (Control) key and then press an arrow key, the insertion pointer moves in larger increments. The invigorated insertion pointer leaps desperately in all four directions:

Press This Key Combo	To Move the Insertion Pointer
Ctrl+↑	Up to the start of the previous paragraph
Ctrl+↓	Down to the start of the next paragraph
Ctrl+→	Right to the start (first letter) of the next word
Ctrl+←	Left to the start (first letter) of the previous word

You can use either set of arrow keys on the computer keyboard, but when using the numeric keypad, ensure that the Num Lock light is off, (If it's on, press the Num Lock key.) If you don't, you see numbers in your text rather than the insertion pointer dancing all over — like444this.

Moving from beginning to end

The insertion pointer also bows to pressure from those cursor keys without arrows on them. The first couple consists of End and Home, which move the insertion pointer to the start or end of something, depending on how End and Home are used:

Press This Key or Combination	*To Whisk the Insertion Pointer*
End	To the end of a line of text
Home	To the start of a line of text
Ctrl+End	To the end of the document
Ctrl+Home	To the tippy-top of the document

The remaining cursor keys are the Page Up, or PgUp, key and the Page Down, or PgDn, key. As you might suspect, using these keys doesn't move up or down a page in your document. Nope. Instead, they slide through your document one screen at a time. Here's the roundup:

Press This Key or Combination	*To Whisk the Insertion Pointer*
PgUp	Up one screen or to the tippy-top of your document if you're near there
PgDn	Down one screen or to the end of the document if you're near there
Ctrl+Alt+PgUp	To the top of the current screen
Ctrl+Alt+PgDn	To the bottom of the current screen

The key combinations to move to the top or bottom of the current screen are Ctrl+Alt+PgUp and Ctrl+Alt+PgDn, respectively. That's Ctrl+Alt, not just the Ctrl key. And yes, few people use these commands.

What about Ctrl+PgUp and Ctrl+PgDn?

The Ctrl+PgUp and Ctrl+PgDn keyboard shortcuts are the Browse Previous and Browse Next commands, respectively. Their function changes based on what you've recently done in Word.

For example, the Ctrl+PgDn keyboard shortcut repeats the Find Next command. It might also repeat the Go To command, or a number of other Word commands that move the insertion pointer.

Because of their changing behavior, I don't recommend using Ctrl+PgUp or Ctrl+PgDn as a consistent way to move the insertion pointer.

Go Back to Where You Once Edited

Considering all the various commands for moving the insertion pointer, it's quite possible to make a mistake and not know where you are in a document. Yea, verily, the insertion pointer has gone where no insertion pointer has gone before.

Rather than click your heels together three times and try to get back the wishful way, just remember this keyboard combination:

Shift+F5

Pressing the Shift+F5 keyboard shortcut forces Word to return you to the last spot you edited. You can use this keyboard shortcut as many as three times before the cycle repeats. But the first time should get you back to where you were before you got lost.

Sadly, the Shift+F5 keyboard shortcut works only in Word; you can't use this command in real life.

Go to Wherever with the Go To Command

Word's Go To command allows you to send the insertion pointer to a specific page or line or to the location of a number of interesting items that Word can potentially cram into your document. The Go To command is your word-processing teleporter to anywhere.

To use the Go To command, follow these steps:

1. **Click the Home tab.**

2. **In the Editing group, choose the Go To command.**

   The Find and Replace dialog box appears with the Go To tab forward, as shown in Figure 3-2.

Figure 3-2: Telling Word to Go To you-know-where.

And now the shortcut: Press Ctrl+G to quickly summon the Find and Replace dialog box's Go To tab.

To whisk the insertion pointer to a specific location, choose it from the Go to What list. For example, choose Page to visit a specific page. Type the page number in the Enter Page Number box, and then click the Go To button to go to that page in your document.

✔ The Enter Page Number box also accepts relative pages as input. For example, to go three pages forward, type **+3**. To go 12 pages backward, type **-12** in the box.

✔ The last item you chose from the Go to What list affects the behavior of the Ctrl+PgUp and Ctrl+PgDn keyboard shortcuts. For example, if you choose Page and click the Go To button, the Ctrl+PgUp and Ctrl+PgDn keyboard shortcuts navigate through your document a page at a time.

Chapter 4

Text Editing

Writing is about creating text. Part of the process also includes reviewing and editing your words. My advice is to concentrate first on writing. In fact, one of the reasons people get stuck is that they spend more time editing than writing.

To accommodate your text-editing desires, Word comes with a host of commands to chop, slice, stitch, and otherwise decimate your text. The commands are a necessary part of the writing process, but they work best when you have oodles of text to edit. So, again, write first and edit second.

Remove Text You Don't Want

Credit the guy who put the eraser on the end of the pencil: It's a given that human beings make mistakes. The round, soft eraser counterbalances the sharp point of the pencil in more ways than one.

In Word, you use the keyboard to both create and destroy text. The majority of keys create text. Only two keys delete: Backspace and Delete. These keys gain more power when used with other keys — and even the mouse — that help them to delete great swaths of text.

✔ As text is deleted, the remaining text in the line, in the paragraph, or on the page scoots up to fill the void. Deleting text doesn't leave a hole in your document.

✔ Document fields cannot be deleted like regular text. When you attempt to remove a field, Word highlights the field's text as a warning. To continue and remove the field, press the Delete or Backspace key. See Chapter 23 for more information on fields.

Deleting single characters

Use the Backspace and Delete keys to delete single characters:

✔ Backspace deletes the character to the left of the insertion pointer.

✔ Delete deletes the character to the right of the insertion pointer.

In the following example, the insertion pointer is flashing (okay, it *would* be flashing on a monitor) between the *v* and the *e* in *loved*. Pressing the Backspace key deletes the *v;* pressing the Delete key deletes the *e:*

```
Martin lov|ed Karen with all his heart; that
she didn't know he existed was inconsequential.
```

You can press and hold down Backspace or Delete to machine-gun-delete characters. Release the key to halt such wanton destruction, although I recommend that you use other delete commands (covered in this chapter) rather than the machine-gun approach.

Deleting a word

To gobble up an entire word, use the Ctrl key with the Backspace or Delete key:

✔ Ctrl+Backspace deletes the word to the left of the insertion pointer.

✔ Ctrl+Delete deletes the word to the right of the insertion pointer.

These keyboard shortcuts work best when the insertion pointer is at the start or end of a word. When the pointer is in the middle of the word, these commands delete only from that middle point to the start or end of the word.

When you use Ctrl+Backspace to delete a word to the left, the insertion pointer sits at the end of the preceding word (or paragraph). When you use Ctrl+Delete to remove a word, the cursor sits at the start of the next word. This positioning is done to facilitate the rapid deletion of several words in a row.

No mere pencil eraser can match Ctrl+Delete or Ctrl+Backspace for sheer speed and terror!

Deleting more than a word

To remove chunks of text larger than a character or a word, the keyboard must pal up with the mouse. The process involves selecting a chunk of text and then deleting that chunk. See Chapter 6 for more information on selecting text.

Delete a line of text

A line of text starts at one side of the page and goes to the other. It's not really a sentence or a paragraph, but the line can be removed. Follow these steps:

1. Move the mouse pointer into the left margin next to the line of text.

You know you've found the sweet spot when the mouse pointer changes into a northeast-pointing arrow.

2. Click the mouse.

The line of text is selected and appears highlighted on the screen.

3. Press the Delete key to send that line into oblivion.

Delete a sentence

A sentence is a grammatical thing. You know: Start with a capital letter and end with a period, a question mark, or an exclamation point. You probably mastered this concept in grammar school, which is why they call it grammar school anyway.

Making a sentence go bye-bye is cinchy:

1. Position the mouse pointer at the offending sentence.

2. Press and hold down the Ctrl key and click the mouse.

The Ctrl and mouse click combination selects a sentence of text.

You can release the Ctrl key.

3. Press the Delete key.

Delete a paragraph

A paragraph is one or more sentences, or a document heading, ending with a press of the Enter key. Here's the fastest way to delete a full paragraph:

1. **Click the mouse button thrice.**

   Thrice means "three times." The triple click selects a complete paragraph of text.

2. **Press the Delete key.**

Another way to select a paragraph is to click the mouse twice in the left margin next to the paragraph.

Delete a page

A page of text includes everything on a page, top to bottom. To remove a page full of text requires some legerdemain with multiple Word commands. Follow these steps:

1. **Press Ctrl+G.**

   The Find and Replace dialog box appears, with the Go To tab forward.

2. **From the Go to What list, click to select Page.**

3. **Type the number of the page you want to delete.**

4. **Click the Go To button and then click the Close button.**

   The insertion pointer is positioned at the top of the page.

5. **Press the F8 key.**

   Word enters extended selection mode.

6. **Press Ctrl+PgDn.**

   PgDn is the Page Down key.

   The entire page is now selected.

7. **Press the Delete key.**

All text is removed from the page.

- ✔ If the page remains, but it's blank, you might be dealing with a hard page break. See Chapter 13.

- ✔ If you're trying to delete a blank page at the end of a document, see Chapter 9.

- ✔ Chapter 3 offers more information on the Go To command.

- ✔ The F8 key activates extended selection mode. See Chapter 6 for more F8 key tricks.

Delete an odd-size chunk of text

Word lets you delete any old odd-size chunk of text anywhere in your document. The key is to select that text as a block. After the block is marked, you can press the Delete key to zap it to Kingdom Come. Refer to Chapter 6 for more information on selecting blocks of text.

Split and Join Paragraphs

A paragraph is both a grammatical and formatting concept. It's a collection of sentences that collectively express some thought, idea, or theme. In Word, a paragraph is a chunk of text that ends when you press the Enter key. While grammarians and software engineers duke it out over the different meanings, you can redefine a paragraph in a document by splitting or joining text.

Making two paragraphs from one

To split a single paragraph in twain, follow these steps:

1. **Click the mouse at the point where you want the new paragraph to begin.**

   Ideally that point is at the start of a sentence.

2. **Press the Enter key.**

   Word splits the paragraph in two; the text above the insertion pointer becomes its own paragraph, and the text following it then becomes the next paragraph.

Depending on how the paragraph was torn asunder, you may need to delete an extra space lingering at the end of the first paragraph or dawdling at the start of the next.

Making one paragraph from two

To join two paragraphs and turn them into one, follow these steps:

1. **Place the insertion pointer at the start of the second paragraph.**

   Use the keyboard to position the insertion pointer, or click the mouse.

2. **Press the Backspace key.**

   The Enter character from the preceding paragraph is removed, which joins two paragraphs into one.

Depending on how neatly the paragraphs were joined, you may need to add a space between the sentences at the spot where the paragraphs were glued together.

Soft and Hard Returns

Word defines a paragraph as a chunk of text ending with a hard return. That hard return character is produced by pressing the Enter key. The paragraph ends, and then a new paragraph starts. And so it goes throughout the document.

You can end a line of text also by typing a soft return, also known as a manual line break. To do so, press Shift+Enter. The current line of text stops and the insertion pointer hops to the start of the next line. Keep typing at that point and, eventually, press Enter to end the paragraph.

The soft return is used to split titles and headings. It's also used to type addresses. That way, you can keep the text together in a single paragraph. For example:

```
Mr. President
1600 Pennsylvania Ave.
Washington, DC 20500
```

The text above is a single paragraph with soft returns separating each line.

To help you see hard returns and soft returns, use the Show/Hide command: Click the Home tab, and in the Paragraph Group, click the Show/Hide command button. The button is adorned with the paragraph symbol (¶).

When the Show/Hide command is active, the soft return appears as a right-angle arrow, similar to what you see on the keyboard's Enter key: ↵

The hard return appears as the paragraph mark: ¶

Figure 4-1 illustrates how these two characters appear in a document with the Show/Hide command enabled.

✔ See Chapter 2 for additional details on the Show/Hide command and seeing hidden characters in your text.

✔ While soft returns keep text close, the text is still affected by the paragraph's line spacing. See Chapter 11 for more information on paragraph formatting.

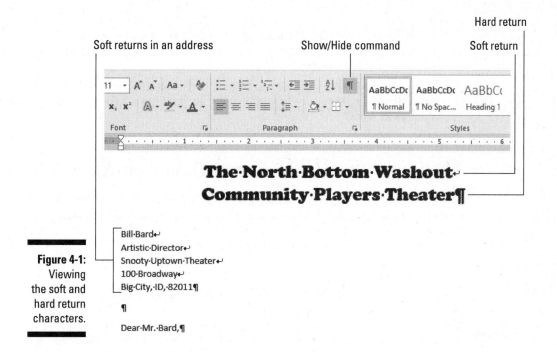

Soft returns in an address   Show/Hide command   Hard return / Soft return

Figure 4-1:
Viewing
the soft and
hard return
characters.

Undo Mistakes with Undo Haste

That quaffing and drinking will undo you.

— *Richard II,* William Shakespeare

The Undo command undoes anything you do in Word, which includes formatting text, moving blocks, typing and deleting text — the whole enchilada. You have two handy ways to unleash the Undo command:

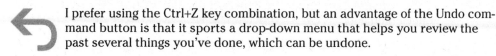

- ✔ Press Ctrl+Z.
- ✔ Click the Undo command button on the Quick Access toolbar.

I prefer using the Ctrl+Z key combination, but an advantage of the Undo command button is that it sports a drop-down menu that helps you review the past several things you've done, which can be undone.

- ✔ Regrettably, you cannot pick and choose from the Undo command button's drop-down menu; you can merely undo multiple instances of things all at one time.

- ✔ The Undo command works sporadically sometimes. Before this happens, Word warns you. For example, you may see a message such as "There is not enough memory to undo this operation, Continue?" Proceed at your own peril.
- ✔ The Undo command doesn't work when there's nothing to undo or if something simply cannot be undone. For example, you cannot undo a document save.

Undoing the Undo command with Redo

If you undo something and — whoops! — you didn't mean to, use the Redo command to set things back to the way they were. For example, you may type some text and then use Undo to "untype" the text. You can use the Redo command to restore the typing. You have two choices:

- ✔ Press Ctrl+Y.
- ✔ Click the Redo command button on the Quick Access Toolbar.

The Redo command does exactly the opposite of whatever the Undo command does. So, if you type text, Undo untypes the text and Redo recovers the text. If you use Undo to recover deleted text, Redo deletes the text again.

Using the Repeat command

When the Redo command has nothing left to redo, it changes functions and becomes the Repeat command. On the Quick Access toolbar, the command changes as shown in the margin. The Repeat command's duty is to repeat the last thing you did in Word, whether it's typing text, applying a format, or doing a variety of other things.

Lamentably, you can't use the Repeat command to ease your typing chores. That's because it repeats only the last single character you typed.

The keyboard shortcut for the Repeat command is Ctrl+Y, the same as the Redo command.

Chapter 5

Search for This, Replace It with That

*L*ittle Bo Peep has lost her sheep. Too bad she doesn't know about Word's Find and Replace commands. She could find the misplaced ruminants in a matter of nanoseconds. Not only that, she could use search and replace to, say, replace all the sheep with real estate. It's all cinchy after you understand and use the various Find and Replace commands. Sadly, it's only words that are replaced. True, if Word could search and replace real things, there'd be a lot less sheep in the world.

Text Happily Found

Finding text is one of the most basic and ancient tools available in a word processor. The only issue has been whether the command is called Find or Search. The terms Relentlessly Hunt Down and Fiendishly Locate were never considered.

In Word, finding duties are split between the traditional Find dialog box and the Navigation pane.

Finding a tidbit o' text

Don't bother with the Ribbon! To find text in your document, press Ctrl+F, the memorable keyboard shortcut for the Find command. You see the Navigation pane, similar to what's shown in Figure 5-1.

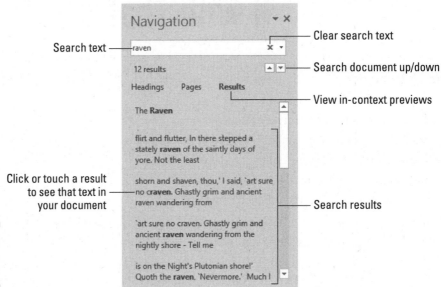

Search text ——

Click or touch a result to see that text in your document ——

Clear search text

Search document up/down

View in-context previews

Search results

Figure 5-1:
The Navigation pane.

In the Search Document box, type the text you want to locate. As you type instances of the text are highlighted in the document. In-context chunks of text appear in the Navigation pane under the Results heading, as illustrated in Figure 5-1.

To peruse found text, use the up and down arrows in the Navigation pane, as illustrated in Figure 5-1.

When text can't be found, the Navigation pane explains that it can't find the text. It uses the pronoun *we,* which I find disturbing.

✔ To clear text from the Search Document box, click the X button found at the right end of the box.

✔ Do not end the text with a period unless you want to find the period, too. Word's Find command is persnickety.

✔ Word finds text only in the current document (the one you see in the window). To find text in another document, switch to that document's window and try searching again. Or you can use the Find command in Windows, which is not covered in this book.

✔ Word does host the Find command on the Ribbon's Home tab. Seriously, press the Ctrl+F key. It's faster.

Scouring your document with Advanced Find

The Navigation pane is a handy tool for locating text. In fact, I keep it open for all my documents. When it comes to exercising some Find command muscle, however, you must turn to a more specific tool. That's the traditional Find dialog box, called the Find and Replace dialog box, shown in Figure 5-2.

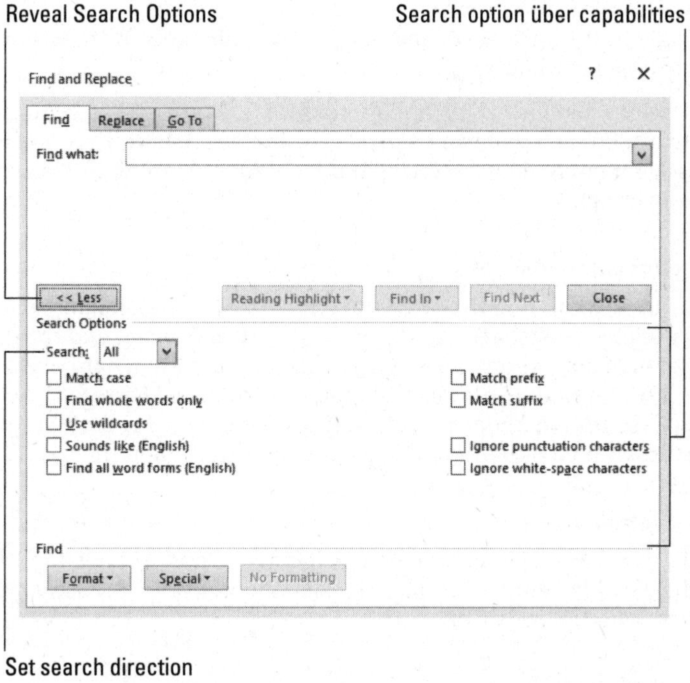

Reveal Search Options   Search option über capabilities

Figure 5-2:
The Find and Replace dialog box.

Set search direction

Follow these steps to conjure forth the Find and Replace dialog box:

1. **Click the Home tab.**

2. **In the Editing group, choose Find ⇨ Advanced Find.**

   The Find and Replace dialog box appears, with the Find tab forward. You may see only the top part of the dialog box. So:

3. **Click the More button to reveal the dialog box's powerful bits.**

   What you see now appears just like Figure 5-2.

4. Type the search text in the Find What text box.

5. Use the dialog box's controls to make further adjustments.

Examples for using the various controls are found throughout this chapter.

6. Click the Find Next button to locate the text.

Once the text is found, you can do whatever to it: Edit it, change it, or click the Find Next button to continue looking for text.

After the Find command has scoured the entire document, you see an info box explaining that the search is finished. Click OK, and then click the Cancel button to dismiss the Find and Replace dialog box.

- ✔ It's possible to reassign the keyboard shortcut Ctrl+F from the Navigation pane to the Advanced Find dialog box. This bit of Word wizardry is divulged in Chapter 31.

- ✔ Options set in the Find and Replace dialog box remain set until deactivated. When you can't seem to locate text that you *know* is in your document, review the dialog box's settings. Turn off the ones you no longer need.

Find case-sensitive text

When you want to find Pat in your document, the Find command needs to know the difference between *Pat* and *pat.* One is a name, and the other is to lightly touch something. To use the Find command to locate one and not the other, use the Find and Replace dialog box (refer to Figure 5-2). Select the Match Case option under Search Options. That way, *Pat* matches only words that start with an uppercase *P* and have lowercase *at* in them.

Find a whole word

Word's Advanced Find command can locate *Pat* and not *pat*, but it might also flag the word *Pattern* at the start of a sentence. To avoid that situation, select the Find Whole Words Only option.

Find word variations

Two options in the Find and Replace dialog box assist you with finding words that may not be exactly what you're looking for.

The Sounds Like (English) option allows you to search for *homonyms,* or words that sound the same as the search word. These words include *their* and *there, deer* and *dear,* and *hear* and *here.* The command doesn't, however, locate rhyming words.

The Find All Word Forms (English) option expands the search to include different forms of the same word. With this option set, you can search for the word *hop* and also find matches with *hops, hopped,* and *hopping.*

Search this way or that

The Find command searches from the insertion pointer's position to the end of a document and then back 'round the top again. To override its sense of direction, use the Search drop-down list, as illustrated in Figure 5-2. You see three options:

- ✔ **Down:** The Find command searches from the insertion pointer's location to the end of your document, and then it stops.

- ✔ **Up:** The Find command searches from the insertion pointer's location to the start of your document. Then it stops.

- ✔ **All:** The Find command searches the entire document, from the insertion pointer's location down to the end of the document, back up to the beginning, and then stops at the point where the search began.

You can use keyboard shortcuts to search up or down. The Ctrl+PgDn key combination repeats the last search downward; the Ctrl+PgUp key combination repeats the most recent search upward.

Finding stuff you can't type

The Find command is brilliant enough to locate items in your document such as tab characters or text colored red. The puzzle is how to input that type of information in the Find and Replace dialog box. The secret is to use the Format and Special buttons lurking near the bottom of the dialog box (refer to Figure 5-2).

Find special characters

To hunt down untypeable characters in your document, click the Special button in the Advanced Find dialog box. Up pops a list of 22 items that Word can search for but that you would have a dickens of a time typing.

Despite the exhaustive list, here are the few items you'll eventually (if ever) use:

- ✔ **Any Character, Any Digit,** and **Any Letter** are special characters that represent, well, just about anything. These items can be used as wild cards for matching lots of stuff.

- ✔ **Caret Character** allows you to search for a caret (^) symbol, which may not seem like a big deal, but it is: Word uses the ^ symbol in a special way for finding text; see the next section.

✔ **Paragraph Mark** (¶) is a special character that's the same as the Enter character — the one you press to end a paragraph.

✔ **Tab Character** moves the insertion pointer to the next tab stop.

✔ **White Space** is any number of blank characters: one or more spaces, tabs, empty lines, or a combination thereof.

Choose an item from the list to search for that special character. When you do, a special, funky shorthand representation for that character appears. The shorthand involves the ^ character and then another character, such as ^t to search for the tab character.

Find formatting

In its most powerful superhero mode, the Find command can scour your document for text and formatting. You can search for the formatting information itself or use it with text to locate specifically formatted text.

The secret to hunting down text formats is to use the Format button, found at the bottom of the Find and Replace dialog box, as shown in Figure 5-2. Click that button to view a menu full of formatting categories, such as Font, Paragraph, and Tabs. Choose a category to pluck out a specific format.

For example, suppose that you want to find the text *red herring* in your document. The text is italic and colored red. Follow these steps:

1. **Click the Home tab.**

2. **In the Editing group, choose Find ⇨ Advanced Find.**

   The Find and Replace dialog box appears.

3. **Type the text you're searching for.**

   In this example, that would be *red herring.*

4. **Ensure that the dialog box details are displayed; click the More button if necessary.**

5. **Click the No Formatting button to remove any previously applied formatting.**

   The No Formatting button is available when you've previously searched for format attributes.

6. **Click the Format button and choose Font from the pop-up list.**

   The Find Font dialog box appears

7. **Choose Italic as the font style.**

8. **Select Red from the Font Color menu.**

   Yes, many shades of red dwell on the menu. Pick the correct one.

9. Click OK.

The Find Font dialog box goes away and you return to the Find and Replace dialog box. Below the Find What text box appears the search format. It lists which attributes the Advanced Find command is looking for.

10. Click the Find Next button to locate the formatted text.

If you want to search only for a format, leave the Find What text box blank (refer to Step 3). That way, you can search for formatting attributes without regard to what the text reads.

The Find command remembers your formatting options! The next time you want to search for plain text, click the No Formatting button (Step 5). Doing so removes the formatting attributes and allows you to search for text in any format.

Replace Found Text

The Find command is good only for finding stuff. When you want to find something and replace it with something else, you use the Find and Replace command. That will help Little Bo Peep establish her real estate empire.

Replacing one thing with another

To find a bit of text and then replace it with another bit of text, use the Replace command. Follow these steps:

1. Click the Home tab.

2. In the Editing group, click the Replace command button.

When the Replace command button isn't visible in the Editing group, click the Editing button, and then choose the Replace command button from the pop-up group of command buttons that appears.

Choosing the Replace command button summons the Find and Replace dialog box with the Replace tab forward, shown in Figure 5-3.

3. In the Find What box, type text you want to replace.

For example, if you're finding *coffee* and replacing it with *tea,* type **coffee**.

4. In the Replace With box, type the replacement text.

To continue from the example in Step 3, you type **tea** here.

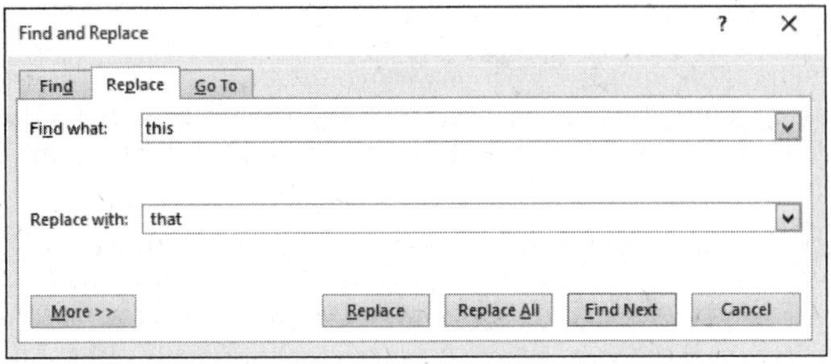

Find and Replace   ?   ✕

Find   Replace   Go To

Find what: this   ▼

Replace with: that   ▼

More >>   Replace   Replace All   Find Next   Cancel

Figure 5-3: The Replace tab in the Find and Replace dialog box.

5. **Click the Find Next button.**

   At this step, the Replace command works just like the Find command: Word scours your document for the text you typed in the Find What box. If the text is found, proceed with Step 6. If nothing is found, start over again with Step 3 or just abandon your efforts and close the dialog box.

6. **Click the Replace button.**

   The found word, highlighted on the screen, is replaced.

After you click the Replace button, Word immediately searches for the next instance of the text, at which point you repeat Step 6 until the entire document has been searched.

✔ The Replace command's dialog box also sports a More button, which can be used exactly like the More button for the Find command. See the section "Scouring your document with Advanced Find," earlier in this chapter.

✔ Word may find and replace your text in the middle of another word, such as *use* in *causes.* Oops! Click the More button and select the Find Whole Words Only option to prevent such a thing from happening.

✔ If you don't type anything in the Replace With box, Word replaces your text with *nothing!* It's wanton destruction!

✔ Speaking of wanton destruction, the Undo command restores your document to its preceding condition if you foul up the Replace operation. See Chapter 4 for more information.

✔ The keyboard shortcut for the Replace command is Ctrl+H. The only way I can figure that one out is that Ctrl+F is the Find command and Ctrl+G is the Go To command. F, G, and H are found together on the computer keyboard, and Find, Replace, and Go To are found together in the Find and Replace dialog box. Go figure.

Replacing it all at once

I confess that it's tedious to use the Replace button when replacing text. Sure, sometimes it's handy, especially when you don't want to replace everything. But if you've changed your novel's main character name from Xlaborded to Zlaborded, you can probably and safely replace every instance all at once. That's why the Replace command's dialog box sports the handy Replace All button.

The Replace All button directs the Replace command to find all instances of the Find What text and — without question or pause — replace it with the Replace With text.

Be doubly certain that you made the proper settings in the Find and Replace dialog box before you click that Replace All button! You can still undo any mistakes, but for a large document, a lot of text can be found and replaced in a manner most merciless.

Finding and replacing formatting

Perhaps the trickiest thing to replace in a document is formatting. Say you work at the DMV and you've been directed to change all underline text to italic. That trick is possible, but it runs the risk of screwing up the document's formatting.

The general steps for replacing a format are as follows:

1. **Summon the Find and Replace dialog box (press Ctrl+H).**

2. **Clear all text and formatting from the Find What and Replace With text boxes.**

3. **Click the Find What text box, and then click the Format button to choose a format to find.**

4. **Click the Replace With text box, and then use the Format button to select a replacement format.**

   For some font attributes, you must also remove the original text format, which can be tricky.

5. **Click the Replace or Replace All buttons.**

Better than the preceding generic steps, consider a specific example. Follow these steps to replace underline with italics:

1. **Press Ctrl+H to summon the Find and Replace dialog box.**

2. **Click the More button, if necessary, to display the full dialog box.**

3. **Click the Find What text box and erase any text there.**

4. **If it's available, click the No Formatting button.**

   You want to direct the Replace command to ignore any previous formatting searches.

5. **Click the Format button and choose Font.**

   The Find Font dialog box appears.

6. **Choose the solid underline from the Underline Style menu.**

   It's the third item in the menu, right above the double underline.

7. **Click OK to close the Find Font dialog box.**

   The text *Format: Underline* appears below the Find What box.

8. **Click the Replace With text box and erase any text.**

9. **Click the No Formatting button, if necessary, to remove any previous formatting.**

10. **Choose Font from the Format button's pop-up list.**

    The Find Font dialog box appears.

11. **From the Font Style list, choose Italic.**

12. **From the Underline Style list, choose (none).**

    If you just chose the Italic style, Word would simply underline italic text. Instead, by choosing (none) as the underline style, Word removes any previously applied underline format.

13. **Click OK to close the Find Font dialog box.**

    The text *Format: Font: Italic, No underline* appears below the Replace With box.

14. **Cross your fingers**

15. **Click the Replace All button.**

    Word scours your document and replaces any italic text with underline.

16. **Close the Find and Replace dialog box.**

The key to replacing formatting is not only to replace one format with another but also to peel off the existing format. To do so, you replace an underline style with (none), or Italic with Not Italic, or Bold with Not Bold, and so on. That way, the text formatting is replaced, not added to.

> ✔ An easier way to update formatting in a document is to use and apply *styles*. Refer to Chapter 15 for details.

> ✔ Don't forget about the No Formatting button! You need to click it if you want to change the formats or replace text without paying attention to formats.

Chapter 6

Blocks o' Text

· ·

· ·

*W*riting is about blocks. From the moveable blocks used by the ancient Chinese for printing to the inevitable writer's block. In Word, *blocks* refer to selected chunks of text in a document, which I believe you'll find more useful than the other types of blocks.

Meet Mr. Block

"Hello, Mr. Block! How do you do?"

"Well! I'm a block of text. I have a beginning and an end. I can be any size, from a single character to the entire document."

To create Mr. Block, you select text. You can use the keyboard. You can use the mouse. You can use both at once, or employ some of Word's more esoteric text-selection commands.

A block of selected text appears highlighted in a document, similar to what's shown in Figure 6-1.

Once a block of text is selected, you can perform certain actions that affect only the text in that block. You can also copy, move, or delete the block.

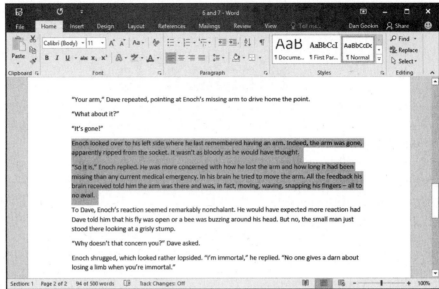

Figure 6-1:
A block
of text is
selected.

To help format a selected block of text, the mini toolbar appears, as shown in Figure 6-2.

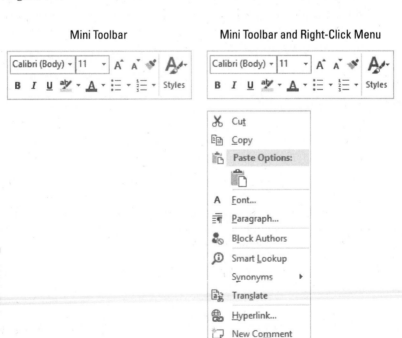

Figure 6-2:
The mini
toolbar and
block pop-
up menu.

The mini toolbar hosts popular commands found on the Ribbon, allowing you to quickly format the block of text. You can also right-click the selected text, in which case you see both the mini toolbar as well as a shortcut menu, also shown in Figure 6-2.

- ✔ A block of text in Word includes text and the text formatting.

- ✔ Graphics and other nontext elements can also be selected as a block. In fact, you can select graphics along with text in the same block.

- ✔ When the status bar is displaying a word count, the number of words selected in the block of text is displayed, next to the total number of words in the document. (Refer to Figure 6-1.)

- ✔ When the Find command locates text, the found text is selected as a block. Refer to Chapter 5 for more information on the Find command.

- ✔ The mini toolbar disappears after a few moments of neglect. Refer to Chapter 33 for information on disabling the mini toolbar.

- ✔ Selecting text also means selecting characters such as tabs and the Enter character that marks the end of a paragraph. Word shows the Enter character as an extra blank space at the end of a paragraph. When you select that blank, you select the whole paragraph as a paragraph. To avoid selecting the Enter character, don't select the blank space at the end of a paragraph.

Mark a Block of Text

Before you can work with a block of text, you must tell Word where the block starts and where it ends. The process is known as marking a block of text or selecting text.

Using the keyboard to select text

The keyboard's cursor keys are used to select text, but only when you know the secret: Press and hold down the Shift key as you move the cursor. When the Shift key is down, Word's standard cursor key commands not only move the insertion pointer but also select chunks of text. Table 6-1 lists common key combinations.

Although you can use any keyboard cursor-movement command, including some that move the insertion pointer a great distance, I recommend using this Shift key technique for selecting only small chunks of text. Otherwise, you may end up tying your fingers into knots.

Table 6-1	Keyboard Selection Wizardry
To Select This	*Press This*
A character at a time to the right of the insertion pointer	Shift+→
A character at a time to the left of the insertion pointer	Shift+←
A block of text from the insertion pointer to the end of the line	Shift+End
A block of text from the insertion pointer to the beginning of the line	Shift+Home
A block of text from the insertion pointer to a line above	Shift+↑
A block of text from the insertion pointer to a line below	Shift+↓

- ✔ See Chapter 3 for the full list of Word's cursor key commands.

- ✔ Either Shift key works, although I prefer to use the left Shift key and then work the arrow keys on the right side of the keyboard.

Marking a block with the mouse

Mickey may rule a kingdom, but your computer's mouse rules over text selection in your computer.

Drag over text to select it

Position the mouse pointer at the start of the text block, and then drag the mouse over the text you want to select. As you drag, the text becomes highlighted or selected.

- ✔ This technique works best when you use the mouse to drag over only the text you can see on the screen. When you try to select text beyond what you see on the screen, you have to select and scroll, which can be unwieldy.

- ✔ Also see Chapter 33, which covers how to adjust Word so that you can use the mouse to select individual letters instead of entire words at a time.

Click the mouse to select text

A speedy way to select specific sizes of chunks of text is to match the power of the mouse with the dexterity of your index finger. Table 6-2 explains some clicking-and-selecting techniques worth noting.

Table 6-2	Mouse-Selection Arcana
To Select This Chunk of Text	*Click the Mouse Thusly*
A single word	Double-click the word.
A line	Move the mouse pointer into the left margin beside the line you want to select. The mouse pointer changes to an arrow pointing northeastward. Click the mouse to select a line of text. Drag the mouse up or down to select several lines.
A sentence	Position the insertion pointer over the sentence and Ctrl+click. (Press the Ctrl key and click the mouse.)
A paragraph	Point the mouse somewhere in the paragraph's midst and click thrice (triple-click).

Select text with the old poke-and-point

Here's the best way to select a chunk of text of any size, especially when that chunk of text is larger than what you can see on the screen at one time:

1. **Click the mouse to set the insertion pointer wherever you want the block to start.**

   I call this location the anchor point.

2. **Scroll through your document.**

   You must use the scroll bar or the mouse wheel to scroll through your document. If you use the cursor-movement keys, you reposition the insertion pointer, which isn't what you want.

3. **Hold down the Shift key and click the mouse where you want the block to end.**

   The text from the insertion pointer to wherever you clicked the mouse is selected as a block.

Using the F8 key to mark a block

A relic from the old days, the F8 key is known as Word's Extend Selection command. Press that key to activate this feature: Word drops anchor at the insertion pointer's location. Use either the mouse or the cursor keys to select text. In fact, you cannot do anything but select text in extend selection mode.

You exit extend selection mode by either doing something with the block of text or pressing the Esc key.

- ✔ To help you with the F8 key and extend selection mode, right-click the status bar and choose the item Selection Mode. The text *Extend Selection* appears on the status bar when this mode is active.

- ✔ Not only can you use the cursor keys while in extend selection mode, any of the character keys work as well; text is selected from the anchor point to the character you type. Type an *N,* for example, and all text between the insertion pointer and the next letter *N* is selected.

- ✔ You can also use the Find command to locate a specific bit of text in extend selection mode. Word marks all text between the anchor and the text that the Find command locates.

- ✔ Press the F8 key twice to select the current word.

- ✔ Press the F8 key thrice (three times) to select the current sentence.

- ✔ Press the F8 key four times to select the current paragraph as a block of text.

- ✔ Press the F8 key five times to select the entire document, from top to bottom.

- ✔ No matter how many times you press F8, be aware that it always drops anchor. So pressing F8 once or five times means that Word is still in Extend Selection mode. Do something with the block or press Esc to cancel that mode.

Blocking the whole dang-doodle document

The biggest block you can mark is an entire document. Word has a specific command to do it. Follow these steps:

1. **Click the Home tab.**

2. **In the Editing group, choose Select⇨Select All.**

   The entire document is marked as a single block o' text.

And now, the keyboard shortcut: Press Ctrl+A to select an entire document as a block.

Deselecting a block

When you mark a block of text and change your mind, you must unmark, or *deselect,* the text. Here are a few handy ways to do it:

- ✔ **Move the insertion pointer.** It doesn't matter how you move the insertion pointer, with the keyboard or with the mouse, but doing so deselects the block.

- ✔ **Press the Esc key and then the ← key.** This method works to end Extend Selection mode.

- ✔ **Press Shift+F5.** The Shift+F5 key combo is the "go back" command (see Chapter 3), but it also deselects a block of text *and* returns you to the text you were editing before making the selection.

Manipulate the Block of Text

You can block punches, block hats, block and tackle, play with building blocks and engine blocks, take nerve blocks, suffer from mental blocks, jog for blocks, and, naturally, block text. But what can you do with those marked blocks of text?

Why, plenty of things! You can apply a format to all text in the block, copy a block, move a block, search through a block, proof a block, print a block, and even delete a block. The information in this section explains a few of those tricks.

- ✔ Blocks must be selected before you can manipulate them. See the first half of this chapter.

- ✔ When a block of text is marked, various Word commands affect only the text in that block.

- ✔ To replace a block, type some text. The new text (actually, the initial character) replaces the entire block.

- ✔ To delete a block, press the Delete or Backspace key. Thwoop! The block is gone.

- ✔ Formatting commands can be applied to any marked block of text — specifically, character and paragraph formatting. See Part III of this book.

- ✔ Also see Chapter 32 for information on Word's bizarre yet potentially useful Collect and Paste feature.

Copying a block

After a block is marked, you can copy it to another part of your document to duplicate the text. The original block remains untouched by this operation. Follow these steps to copy a block of text from one place to another:

1. **Mark the block.**

   Detailed instructions about doing this task are offered in the first part of this chapter.

2. **Click the Home tab.**

3. **In the Clipboard group, click the Copy command button.**

   You get no visual clue that the text has been copied; it remains selected.

4. **Click to set the insertion pointer at the position where you want to place the block's copy.**

   Don't worry if there's no room! Word inserts the block into your text.

5. **Click the Paste command button.**

   The block of text is inserted into your text just as though you had typed it there by yourself.

The keyboard shortcuts for copy and paste are Ctrl+C and Ctrl+V, respectively. You'll probably use those keyboard shortcuts more than the command buttons in the Home tab's Clipboard group.

✔ See the later section, "Setting the pasted text format," to find out what to do about the wee li'l clipboard icon that appears by the pasted text.

✔ The Paste command continues to paste the copied text, over and over — that is, until new text is selected and copied (or cut). Pasting text again simply pastes down a second copy of the block, spit-spot (as Mary Poppins would say).

✔ You can paste the block into another document you're working on or even into another application. This is a Windows trick that works in any program that can accept text as input.

Moving a block

To move a block of text, you select the text and then *cut* and paste. This process is almost the same as copying a block, described in the preceding section, although in Step 3 you choose the Cut tool (shown in the margin) or press Ctrl+X rather than choose the Copy tool. Otherwise, all steps are the same.

Don't be alarmed when the block of text vanishes! That's cutting in action; the block of text is being *moved,* not copied. You see the block of text again when you paste it.

If you screw up, the Ctrl+Z Undo shortcut undoes a block move.

Setting the pasted text format

When you paste text in Word, you see the Paste Options icon shown in the margin. It appears near the pasted block of text. Don't let it annoy you! That button allows you to select formatting for the pasted block because occasionally the block may contain formatting that, well, looks quite ugly after it's pasted.

To work the Paste Options button, click it with the mouse or press and release the Ctrl key on the keyboard. You see a menu of options, illustrated in Figure 6-3.

Press Ctrl to see the menu

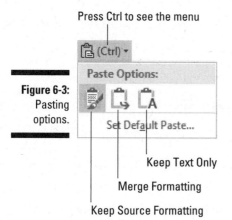

Figure 6-3:
Pasting
options.

Keep Text Only

Merge Formatting

Keep Source Formatting

Table 6-3 summarizes the available paste options.

To keep only text with a copied or cut block (no formatting), press the Ctrl key and then the T key after pasting. That's two separate keys, not Ctrl+T.

Using the Paste Options icon is utterly optional. In fact, you can continue typing or working in Word and the icon bows out, fading away like some

Table 6-3		**Paste Option Options**	
Icon	*Keyboard Shortcut*	*Name*	*Description*
	K	Keep Source Formatting	The formatting is okay; don't do a thing.
	M	Merge Formatting	Reformat the pasted block so that it matches the text it's being pasted into.
	T	Keep Text Only	Just paste in the text — no formatting.

nebbish who boldly asked a power blonde to go out with him and she utterly failed to recognize his existence. Like that.

(TECHNICAL STUFF) Click the Set Default Paste text to direct Word to permanently deal with pasted text. It's a handy trick, especially when you find yourself repeatedly choosing the same Paste Options format.

Copying or moving a block with the mouse

When you have to move a block only a short distance, you can use the mouse to drag-move or drag-copy the block.

 To move any selected block of text, hover the mouse pointer anywhere in the blocked text, and then drag the block to its new location. As you drag the block, the mouse pointer changes, as shown in the margin. That means you're moving a block of text.

 To copy a block of text, point the mouse pointer at the block — just as if you were going to move the block — but press and hold down the Ctrl key as you drag. When you drag the block, the mouse pointer changes to resemble the icon shown in the margin. That's your clue that the block is being copied and not just moved.

This trick works best when you're moving or copying a block to a location that you can see right on the screen. Otherwise, you're scrolling your document with the mouse while you're playing with blocks, which is like trying to grab an angry snake.

- ✔ When you drag a block of text with the mouse, you're not copying or cutting it to the Clipboard. You cannot use the Paste (Ctrl+V) command to paste in the block again.

- ✔ To create a *linked copy* of the block, drag the mouse and hold down *both* the Shift and Ctrl keys. When you release the mouse button, the copied block plops down into your document with a dark highlight. It's your clue that the copy is linked to the original; changes in the original are reflected in the copy and vice versa. If the linked copy doesn't update, right-click the text and choose the Update Link command.

Viewing the Clipboard

All text you copy or cut is stored in a location called the Clipboard. That's the standard cut/copy/paste holding bin for text, but in Word the Clipboard is more powerful than in other Windows programs. Specifically, you can use the Clipboard task pane to examine items cut or copied, and paste them again in your document in any order.

To copy a chunk of text from the task pane to your document, heed these steps:

1. **Place the insertion pointer in your document where you want the pasted text to appear.**

2. **Click the Home tab.**

3. **In the Clipboard group, click the dialog box launcher.**

    You see the Clipboard task pane, along with all text cut or copied since you've started the Word program, similar to what's shown in Figure 6-4.

4. **Position the mouse pointer at an item in the task pane.**

    A menu button appears to the right of the item.

5. **Click the menu button and choose the Paste command.**

    The text is pasted into your document.

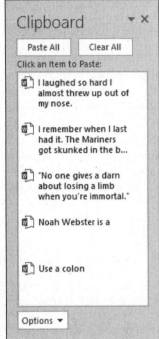

Figure 6-4:
The Clip-
board task
pane.

Unlike using the Ctrl+V keyboard shortcut, or the Paste button on the Ribbon, you can paste text from the Clipboard in any order, and even summon text you copied or cut hours ago or text you copied or cut from other Microsoft Office programs.

Also see Chapter 32 for information on using the Collect and Paste feature, which takes advantage of the Clipboard task pane.

Chapter 7

Spell It Write

· ·

In This Chapter

▶ Dealing with typos and spelling errors

▶ Adding or ignoring unknown words

▶ Correcting words automatically

▶ Checking AutoCorrect settings

▶ Fixing grammatical boo-boos

▶ Reviewing your document

▶ Customizing proofing options

· ·

Spell checking is a feature forced upon Word, and I know who to blame. Historically, the notion of proper English spelling wasn't considered a necessity. That was, until Noah Webster developed the dictionary. Thanks, pal.

Actually, I'm doing Webster a disservice. He fixed a lot of English spelling that would truly drive you batty. So he's not to blame. Regardless, Word offers kind and subtle spell and grammar checking. Use it or suffer the consekwensis.

Check Your Spelling

Word's spell-check feature works the second you start typing. Offending or unknown words are immediately underlined with the red zigzag of shame. Leave the word be, correct it, or add it to your own dictionary just to spite Mr. Webster.

✔ Spell checking works thanks to a digital dictionary stocked with zillions of words, all spelled correctly. Every time you type a word, it's checked against that dictionary. When the word isn't found, it's marked as suspect in your document.

✔ Don't let the red zigzag of a failed elementary education perturb you. My advice is to keep typing. Focus on getting your thoughts on the page. Go back later to fix the inevitable typos.

✔ The spell-check feature also flags repeated words by underlining them with a red zigzag. Your choice is to either delete the repeated word or just ignore it.

✔ Word doesn't spell-check certain types of words, such as words with numbers in them or words written in all capitals, which are usually abbreviations.

✔ To disable automatic spell checking, see the section, "Spell-check and grammar settings."

✔ An alternative to on-the-fly spell checking is to perform a manual spell check. See the section, "All-at-Once Document Proofing."

Fixing a misspelled word

Don't let that red zigzag of shame vex you any longer! Follow these steps:

1. **Right-click the misspelled word.**

   Up pops a shortcut menu, as shown in Figure 7-1.

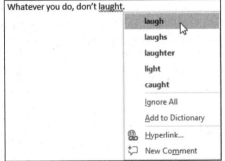

Figure 7-1:
Deal with
that typo.

2. **Choose from the list the word you intended to type.**

   In Figure 7-1, the word *laugh* fits the bill. Click that word and it replaces the spurious word.

If the word you intended to type isn't on the list, don't fret: Just take another stab at spelling the word phonetically and then correct it again. Or, what the hey: Use a traditional dictionary (the paper kind).

Yew right grate

Word's document-proofing tools are as technologically advanced as the programmers at Microsoft can make them. As the title of this sidebar suggests, however, there's something to be said about context.

Just because your document appears to contain no errors doesn't mean that everything is perfect. You have no better way to proof a document than to read it with human eyes.

Dealing with incorrectly flagged words

Occasionally, Word's spell checker bumps into a word it doesn't recognize, such as your last name or perhaps your city. Word dutifully casts doubt on the word by underlining it with the notorious red zigzag. Yes, this is one of those cases where the computer is wrong.

To correct the incorrect spell check, right-click the word. Choose one of two options on the shortcut menu (shown earlier in Figure 7-1):

Ignore All: Select this command when the word is properly spelled and you don't want Word to keep flagging it as misspelled in the current document.

Add to Dictionary: This command adds the word to a custom dictionary. The word is no longer flagged as misspelled in the current document or any other documents.

If the word is intentionally misspelled and you don't want to ignore all instances or add it to the custom dictionary, just leave it be.

- ✔ See the section, "Undoing the Ignore All command," later in this chapter, for information on reversing your decision to ignore a spelling error.
- ✔ For information on viewing or editing the custom dictionary, see the section, "Customizing the custom dictionary."

The 25 most frequently misspelled words

a lot	atheist	gauge	maneuver	ridiculous
accidentally	collectible	grammar	no one	separate
acquire	consensus	independent	occurrence	supersede
amateur	definite	kernel	realize	their
argument	embarrass	liaison	receive	weird

AutoCorrect in Action

Sometimes you may never see the embarrassing red zigzag. That's because Word quickly fixes hundreds of common typos and spelling errors on-the-fly. The AutoCorrect feature is responsible, and you have to be quick to see it.

For example, in Word you can't type the word *mispell* (with only one *s*). That's because AutoCorrect fixes that typo the split second that you press the spacebar.

AutoCorrect also converts common text shortcuts into their proper characters. For example, type **(C)** and AutoCorrect properly inserts the © copyright symbol. Ditto for **(TM)** for the trademark. Typing --> is translated into an arrow, and even **:)** becomes a happy face.

Beyond spelling, AutoCorrect fixes common punctuation. It automatically capitalizes the first letter of a sentence. AutoCorrect capitalizes *I* when you forget to, properly capitalizes the names of days, fixes the iNVERSE cAPS lOCK pROBLEM, plus other common typos.

Undoing an AutoCorrect correction

You can reverse AutoCorrect instant changes, but only when you're quick. The secret is to press Ctrl+Z (the Undo command) immediately after AutoCorrect makes its correction. The change is gone.

Even when you're not quick with the Undo command, you can peruse AutoCorrect changes. These are flagged by a blue rectangle that appears under the corrected text's first letter, as shown in Figure 7-2. Position the mouse pointer at that rectangle, and click to see various AutoCorrect options, also illustrated in Figure 7-2.

Point the mouse pointer

Blue rectangle/AutoCorrect hint

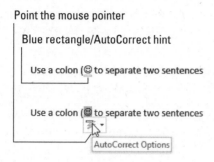

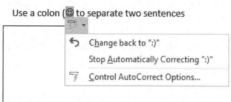

Click to display the menu

To restore the text to how it was typed originally, choose the option Change Back to *whatever*, where *whatever* is the original text, such as :) shown in Figure 7-2.

To prevent AutoCorrect from ever making the change again, choose the option Stop Automatically Correcting *whatever*. Although the text won't be corrected, it may still show up as a typo or a spelling error.

See the next section for information on the final option, Control AutoCorrect Options.

Adjusting AutoCorrect settings

To control how AutoCorrect behaves, as well as review — or even add — words it corrects, follow these steps:

1. **Click the File tab.**

2. **Choose Options.**

   The Word Options dialog box appears.

3. **Click the Proofing category on the left side of the window.**

4. **Click the AutoCorrect Options button.**

   The AutoCorrect dialog box appears, with the AutoCorrect tab forward.

The AutoCorrect tab lists all problems that AutoCorrect fixes for you, plus common typo corrections. That's also where you can remove the AutoCorrect entries you detest:

To remove an entry in the AutoCorrect list, scroll to find that item, such as :) for the happy face. Click to select the entry, and then click the Delete button.

To add an entry, use the Replace and With text boxes. For example, to replace *kludge* with *kluge*, type **kludge** in the Replace box and **kluge** in the With box.

Click the OK button when you're done making adjustments, and then close the Word Options dialog box.

Also see Chapter 33 for information on disabling various AutoCorrect and AutoFormat features.

Grammar Be Good

Mark Twain once referred to English spelling as "drunken." If that's true, English grammar must be a hallucination. To help you to detox, Word offers on-the-fly grammar checking. It's just like having your eighth-grade English teacher inside your computer — only it's all the time and not just during third period.

Word's grammar checker works like the spell checker. The main difference is that offenses are underlined with a blue zigzag, such as the one shown in Figure 7-3 (although the zigzag looks gray in this book). That's your hint of Word's sense of grammatical justice. Even then, the offense is most likely mild and, given the illusionary nature of English grammar, can probably be ignored.

Right-click the grammatical error

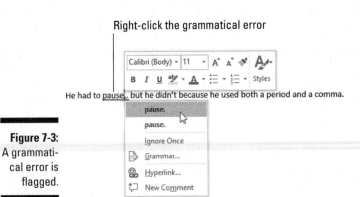

Figure 7-3:
A grammatical error is flagged.

To address a grammar issue, right-click the blue-underlined text, as shown in Figure 7-3. Use the pop-up menu to discover what's wrong or to choose an alternative suggestion. You also have the option to ignore the error, which I find myself using quite often.

- ✔ The most common source of grammatical woe in English is verb agreement, or matching the subject to the correct verb.

- ✔ The grammar checker is excellent at spotting two spaces between words when you need only one space. It's not so good at spotting fragments.

- ✔ You may see false grammar errors when using Word's revision-tracking feature while the No Markup setting is enabled. Reveal all the revision marks to see what's up. Refer to Chapter 26 for details.

- ✔ You can customize or even turn off grammar checking. Refer to the sections "Disabling automatic spell check" and "Curtailing grammar checking," later in this chapter.

All-at-Once Document Proofing

If you prefer to ignore the red zigzag underline of shame, or perhaps you've disabled that feature, you can resort to performing a final document proof. It's an all-in-one spelling- and grammar-checking process, which is how spell check worked before it became an on-the-fly feature.

To perform all-at-once document proofing, follow these steps:

1. **Click the Review tab.**

2. **In the Proofing group, click the Spelling & Grammar button.**

   Errors are shown one at a time as they occur in your document. You must deal with them sequentially.

3. **Deal with the offense.**

   Depending on the offense, either the Spelling pane or Grammar pane appears. Options presented let you deal with each offense:

   - **Ignore:** Click this button to ignore the error once. You will be reminded of the same spelling error or similar grammatical errors again.

   - **Ignore All:** Use this button to direct Word to merrily skip the spelling error through the entire document.

   - **Add:** Use this button to thrust the word into the custom dictionary. It won't be flagged as incorrect ever again. Well, unless you edit the dictionary, as described elsewhere in this chapter.

- **Change:** For spelling boo-boos and grammatical flubs, click to select a correct option from the list presented and then click the Change button to replace the offending text.

- **Change All.** For spelling errors only, click the correct word and then click Change All to replace all instances of your spelling mistake.

4. **Continue checking your document.**

5. **Click the OK button once the checking is done.**

You can easily enter a trancelike state while you're document proofing. You might find yourself clicking the Ignore button too quickly. My advice: Use the Undo command, Ctrl+Z. It lets you go back and change text that you may not have paid attention to.

✔ Another way to sequentially peruse spelling and grammar errors is to use the Spelling and Grammar Check button on the status bar (shown in the margin). To proof your document, click that button to hop from one spelling or grammar error to the next.

✔ Word disables its on-the-fly proofing when your document grows larger than a certain size, say 100 pages. You'll see a warning message when this change happens. At that point, you must perform an all-at-once document check, as described in this section.

Spell Check and Grammar Settings

Whether you adore or detest Word's capability to ridicule your language abilities, you have the final say-so. Plenty of settings and options are available to control Word's spelling- and grammar-checking tools.

Undoing the Ignore All command

Whoops! I've done it too: Clicked that Ignore All command when, in fact, Word was correct and my spelling was all wrong. Now that horribly misspelled word litters my document like the pox.

Fret not, gentle reader. You can undo the Ignore All spelling directive. Follow these steps:

1. **Click the File tab.**

2. **Choose the Options command.**

The Word Options dialog box appears.

3. **Choose Proofing on the left side of the dialog box.**

4. **Click the Recheck Document button.**

   A warning dialog box appears, reminding you of what you're about to do.

5. **Click the Yes button.**

   Everything you've told Word to ignore while proofing your document is now ignored.

6. **Click the OK button to close the Word Options dialog box and return to your document.**

The Ignore All command affects only the current document. If you've accidentally added a word to the custom dictionary, see the next section.

Customizing the custom dictionary

You build the custom dictionary by adding properly spelled words that are flagged as misspelled. You can also manually add words, remove words, or just browse the dictionary to see whether or not you're making old Noah Webster jealous. Follow these steps:

1. **Click the File tab.**

2. **Choose Options to display the Word Options dialog box.**

3. **Choose Proofing.**

4. **Click the Custom Dictionaries button.**

   The Custom Dictionaries dialog box appears.

   Word 2016 uses the RoamingCustom.dic file as the custom dictionary. You may see other files in the list, especially if you've upgraded from older versions of Microsoft Word.

5. **Select the item RoamingCustom.dic (Default).**

6. **Click the button labeled Edit Word List.**

   You see a scrolling list of words you've added to the custom dictionary.

To add a word to the custom dictionary, type it in the Word(s) text box. Click the Add button.

To remove a word from the custom dictionary, select the word from the scrolling list. Click the Delete button.

Click the OK button when you're done with the custom dictionary. Then click the OK button to close the Word Options dialog box.

Disabling automatic spell check

To banish the red zigzag underline from your document, which effectively disables on-the-fly spell checking, follow these steps:

1. **Click the File tab and choose Options.**

   The Word Options dialog box appears.

2. **On the left side of the dialog box, choose Proofing.**

3. **Remove the check mark by the item Check Spelling as You Type.**

4. **Click the OK button.**

If you also want to banish the blue zigzag of messed-up grammar, repeat these steps but in Step 3 remove the check mark by the item Mark Grammar Errors as You Type.

Curtailing grammar checking

I find Word's grammar checker to be insistently incorrect. After all, English is fluid. Especially if you're writing poetry or you just know the rules and prefer to bend them or toss them asunder, consider throttling back some of Word's more aggressive grammar flags.

To adjust grammar settings, follow these steps:

1. **Click the File tab.**

2. **Choose Options to display the Word Options dialog box.**

3. **Choose Proofing.**

4. **By the Writing Style item, click the Settings button.**

   The Grammar Settings dialog box appears.

5. **Uncheck those items you no longer desire Word to mark as offensive.**

   The categories are pretty general, which makes deselecting a rule difficult. That's because when Word flags a grammar error, you see a specific rule and not the general ones listed in the Grammar Settings dialog box.

6. **Click the OK button to dismiss the Grammar Settings dialog box.**

7. **Click OK to close the Word Options dialog box.**

If you prefer to disable all the rules, instead deactivate grammar checking altogether. See the preceding section.

Chapter 8

Documents New, Saved, Opened, and Closed

In This Chapter

▶ Understanding terms

▶ Creating a new document

▶ Saving documents

▶ Updating (resaving) a document

▶ Opening a document

▶ Inserting one document inside another

▶ Retrieving a lost document

I like the word *document*. It's elegant. It's much better than saying "a file" or "that thing I created with my word processor." A document could include everything from a quick shopping list to a vast cycle of medieval fantasy novels you keep reading despite knowing that your favorite protagonist will die a sudden, horrific death.

Regardless of size or importance, a word-processing file is called a *document*. It's the end result of your efforts in Word. You create new documents, save them, open up old documents, and close documents. That's the document cycle.

Some Terms to Get Out of the Way

To best understand the document concept, you must escape the confines of Word and wander into the larger dominion of computer storage. A basic understanding of files and storage is necessary if you're to get the most from your word-processing efforts.

File: A Word document is a file. A *file* contains information stored for the long term, which can be recalled again and shared with others. Windows manages files and their storage, backup, copying, moving, and renaming.

Folder: Files dwell in containers called folders. A *folder* is nothing more than storage for various files, although folders play a role in how files are organized.

Local storage: The file crated when you save a document must be kept somewhere for the long term. When it's saved on your computer's hard drive, it's kept on local storage. Because some computers use a solid-state drive (SSD) instead of a hard drive, the term *local storage* is used instead of hard drive or disk drive.

Cloud storage: Also available for saving documents is storage available on the Internet, commonly referred to as *cloud storage.* Specifically, Word is integrated to use Microsoft's OneDrive cloud storage. Files saved to cloud storage are available to your computer and also to any computer connected to the Internet. Yes, you need to log into the cloud storage; not just anyone can pilfer your files.

You can use other cloud storage services with Word, such as Dropbox or Google Drive. These locations are accessed through their shadow copies on local storage.

Behold! A New Document

To summon a new document, click the Blank Document template thumbnail found on the Word Start screen. Or if the Start screen has been disabled (per the directions in Chapter 33), Word starts by displaying a blank document.

After Word has started, you can summon a new document by obeying these steps:

1. **Click the File tab.**

   The File screen appears.

2. **Choose the New command from the left side of the window.**

   The New screen lists the same templates that appear on the Start screen. Category tabs are Featured and Personal for Word's templates and your own templates, respectively.

3. **Click the Blank Document thumbnail.**

   A new Word window appears and you see a blank page, ready for typing.

How long can a Word document be?

The quick answer is that no length limit is assigned to a Word document. If you like, your document can be thousands of pages long. Even so, I don't recommend putting that limit to the test.

The longer a document, the more apt Word is to screw up. For most documents, the length is fine. For larger projects, however, I recommend splitting your work into chapter-sized chunks. Organize those chapter documents in their own folder.

To stitch together several documents into a larger document, use Word's master document feature, as described in Chapter 25.

Ah, the shortcut: Press Ctrl+N to quickly summon a new, blank document in Word.

- ✔ You can produce as many new documents as are needed. Word lets you work with several documents at a time. See Chapter 24 for information on multiple-document mania.
- ✔ Refer to Chapter 1 for information on the Word Start screen.
- ✔ Refer to Chapter 16 for information on templates.

Save Your Stuff!

It doesn't matter whether you're writing the next Great American Novel or you're jotting down notes for tonight's PTA meeting, the most important thing you can do to a document is *save it*.

Save! Save! Save!

Saving creates a permanent copy of your document, encoding your text as a file on the computer's storage system. That way, you can work on the document again, publish it electronically, or have a copy ready in case the power goes *poof*. All these tasks require saving.

Saving a document the first time

Don't think that you have to wait until you finish a document to save it. In fact, you should save almost immediately — as soon as you have a few sentences or paragraphs.

To save a document for the first time, follow these steps:

1. Click the File tab.

2. Choose the Save As command.

The Save As screen appears, similar to the one shown in Figure 8-1. This screen is part of Word's Backstage, which is an alternative to the traditional Windows Save As dialog box.

3. Choose a location for the document.

To use local storage, choose This PC.

To use cloud storage on OneDrive, choose OneDrive.

A list of recent folders appears on the right side of the screen. Click a folder to choose it as the storage location.

After choosing a location, the traditional Save As dialog box appears. Or you can quickly summon that dialog box by clicking the Browse button, as illustrated in Figure 8-1.

If the specific folder you need wasn't shown on the Save As screen, use the Save As dialog box to navigate to that folder — or create a folder by clicking the New Folder button in that dialog box.

Locations to save your document · · · · · · Choose a recent folder

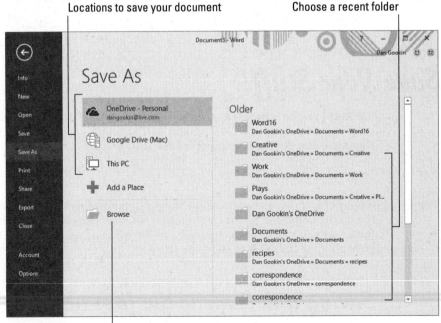

Figure 8-1:
The Save As screen.

Summon the traditional Save As dialog box

4. Type a name for your document in the File Name box.

Word automatically selects the first several words of your document as a filename and places that text in the File Name box. If that's okay, you can move to Step 5. Otherwise, type a better name.

Be descriptive! The more concisely you name your document, the easier it is to recognize it by that name in the future.

5. Click the Save button.

The file is now safely stored.

The document doesn't close after you save. You don't need to quit Word. You can keep working.

As you work, continue to save. See the section "Saving or updating a document."

✔ You can skip the File tab process by instead clicking the Save button on the Quick Access toolbar. If the document hasn't yet been saved, the Save As screen appears.

✔ Your clue that the document is saved successfully is that its filename appears on the document's title bar, top center of the Word window.

✔ The Save As command can also be used to save a document with a new name, to a different location, or in a different format. See Chapter 24.

✔ Do not save a document to removable media, such as an optical disc or a memory card. Instead, save the document to the computer's main storage device, the hard drive or SSD. If you save to removable media and that media is accidentally removed, you may lose your document or the computer may crash.

✔ To place your document file on removable media, save and close the document. Copy the file from the computer's primary storage to the removable storage. This operation is done in Windows, not Word.

✔ As an alternative to using removable media, save your document to cloud storage. Documents saved to OneDrive can be shared with others. See Chapter 26 for collaboration information.

Dealing with document-save errors

Saving a document involves working with both Word and the Windows operating system. This process doubles the chances of something going wrong, so it's high time for an error message. One such error message is

The file *whatever* already exists

You have three choices:

> ✔ **Replace Existing File:** Nope.
>
> ✔ **Save Changes with a Different Name:** Yep.
>
> ✔ **Merge Changes into Existing File:** Nope.

Choose the middle option and click OK. Type a different filename in the Save As dialog box.

Another common problem occurs when a message that's displayed reads something like this:

> The file name is not valid

That's Word's less-than-cheerful way of telling you that the filename contains a boo-boo character. To be safe, use letters, numbers, and spaces when naming a file. Check the nearby sidebar, "Trivial — but important — information about filenames."

Saving or updating a document

As you continue to work on your document, you should save again. That way, any changes you've made since the last time you saved are recorded on the computer's storage system. Saving a document multiple times keeps it fresh.

Trivial — but important — information about filenames

Be creative in your document, but also be creative when saving the document and christening it with a name. These names must abide by the Windows rules and regulations for all filenames:

✔ A filename can be longer than 200 ridiculous-something characters; even so, keep your filenames short but descriptive.

✔ A filename can include letters, numbers, and spaces, and can start with a letter or a number.

✔ A filename can contain periods, commas, hyphens, and even underlines.

✔ A filename cannot contain any of these characters: \ / : * ? " < > |.

Word automatically appends a *filename extension* to all documents you save — like a last name. You may or may not see the filename extension, depending on how you've configured Windows. Either way, don't type the extension. Only concern yourself with giving the document a proper and descriptive filename.

To resave a document that has already been saved, follow these steps:

1. **Click the File tab.**

2. **Choose the Save command.**

   You get no feedback, and the Save As dialog box doesn't show up. That's because you already gave the file a name; the Save command merely updates the existing file.

 The fastest, and most common, way to save or update a document is to press the Ctrl+S keyboard shortcut. You can also click the Save button on the Quick Access toolbar.

- ✔ I save my documents dozens of times a day — usually when the phone rings, when I need to step away and the cat is lurking too closely to the keyboard, or often when I'm just bored.

- ✔ If you haven't yet saved a document, using the Save command, Ctrl+S, or the Save button on the Quick Access toolbar brings up the Save As screen, as described earlier in this chapter.

Forgetting to save before you quit

When you're done writing in Word, you close the document, close the window, or quit Word outright. No matter how you call it quits, when your document hasn't yet been saved, or was changed since the last save, you're asked to save one last time before leaving.

The warning dialog box that appears when you attempt to leave before saving features three options:

Save: Click this button to save the document and close. If you've been bad and haven't yet saved the document, the Save As screen appears.

Don't Save: When you click this button, the document is closed without saving. It might still be available for later recovery. See the later section, "Recover a Draft."

Cancel: Click this button to forget about saving and return to the document for more editing and stuff.

I recommend that you choose the Save option.

Open a Document

Saving a document means nothing unless you have a way to retrieve that document later. As you might suspect, Word offers multiple ways to *open* a document either on local storage or on cloud storage.

Using the Open command

Open is the standard computer command used to fetch an existing document. Once you find and open the document, it appears in Word's window as though it had always been there.

To open a document in Word, follow these steps:

1. **Click the File tab.**

2. **Choose the Open command.**

   The Open screen materializes, similar to what's shown in Figure 8-2.

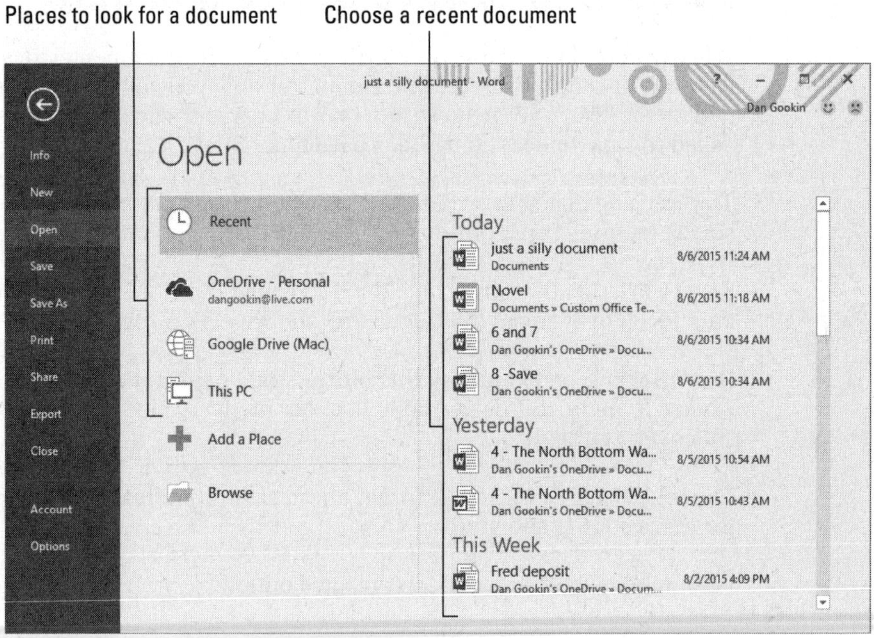

Places to look for a document   Choose a recent document

Figure 8-2:
The Open
screen.

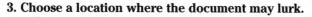

3. **Choose a location where the document may lurk.**

Your choices are Recent Documents, which is shown in Figure 8-2, cloud storage such as OneDrive, or local storage titled This PC.

If you spy the desired document lurking in the Recent list, click it. The document opens on the screen. Congratulations — you're done.

4. **Choose a recent folder from the list.**

5. **Click a document when you find it.**

The document opens, ready for editing.

6. **If you can't find the document, or you just yearn to use the traditional Open dialog box, click the Browse button.**

The traditional Open dialog box appears, which you can use to locate the file you want to open: Click to select the file, and then click the Open button.

The file you open appears in the Word window. Word may highlight the last location where you were writing or editing, along with a *Welcome back* message.

After the document is open, you can edit it, look at it, print it, or do whatever you want.

- ✔ The shortcut key to access the Open screen is Ctrl+O. Also, an Open command button appears on the Quick Access toolbar.

- ✔ You can open a document also by locating its icon in a folder window, which happens in Windows, not in Word. Double-click the icon to open the document. See Chapter 1 for information.

- ✔ To access recently opened documents, right-click the Word icon on the taskbar. Choose a document from the pop-up list (called the *jump list*) to open it.

- ✔ Opening a document doesn't erase it from storage. In fact, the file stays on the storage system until you use the Save command to save and update the document with any changes.

- ✔ When you position the mouse pointer at a recently opened document on the Open screen, you see a pushpin icon, similar to what's shown in the margin. Click that icon to make the document "stick" to the Open screen. That way, it's always available for quick access later.

- ✔ To remove a document from the Recent list, right-click the document's entry. Choose the command Remove from List.

✔ Avoid opening a file on any removable media, such as a digital memory card or an optical disc. Although it's possible, doing so can lead to head-aches later should you remove the media before Word is done with the document. Because of that, I recommend that you use Windows to copy the document from the removable media to the computer's main storage device. Then open it in Word.

Opening one document inside another

It's possible in Word to open one document inside another. Doing so isn't as odd as you'd think. For example, you may have your biography, résumé, or curriculum vitae document and want to add that information to the end of a letter begging for a new job. If so, or in any other circumstances that I can't think of right now, follow these steps:

1. **Position the insertion pointer where you want the other document's text to appear.**

   The text is inserted at that spot.

2. **Click the Insert tab.**

3. **From the Text group, click the Object button.**

   The Object button is shown in the margin. After clicking the button, you see a menu.

4. **Choose the menu item Text from File.**

   The Insert File dialog box appears. It's similar to the Open dialog box.

5. **Locate and select the document you want to insert.**

   Browse through the various folders to find the document icon. Click to select that icon.

6. **Click the Insert button.**

The document's text is inserted into the current document, just as if you had typed and formatted it yourself.

✔ The resulting combined document still has the same name as the first document; the document you inserted remains unchanged.

✔ You can insert any number of documents into another document, one at a time. There's no limit.

✔ Inserting text from one document into another is often called *boilerplating*. For example, you can save a commonly used piece of text in a document and then insert it into other documents as necessary. This process is also the way that sleazy romance novels are written.

✔ Biography. Résumé. Curriculum vitae. The more important you think you are, the more alien the language used to describe what you've done.

Close a Document

When you've finished writing a document, you need to do the electronic equivalent of putting it away. That electronic equivalent is the Close command: Press Ctrl+W.

✔ Because closing a document may also quit Word, more information on this topic is found in Chapter 1, which covers quitting Word.

✔ If you haven't saved your document, you'll be prompted to do so. See the early section, "Forgetting to save before you quit."

Recover a Draft

When you forget to save a document, or the computer crashed, or the power went out, you can recover some — but perhaps not all — of an unsaved document. Valiantly make this attempt:

1. **Press Ctrl+O to summon the Open screen.**

2. **Ensure that Recent is chosen as the file location.**

3. **Click the Recover Unsaved Documents button, found at the bottom of the list of recent files.**

   You may have to scroll the list of recent files a bit to locate the button

   The Open dialog box appears, listing the contents of a special folder, UnsavedFiles. It's Word's graveyard of sorts. Actually, it's more like a morgue in a county with a lousy EMS.

4. **Click to select a document to recover.**

   The document may have an unusual name, especially when it has never been saved.

5. **Click the Open button to open and recover the document.**

The document you recover might not be the one you wanted it to be. If so, try again and choose another document.

You might also find that the recovered document doesn't contain all the text you typed or thought would be there. You can't do anything about it, other than *remembering to save everything* in the first place!

The recovery of drafts is possible because of Word's AutoRecover feature. Refer to Chapter 31 for more information on AutoRecover.

Chapter 9

Publish Your Document

· ·

· ·

*A*fter writing, editing, formatting, and proofing (with lots of document saving along the way), the final step in document preparation is publishing. Don't get all excited: Publishing in Word has nothing to do with seeing your book on the *New York Times* bestseller list (although it could). Publishing is a general topic that includes printing a document to paper but also generating an electronic document you can share online. Times have changed.

Your Document on Paper

The word processor, the best writing tool ever invented. It's also the first writing tool that avoids paper until your document is complete. At that point, if you desire, you can generate a dead-tree version of the document, also called a *printout* or a *hard copy*.

✔ Configuring the printer is done in Windows, not Word. Use the Control Panel or Settings app to control the printer.

✔ I assume that your computer has a printer attached or available on a network and that everything is set up just peachy. That setup includes stocking the printer with ink or toner and plenty of paper.

Previewing before printing

Before you print, preview the look of the final document. Yeah, even though your document is supposed to look the same on the screen as it does on paper, you may still see surprises: missing page numbers, blank pages, screwy headers, and other jaw-dropping blunders, for example.

Fortunately, a print preview of your document appears as part of the Print screen, as shown in Figure 9-1.

To preview your document, follow these steps:

1. Save your document.

Yep — always save. Saving before printing is a good idea.

2. Click the File tab.

3. Chose the Print item from the left side of the File screen.

The Print screen appears, similar to what's shown in Figure 9-1.

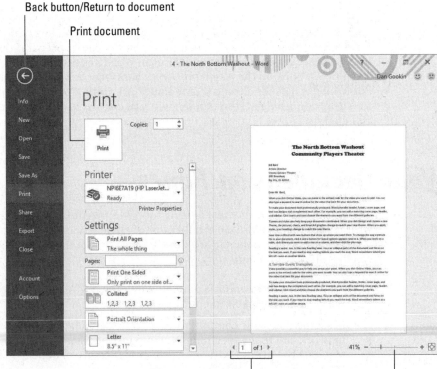

Back button/Return to document

Print document

Page through preview

Zoom control

Figure 9-1:
The Print
screen.

4. Use the buttons at the bottom of the screen to page through your document.

You can use the Zoom control (refer to Figure 9-1) to enlarge or reduce the image. Look at the margins. If you're using footnotes, headers, or footers, look at how they lay out. The idea is to spot anything that's dreadfully wrong *before* you print.

When you're ready, you can print the document. Details are offered in the next section, but basically you click the big Print button, labeled in Figure 9-1. Or when things need to be repaired, click the Back button to return to your document.

Printing the whole document

Printing the document is easy:

1. Make sure that the printer is on and ready to print.

Printing works fastest when the printer is on.

2. Save your document.

Click the little Save button on the Quick Access toolbar for a quickie save.

3. Click the File tab.

4. Choose the Print command from the File tab's window.

The Print screen appears (refer to Figure 9-1).

5. Click the big Print button.

The Print screen closes, and the document spews forth from the printer.

Printing speed depends on the complexity of the document and how dumb the printer is. Fortunately, you can continue working while the document prints.

✔ The keyboard shortcut to display the Print screen (Steps 3 and 4) is Ctrl+P.

✔ Obligatory Ctrl+P joke goes here.

✔ If nothing prints, don't use the Print command again! Most likely nothing is awry; the computer is still thinking or sending information to the printer. If you don't see an error message, everything will probably print, eventually.

Delete that extra blank page at the end of a document

Occasionally, you may be surprised when your document prints one extra page — a blank page. And you're not only bothered because you forgot to preview before printing (which I recommend in this chapter) but also vexed because you cannot get rid of it! Until now.

To remove the ugly, blank page that often roots at the end of your document, press Ctrl+End.

With the insertion pointer at the end of your document, press the Backspace key repeatedly until the extra page is gone. How can you tell? Keep an eye on the total page count on the status bar. When the page count decreases by one, you know that the extra page is gone.

- ✔ The computer prints one copy of your document for every Print command you incant. If the printer is just being slow and you impatiently click the Print button ten times, you'll end up printing ten copies of your document. (See the section "Canceling a print job," later in this chapter.)
- ✔ When the document format specifies a unique paper size, the printer prompts you to load that paper size. Stand by to produce and load the proper paper when the printer prompts you.

Printing a specific page

Follow these steps to print only one page of your document:

1. **Move the insertion pointer so that it's sitting somewhere on the page you want to print.**

   Check the page number on the status bar to ensure that you're on the correct page.

2. **Press Ctrl+P.**

3. **Click the Print Range button below the Settings heading.**

   Refer to Figure 9-2 for the button's location.

4. **Choose Print Current Page from the menu.**

5. **Click the Print button.**

The single page prints with all the formatting you applied, including footnotes and page numbers and everything else, just as though you plucked that page from a complete printing of the entire document.

Print the document   Select the printer

Set the number of copies to print

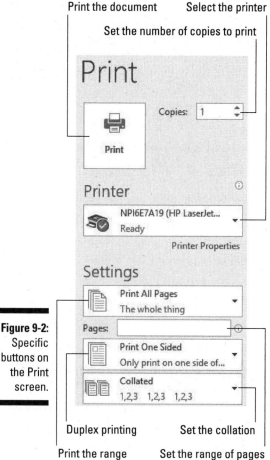

Figure 9-2:
Specific
buttons on
the Print
screen.

Duplex printing   Set the collation

Print the range   Set the range of pages

Printing a single page in this manner is useful when the printer goofs up one page in a document and you need to reprint only that page.

Printing a range of pages

Word enables you to print a range of pages, odd pages, even pages, or a hodgepodge combination of random pages from within your document. To print a range or group of pages, summon the Print screen: Press Ctrl+P.

On the Print screen, look for the Pages text box, illustrated in Figure 9-2. Here are some suggestions for what to type in that text box:

To print pages 3 through 5, type **3-5**.

To print pages 1 through 7, type **1-7**.

To print pages 2 and 6, type **2,6**.

To print page 3, pages 5 through 9, pages 15 through 17, and page 19 (boy, that coffee went everywhere, didn't it?), type **3, 5-9, 15-17, 19**.

Click the big Print button when you're ready to print. Only the pages you specify churn from the printer.

Leave the Pages box blank to print all pages in the document.

Printing on both sides of the page

If your printer is capable of duplex printing, you can direct Word to print your document on both sides of a sheet of paper. If your printer is so blessed, follow these steps:

1. **Press Ctrl+P when you're ready to print the document.**

   I'll assume that the document has just been saved.

2. **Click the Duplex Printing button on the Print screen.**

   Refer to Figure 9-2 for the button's location.

3. **Choose Print on Both Sides, Flip Pages on Long Sides.**

   Don't bother with the Short Sides option unless you plan on binding your document that way.

   If you don't see the Print on Both Sides options, you have to manually print. See the next section.

4. **Make other settings as necessary on the Print screen.**

5. **Click the big Print button to print your document.**

   Both sides of the page are printed.

I've discovered that Word (Windows actually) isn't that smart when it comes to knowing which printers are duplex and which aren't. Alas, when Windows doesn't recognize your duplex printer as such, there's little you can do.

Printing odd and even pages

Say you have a printer that doesn't print on both sides of the page. If so, print all the odd pages in your document. Flip the paper and reinsert it in the printer. Then print all the even pages. The end result is printing on both sides of the page.

Remove the Document Properties sheet

A printing problem that can potentially annoy you is finding the Document Properties sheet printing with your document. This extra sheet of paper prints first, listing information about the document. The Document Properties sheet isn't printed unless its option is set, and for some reason the option gets set on some folks' computers.

To prevent the Document Properties sheet from printing, click the File tab and choose the Options command. In the Word Options dialog box, click the Display item on the left side of the window. In the Printing Options area on the Display screen, remove the check mark by the item Print Document Properties. Click OK.

To print all odd pages or all even pages, follow these steps:

1. **Press Ctrl+P to summon the Print screen.**

2. **Click the Print Range button below the Settings heading.**

   Refer to Figure 9-2 for the button's location.

3. **Choose Only Print Odd Pages from the menu.**

4. **Click the Print button to print odd pages in your document.**

To print even pages, repeat these steps, but in Step 3 choose Only Print Even Pages.

Printing a block

After you mark a block of text in your document, you can beg the Print command to print only that block. Here's how:

1. **Mark the block of text you want to print.**

   See Chapter 6 for all the block-marking instructions in the world.

2. **Press Ctrl+P to summon the Print screen.**

3. **Click the Print Range button below the Settings heading.**

4. **From the menu, choose the item Print Selection.**

   The Print Selection item is available only when a block is selected in your document.

5. **Click the Print button.**

The block you selected prints at the same position, with the same formatting (headers and footers) as though you had printed the entire document.

Printing more than one copy of something

When it comes time to provide a copy of your report to all five members of the cult and the photocopier is broken, just print multiple copies. Here's how:

1. **Press Ctrl+P on the keyboard to summon the Print screen.**

2. **Enter the number of copies in the Copies text box.**

   To print five copies, for example, click the box and type **5**.

3. **Click the big Print button to print your copies.**

Under normal circumstances, Word prints each copy of the document one after the other. This process is known as *collating*. However, if you're printing five copies of a document and you want Word to print seven copies of page 1 and then seven copies of page 2 (and so on), choose the option Uncollated from the Collated menu button, found under the Settings heading on the Print screen.

Choosing another printer

When the computer has more than one printer available, ensure that you're using the proper one. Or perhaps you want to use another printer, such as that fancy color printer that is available on the network even though Ed has hidden it in his office. Either way, follow these steps:

1. **Press Ctrl+P to summon the Print screen.**

2. **Click the Select Printer button below the Printer heading.**

   The button shows the name of the currently selected printer, which is usually the one set by Windows as the default.

3. **Choose another printer from the list.**

4. **Click the Print button to print your document on the selected printer.**

Unfortunately, not every printer features a clear and descriptive name.

Also, not every printer listed is a physical printer. Some are document printers, such as Microsoft Print to PDF, which is covered later in this chapter.

Adding and managing printers falls under the domain of Windows, not Word. To add printers, rename them, or set the default printer, use Windows.

Canceling a print job

The fastest, easiest way to cancel a print job is to rush up to the printer and set it on fire. Lamentably, this method is frequently met with frowns by local fire officials.

If your printer features a Cancel button, use it to stop a print job run amok. The Cancel button typically features an X, often colored red. Touch that button, and the printer stops — maybe not at once, but the button cancels the rest of the document from printing.

For slow printers, or those without a Cancel button, you can attempt to use Windows to halt a print job run amok. Obey these steps

1. **Look on the far right end of the taskbar for the li'l printer icon.**

   If you don't see the li'l printer icon, it's too late to cancel the print job. Otherwise, you see the printer's control window, which lists any queued printing jobs.

2. **Click the name of your Word document job in the list.**

3. **Choose either the Document⇨Cancel command or the Document⇨Cancel Printing command.**

4. **Click Yes or OK to terminate the job.**

5. **Close the printer's control window.**

This method frequently meets with failure simply because the printer is fast and working these steps takes time. Still, it's worth a try, especially when the printer lacks a Cancel button.

✔ It may take a while for the printer to stop printing. That's because print-ers have their own memory, and a few pages of the document may be stored *and* continue to print even after you tell the printer to stop.

✔ Stopping a print job is a Windows task, not one that Word has control over.

Electronically Publishing Your Document

Not every document needs to hit paper. For example, I never print my books. They're sent electronically to the publisher and even edited right on the screen. eBooks don't need to be printed. And sometimes documents can be more effectively distributed by email than any other means. It's all part of electronically publishing your document.

Preparing a document for sharing

Lots of interesting things can be put in your Word document that you don't want published. These items include comments, revision marks, hidden text, and other items useful to you or your collaborators, which would mess up a document you share with others. The solution is to use Word's Check for Issues tool, like this:

1. **Ensure that your document is finished, finalized, and saved.**

2. **Click the File tab.**

   On the File screen, the Info area should be selected. If not, click the word Info.

3. **Click the Check for Issues button.**

4. **Choose Inspect Document.**

   The Document Inspector window shows up. All items are selected.

5. **Click the Inspect button.**

   After a few moments, the Document Inspector window shows up again, listing any issues with your document. The issues shown are explained, which allows you to cancel the Document Inspector to fix individual items.

6. **(Optional) Click the Remove All button next to any issues you want to clear up.**

   Now that you know what the issues are, you can always click the Close button and return to your document to manually inspect them.

7. **Click the Close button, or click Reinspect to give your document another once-over.**

You can go forward with publishing your document or continue working.

Sending a Word document via email

Emailing your Word document is a snap — as long as you're using Microsoft Outlook as your email program. If not, you need to save your document as you normally would, and then use your email program (which isn't Outlook) to create a new message with the document chosen as a file attachment.

If you do use Outlook as your email program, and it's all set up and actually works, follow these steps in Word to send a document via email:

1. **Save your document one more time.**

2. **Click the File tab.**

3. **Choose the Share command.**

4. **Choose the E-Mail item found under the Share heading.**

5. **Click the Send As Attachment button.**

   At this point, Outlook takes over and you compose your email message. When you send the message, your Word document is sent along as well.

Documents saved to your OneDrive cloud storage can be shared with others on the Internet. See chapter 26 for details.

Making a PDF

Word document files are considered a standard. Therefore, it's perfectly acceptable to send one of your document files as an email attachment or make it available for sharing on cloud storage.

It's also possible to save your document in the Adobe Acrobat document format, also known as a PDF file. This type of electronic publishing is secretly a form of printing your document. Obey these steps:

1. **Finish your document.**

   Yes, that includes saving it one last time.

2. **Press Ctrl+P to summon the Print screen.**

3. **Click the Printer button.**

   A list of available printers appears.

4. **Choose Microsoft Print to PDF.**

5. **Click the Print button.**

   Nothing is printed on paper, but the document is "printed" to a new PDF file. That requires the use of the special Save Print Output As dialog box.

6. **Choose a location for the PDF file.**

   Use the dialog box's controls to locate the proper folder.

7. **Type a filename.**

8. **Click the Save button.**

The PDF file is created. The original document remains in the Word window, unchanged by the print-to-PDF operation.

You need a copy of the Adobe Reader program to view PDF files. Don't worry: It's free. Go to get.adobe.com/reader.

Exporting your document

Beyond the Word document format and PDF, you can export your document into other, common file formats. These formats allow for easy document sharing, although they're not as common as they once were.

To export your document into another file format, follow these steps:

1. **Click the File tab.**

2. **Choose Export from the items on the left side of the screen.**

3. **Choose Change File Type.**

   A list of available file types appears on the right side of the screen. These types include Word formats and other file types such as Plain Text, Rich Text Format (RTF), and web page (HTML).

4. **Click to select a file type.**

5. **Click the Save As icon.**

   You may have to scroll down the list to find the Save As icon.

   The Save As dialog box appears. It's the same Save As dialog box as covered in Chapter 8, although the Save As Type menu lists the file type you selected in Step 3.

6. **Work the dialog box to set a folder or other location for the file, or to change its name.**

7. **Click the Save button to export the document by using the alien file type.**

   It may look like the document hasn't changed, but it has! The title bar now specifies that you're working on the exported document, not the original Word document.

8. **Close the document.**

   Press Ctrl+W or otherwise dismiss the document.

By closing the document, you ensure that any changes you make aren't made to the exported copy. To continue working on the original document, open it again in Word.

Part III
Fun with Formatting

Text Effects menu

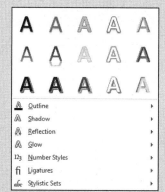

Format Text Effects dialog box
Fill & Outline

Format Text Effects dialog box
Text Effects

In this part . . .

- ✔ Learn how to format your characters by choosing a font, text size, and color.

- ✔ Apply paragraph formats, including line spacing, space before and after, and indenting.

- ✔ Get to know the ruler and all the ways you can use tabs to align your text.

- ✔ Find out how to change page size, orientation, and margins.

- ✔ Get familiar with adding headers, footers, and cover pages.

- ✔ Learn all you need to know about creating and applying styles and using templates.

Chapter 10

Character Formatting

*A*t the atomic level, the most basic element you can format in a document is text — the letters, numbers, and characters you type. You can format text to be bold, underlined, italicized, small or large, in different fonts or colors, and all sorts of pretty and distracting attributes. Word gives you a magnificent amount of control over the appearance of your text.

Text-Formatting Techniques

You can format text in a document in two ways:

✔ Use text-formatting commands as you type, turning them on or off.

✔ Type the text first. Go back and select the text to format. Apply the format.

Either method works, although I recommend you concentrate on your writing first and return to format later.

As an example, suppose you wanted to write and format the following sentence:

```
His toe was really swollen.
```

The first way to format is to type the sentence until the word *really*. Press Ctrl+I to apply the italic format. Type the word. Press Ctrl+I again to turn off the format. Continue typing.

The way I formatted the sentence was to type the entire thing first. Once done, I double-clicked the word *really* to select it, and then pressed Ctrl+I to apply the italic format.

See Chapter 6 for more information on marking blocks of text.

Basic Text Formats

Word stores the most common text-formatting commands on the Home tab, in the Font group, as shown in Figure 10-1.

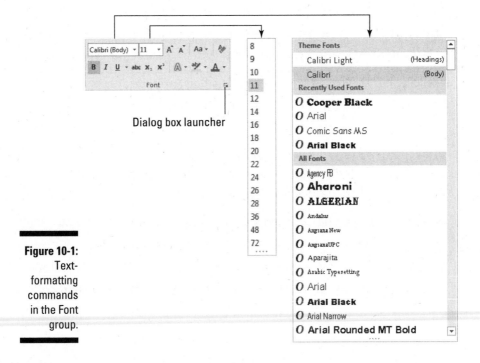

Figure 10-1:
Text-
formatting
commands
in the Font
group.

The Font group's gizmos not only control the text format but also describe the format for currently selected text. So in Figure 10-1, the text format uses the font Calibri, the text size is 11 points, and the Bold attribute is set.

In addition to the Home tab's Font group, text-formatting commands are available on the mini toolbar. It appears whenever text is selected, as described in Chapter 6.

Choosing a font

The base attribute of text is its *typeface,* or *font*. The font sets the way your text looks and its overall style. Although choosing the best font can be ago-nizing (and, indeed, many graphic artists are paid well to choose just the right font), the process isn't too difficult. It generally goes like this:

1. **Click the Home tab.**

2. **In the Font group, click the down arrow by the Font item.**

   A list of fonts appears, similar to what's shown on the right in Figure 10-1.

3. **Select a font.**

   As you point the mouse pointer at a font, text in the document changes to preview the font. Click to choose the font and change the text format.

The Font menu is organized to help you locate the font you need. The top part of the menu lists fonts associated with the document theme. The next section contains fonts you've chosen recently, which is handy for reusing fonts. The rest of the list, which can be quite long, shows all fonts available to Word. The fonts appear in alphabetical order and are displayed as they would appear in the document.

- ✔ To quickly scroll to a specific part of the Font menu, type the first letter of the font you need. For example, type T to find Times New Roman.

- ✔ If you know the exact font name, you can type it in the Font text box, which seems like a horrifically nerdy thing to do.

- ✔ When a font name doesn't appear the Font group (the text box is blank), it means that more than one font is selected in the document.

- ✔ Refer to Chapter 16 for more information on document themes.

- ✔ Fonts are the responsibility of Windows, not Word. Thousands of fonts are available for Windows, and they work in all Windows applications.

✔ Graphic designers prefer to use two fonts in a document — one for the text and one for titles. Word is configured this way as well. The Body font is set for text. The Heading font is set for titles. These two fonts are set as part of the document theme.

Applying character formats

On the lower left side of the Font group you find some of the most common character formats. These formats enhance the selected font or typeface.

B To make text bold, press Ctrl+B or click the Bold command button.

Use **bold** to make text stand out on a page — for titles and captions or when you're uncontrollably angry.

I To make text italic, press Ctrl+I or click the Italic command button.

Italic has replaced underlining as the preferred text-emphasis format. Italicized text is light and wispy, poetic, and free.

<u>U</u> Underline text by pressing Ctrl+U or clicking the Underline command button. You can click the down arrow next to the Underline command button to choose from a variety of underline styles or set an underline color.

The double-underline format is available from the Underline command button's menu, but it does have a keyboard shortcut: Ctrl+Shift+D.

Also available is word-underlining format. <u>Word</u> <u>underlining</u> <u>looks</u> <u>like</u> <u>this</u>. The keyboard shortcut is Ctrl+Shift+W.

a̶b̶c̶ Strike through text by clicking the Strikethrough command button. (A keyboard shortcut is unavailable.)

I don't know why strikethrough text made it to the Font group. If I were king of Microsoft, I would have put small caps up there instead. But who am I? Strikethrough is commonly used in legal documents, when you mean to say something but then ~~change your mind~~ think of something better to say.

X_2 Click the Subscript command button to make text subscript. The keyboard shortcut is Ctrl+= (equal sign).

Subscript text appears below the baseline, such as the 2 in H_2O.

X^2 To make text superscript, click the Superscript command button. The keyboard shortcut is Ctrl+Shift+= (equal sign), which is the shifted version of the subscript keyboard shortcut.

Superscript text appears above the line, such as the 10 in 2^{10}.

Another popular format, but apparently not popular enough to sport a command button in the Fonts group, is small caps. The small caps keyboard shortcut is Ctrl+Shift+K.

Small caps formatting is ideal for headings. I use it for character names when I write a script or play:

> BILL. That's a clever way to smuggle a live grenade into prison.

The All Caps text format sets the text to uppercase letters only. As with small caps, this format doesn't feature a command button, although it has a shortcut key: Ctrl+Shift+A.

To find all these text formats and more, open the Font dialog box. Refer to the section "Behold the Font Dialog Box," later in this chapter.

✔ All character formats work like a toggle switch. Use the command to apply a text format. Use the same command again to remove that format.

✔ Text-formatting commands affect text as you type. They can also be applied to a block of text.

✔ More than one character format can be applied at a time to any text. For example, use Ctrl+B and then Ctrl+I to apply bold and italic formats.

✔ The best way to use superscript or subscript is to write text first and then apply the superscript or subscript format to selected text. So 42 becomes 4^2 and CnH2n+1OH becomes $C_nH_{2n+1}OH$. If you apply superscript or subscript as you type, the text tends to be difficult to edit.

✔ When will the Underline text attribute die? I'm baffled. Honestly, I think we're waiting for the last typewriter-clutching librarian from the 1950s to pass on before underlining is officially gone as a text attribute. And please don't fall prey to the old rule about underlining book titles. It's *Crime and Punishment,* not <u>Crime and Punishment.</u>

Text Transcending Teensy to Titanic

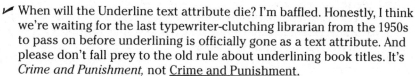

Text size is set in your document based on the ancient typesetter measurement known as *points*. One point is equal to $\frac{1}{72}$ inch. Although that value is mysterious and fun, don't bother committing it to memory. Instead, here are some point pointers:

✔ The bigger the point size, the larger the text.

✔ Most printed text is either 10 or 12 points tall.

✔ Headings are typically 14 to 24 points tall.

✔ In Word, fonts can be sized from 1 point to 1,638 points. Point sizes smaller than 6 are generally too small for a human to read.

✔ A 1-inch-high letter is roughly 72 points.

✔ The point size of text is a measure from the bottom of the descender to the top of the ascender, such as from the bottom of the lowercase *p* to the top of the capital *E*. So the typical letter in a font is smaller than its given point size. In fact, depending on the font design, text formatted at the same size but with different fonts *(typefaces)* doesn't appear to be the same size. It's just one of those typesetting oddities that causes regular computer users to start binge drinking.

Setting the text size

To set the size of text you're about to type, or text in a selected block, heed these steps:

1. **Click the Home tab.**

2. **In the Font group, click the down arrow next to the Font Size box.**

   A menu of font sizes appears, as shown in the center in Figure 10-1.

3. **Choose a font size.**

   As you point the mouse pointer at various values, text in the document (an individual word or a selected block) changes to reflect the size. Click to set the size.

The Size menu lists only common text sizes. To set the text size to a specific value, type the value in the box. For example, to set the font size to 11.5, click in the Size box and type **11.5**.

Nudging text size

Rare is the student who hasn't fudged the length of a term paper by inching up the text size a notch or two. To accommodate those students, or anyone else trying to set text size visually, Word offers two command buttons in the Home tab's Font group.

 To increase the font size, click the Increase Font Size command button. The keyboard shortcut is Ctrl+Shift+>.

The Increase Font Size command nudges the font size up to the next value as listed on the Size menu (refer to Figure 10-1). So if the text is 12 points, the command increases its size to 14 points.

 To decrease the font size, click the Decrease Font Size command button. Its keyboard shortcut is Ctrl+Shift+<.

The Decrease Font Size command works in the opposite direction of the Increase Font Size command: It reduces text size to the next-lower value displayed on the Size menu (refer to Figure 10-1).

 To remember the text size keyboard shortcuts, think of the less-than and greater-than symbols. To make the text size greater than the current size, use the Ctrl+Shift+> shortcut. To make the text size less than its current size, use Ctrl+Shift+<.

To increase or decrease the font size by smaller increments, use these shortcut keys:

Ctrl+]   Makes text one point size larger
Ctrl+[Makes text one point size smaller

More Colorful Text

Adding color to your text doesn't make your writing more colorful. All it does is make you wish that you had more color ink when it's time to print your document. Regardless, you can splash color on your text, without the need to place a drop cloth below the computer.

Coloring the text

To change the color of text in a document, follow these steps:

1. **Click the Home tab.**

 2. **In the Font group, click the Font Color command button.**

The current word, any selected text, or any new text you type is assigned the button's color.

The Font Color button shows which color it assigns to text. To change the color, click the menu triangle to the button's left and choose a color from the menu displayed.

- ✔ To restore the font color, choose Automatic from the Font Color menu. The Automatic color is set by the text style. See Chapter 15 for details on styles.

- ✔ Theme colors are associated with the document theme. Refer to Chapter 16.

- ✔ To craft your own, custom colors, select the More Colors item from the Font Color menu to display the Colors dialog box.

- ✔ The printer companies would love it if you'd use more colored text in your documents. Remember: Colored text works only on a color printer, so buy more ink!

- ✔ Avoid using faint colors for a font, which can make text extremely difficult to read.

- ✔ Don't confuse the Font Color command button with the Text Highlight Color command button, to its left. Text highlighting is used for document markup, as described in Chapter 26.

Shading the background

To set the text background color, use the Shading command. Follow these steps:

1. **Click the Home tab.**

2. **In the Paragraph group, click the Shading command button.**

   The color shown on the button shades the current word or selected block, or sets the background color for new text typed.

To switch colors, click the menu button to the right of the Shading command button. Select a color from the list, or choose More Colors to create a custom color.

- ✔ If you want to remove the background color, choose No Color from the Shading command's menu.

- ✔ The Shading command is used also to shade other objects on the page, such as cells in a table. That's why it dwells in the Paragraph group and not the Font group.

 ✔ To create white-on-black text, first select the text. Change the text color
   to white, and then change the background (shading) to black.

 ✔ If you need to apply a background color to an entire page, use the Page
   Color command. See Chapter 13.

Change Text Case

Text case isn't really a font format, but it's historically related to fonts: Back
in the days of mechanical type, a font came in a case, like a briefcase. The
upper part of the case held the capital letters. The lower part held the non-
capital letters. That's where the terms *uppercase* and *lowercase* originated.

To change the case of text in Word, well, you could just type it the proper
way in the first place. Even I forget to do that. Although Word's AutoCorrect
and AutoFormat features can automatically capitalize text for you, another
command is available. Follow these steps:

1. Click the Home tab.

2. In the Font group, click the Change Case command button.

3. Choose the proper case from the menu.

   The list of menu items reflects how the case is changed, as shown in
   Figure 10-2.

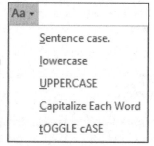

Figure 10-2:
Options for
changing
text case.

The Change Case command is not really a formatting command; its effect
doesn't stick with the text you type.

TIP

The keyboard shortcut for the Change Case command is Shift+F3. Press this
key combination to cycle between three case options: ALL CAPS, lowercase,
and Capitalize Each Word.

Clear Character Formatting

So many Word formatting commands are available that it's possible for your text to look more like a pile of runes than modern text. Word understands this problem, so it offers the Clear Formatting command. Use this command to peel away all formats from your text, just like you peel the skin from a banana.

To remove text formatting, follow these steps:

1. Click the Home tab.

2. In the Font group, click the Clear Formatting command button.

Text formats are removed from selected text or from all new text typed.

The formatting isn't removed as much as it's restored: After issuing the Clear Formatting command, text is altered to represent the defined style. That style includes font, size, and other attributes.

- ✔ The keyboard shortcut for the Clear Formatting command is Ctrl+spacebar.

- ✔ The Clear Formatting command removes the ALL CAPS text format but doesn't otherwise change the text case.

- ✔ You cannot use the Clear Formatting command to remove text highlighting. See Chapter 26.

- ✔ Although you can use the Clear Formatting command to change text color, it doesn't reset the background color. See the section, "Shading the background," earlier in this chapter.

Behold the Font Dialog Box

Word features a single location where all your font-formatting dreams can come true. It's the Font dialog box, shown in Figure 10-3.

To summon the Font dialog box, obey these steps:

1. Click the Home tab.

2. In the Fonts group, click the dialog box launcher button.

The button is found in the lower-right corner of the Font group (refer to Figure 10-1).

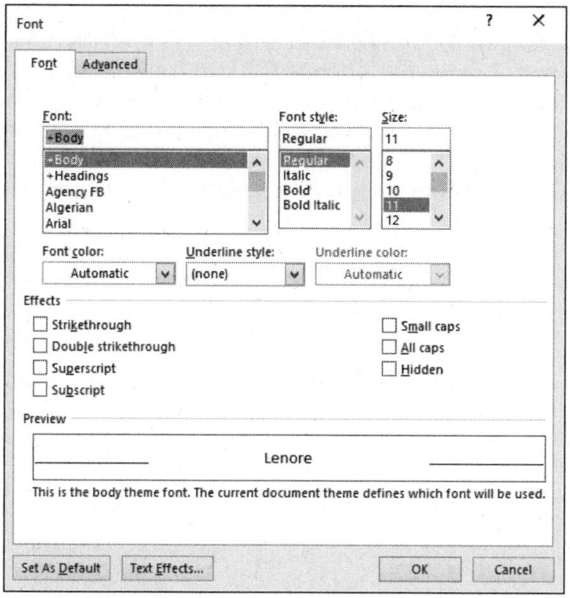

Figure 10-3:
The neatly
organized
Font dialog
box.

The Font dialog box contains *all* the commands for formatting text, including quite a few that didn't find their way into the Font group on the Ribbon. As with all text formatting, the commands you choose in the Font dialog box affect any new text you type or any selected text in your document.

When you've finished setting up your font stuff, click the OK button. Or click Cancel if you're just visiting.

- ✔ Use the Ctrl+D keyboard shortcut to quickly summon the Font dialog box.

- ✔ The best benefit of the Font dialog box is its Preview window, at the bottom. This window shows you exactly how your choices affect text in your document.

- ✔ The Font names *+Body* and *+Heading* refer to the fonts selected by the current document theme. This is done so that you can use Word's theme commands to quickly change body and heading fonts for an entire document all at one time.

- ✔ Click the Font dialog box's Text Effects button to access interesting text attributes such as Shadow, Outline, Emboss, and Engrave. See Chapter 17 for information on this button.

- ✔ The Font dialog box's Advanced tab hosts options for changing the size and position of text on a line.

✔ The Set as Default button in the Font dialog box is used to change the font that Word uses for a new document. If you prefer to use a specific font for all your documents, choose the font (plus other text attributes) in the Font dialog box, and then click the Set as Default button. In the dialog box that appears, choose the option All Documents Based on the Normal Template, and then click the OK button. Afterward, all documents start with the font options you selected.

Chapter 11

Paragraph Formatting

· ·

· ·

*I*f you're after formatting fun, a standard paragraph of text presents you with the most opportunities. Word's paragraph-formatting commands are vast, mostly because so many aspects of a typical paragraph can be adjusted and customized to present text just the way you like.

Paragraph-Formatting Rules and Regulations

Word's paragraph-level formatting commands affect paragraphs in a document. That makes complete sense, but what is a paragraph?

Officially, a *paragraph* is any chunk of text that ends when you press the Enter key. So a single character, a word, a sentence, or a document full of sentences is a paragraph, so long as you press the Enter key.

The paragraph symbol (¶) appears in a document to mark the end of a paragraph. Normally this character is hidden, but you can order Word to display it for you. Follow these steps:

1. **Click the File tab.**

2. **Choose the Options command.**

   The Word Options dialog box appears.

3. **Click Display.**

4. **Place a check mark by Paragraph Marks.**

5. **Click OK.**

Now, every time you press the Enter key, the ¶ symbol appears, marking the end of a paragraph.

Also see Chapter 2 for information on the Show/Hide command, which also displays paragraph symbols in a document (as well as other hidden text).

Formatting a paragraph

You can format a paragraph in several ways:

Change an existing paragraph. With the insertion pointer in a paragraph, use a paragraph-formatting command. Only the current paragraph format is changed.

Change a block of paragraphs. Select one or more paragraphs and then use the formatting command to affect the lot.

Just start typing. Choose a paragraph-formatting command, and then type a paragraph. The chosen format is applied to the new text.

- To format all paragraphs in a document, press Ctrl+A to select all text in the document and then apply the format.

- If your desire is to format several paragraphs in the same manner, consider creating a new style. See Chapter 15.

Locating the paragraph-formatting commands

In a vain effort to confuse you, Word uses not one but *two* locations on the Ribbon to house paragraph-formatting commands. The first Paragraph group is found on the Home tab. The second is located on the Layout tab. Both groups are illustrated in Figure 11-1.

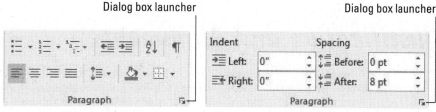

Dialog box launcher   Dialog box launcher

Figure 11-1:
Paragraph
groups.

Home Tab Paragraph Group   Layout Tab Paragraph Group

But wait! There's more.

The Paragraph dialog box, shown in Figure 11-2, can be conjured up by clicking the dialog box launcher button in either of the Paragraph groups (refer to Figure 11-1). In it, you find controls and settings not offered by the command buttons on the Ribbon.

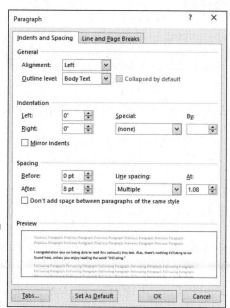

Figure 11-2:
The Para-
graph dialog
box.

The obnoxious keyboard shortcut to summon the Paragraph dialog box is Alt+H, P, G. Don't mock it! You will save time by memorizing this keyboard shortcut.

A smattering of paragraph-formatting commands are found on the mini tool-bar, which shows up after you select text. Refer to Chapter 6 for information on the mini toolbar.

Justification and Alignment

Paragraph alignment has nothing to do with politics, and justification has little to do with the reasons behind putting text in a paragraph. Instead, both terms refer to how the left and right edges of the paragraph look on a page. The four options are Left, Center, Right, and Fully Justified, each covered in this section.

- ✔ All alignment-formatting command buttons are found on the Home tab, in the Paragraph group.
- ✔ The left and right sides of a paragraph are set according to a page's margins. See Chapter 13 for information on setting page margins.

Line up on the left!

Left alignment is considered standard, probably thanks to the mechanical typewriter and, before that, generations of grammar school teachers who preferred text lined up on the left side of a page. The right side of the page? Who cares!

To left-align a paragraph, press Ctrl+L or click the Align Left command button.

- ✔ This type of alignment is also known as *ragged right.*
- ✔ Left-aligning a paragraph is how you undo the other types of alignment.

Everyone center!

Centering a paragraph places each line in that paragraph in the middle of the page, with an equal amount of space to the line's right and left.

To center a paragraph, press Ctrl+E or use the Center command button.

- ✔ Centering is ideal for titles and single lines of text. It's ugly for longer paragraphs and makes reading your text more difficult.
- ✔ You can center a single word in the middle of a line by using the center tab. Refer to Chapter 12 for the details.

Line up on the right!

The mirror image of left alignment, right alignment keeps the right edge of a paragraph even. The left margin, however, is jagged. When do you use this type of formatting? I have no idea, but it sure feels funky typing a right-aligned paragraph.

To flush text along the right side of the page, press Ctrl+R or click the Align Right command button.

> ✔ This type of alignment is also known as *ragged left* or *flush right*.

> ✔ You can right-justify text on a single line by using a right-align tab. Refer to Chapter 12 for more info.

Line up on both sides!

Lining up both sides of a paragraph is *full justification:* Both the left and right sides of a paragraph are neat and tidy, flush with the margins.

To give your paragraph full justification, press Ctrl+J or click the Justify command button.

> ✔ Fully-justified paragraph formatting is often used in newspapers and magazines, which makes the narrow columns of text easier to read.

> ✔ Word makes each side of the paragraph line up by inserting tiny slivers of extra space between words in a paragraph.

> ✔ To line up text even better, activate Word's Hyphenation feature: Click the Layout tab. Click the Hyphenation button and choose Automatic. Word splits long words near the right margin for better text presentation.

Make Room Before, After, or Inside Paragraphs

Sentences in a paragraph can stack as tight as a palette of plywood. Alternatively, you could choose to keep paragraphs all light and airy, like a soft, fluffy cake. Space can cushion above or below the paragraph. These paragraph air settings are illustrated in Figure 11-3.

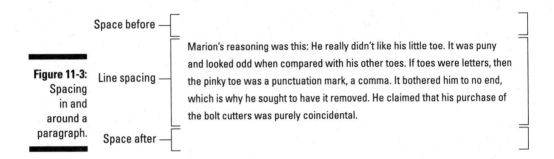

Figure 11-3:
Spacing
in and
around a
paragraph.

Space before

Line spacing

Space after

Marion's reasoning was this: He really didn't like his little toe. It was puny and looked odd when compared with his other toes. If toes were letters, then the pinky toe was a punctuation mark, a comma. It bothered him to no end, which is why he sought to have it removed. He claimed that his purchase of the bolt cutters was purely coincidental.

Commands to control paragraph spacing include the traditional line-spacing commands, as well as the Space Before and Space After commands. These commands are found in the Paragraph groups on both the Home and Layout tabs.

Setting the line spacing

To set the space between all lines in a paragraph, follow these steps:

1. **Click the Home tab.**

2. **In the Paragraph group, click the Line Spacing command button.**

   A menu appears.

3. **Choose a new line spacing value.**

The line spacing is set for the current paragraph or all selected paragraphs. Word adds the extra space below each line of text.

Three keyboard shortcuts are available for the most common line spacing values:

- ✔ To single-space, press Ctrl+1. Use this command to remove other line-spacing styles.

- ✔ To double-space, press Ctrl+2. This setting formats the paragraph with one blank line below each line of text.

- ✔ To use 1½-space lines, press Ctrl+5. Yes, this keyboard shortcut is for 1.5 lines not 5 lines. Use the 5 key in the typewriter area of the computer keyboard. Pressing the 5 key on the numeric keypad activates the Select All command.

Persnickety line-spacing options

For seriously precise line spacing, turn to the Paragraph dialog box: Click the Home tab, and in the lower-right corner of the Paragraph group, click the launcher icon.

In the Paragraph dialog box, the Line Spacing drop-down list features three specific items: At Least, Exactly, and Multiple. These items are used with the At box to indicate line spacing as follows:

At least: The line spacing is set to a minimum value. Word can disobey that value and add more space whenever necessary to make room for larger type, different fonts, or graphics on the same line of text.

Exactly: Word uses the specified line spacing and doesn't adjust the spacing to accommodate larger text or graphics.

Multiple: Use this option to enter line-spacing values other than those specified in the Line Spacing drop-down list. For example, to set the line spacing to 4, choose Multiple from the Line Spacing drop-down list and type **4** in the At box.

Click the OK button to confirm your settings and close the Paragraph dialog box.

The Ctrl+0 (zero) keyboard shortcut applies Word's default line spacing, which is 1.15. According to experts in white lab coats, that extra 0.15-sized chunk of space below each line adds to readability.

When you want text to stack up one line atop another line, such as when typing a return address, use the *soft return* at the end of a line: Press Shift+Enter. See the section in Chapter 4 about soft and hard returns.

Making space between paragraphs

To help separate one paragraph from another, you add space either before or after the paragraph. What you don't do is to press Enter twice to end a paragraph. That's extremely unprofessional and will cause rooms full of people to frown at you.

To add space before or after a paragraph, follow these steps:

1. **Click the Layout tab.**

2. **In the Paragraph group, use the Before gizmo to add space before a paragraph of text or use the After gizmo to add space after the paragraph.**

Measurements are made in points, the same measurement used for font size.

To create the effect of pressing the Enter key twice to end a paragraph, set the After value to a point size about two-thirds the size of the current font. As an example, for a 12-point font, an After value of 8 looks good.

- ✔ The space you add before or after a paragraph becomes part of the paragraph format. Like other formats, it sticks with subsequent paragraphs you type or can be applied to a block of paragraphs.

- ✔ Most of the time, space is added after a paragraph. You can add space before a paragraph, for example, to further separate text from a document heading or subhead

- ✔ Graphics designers prefer to insert more space between paragraphs when the first line of a paragraph isn't indented, as in this book. When you indent the first line, it's okay to have less spacing between paragraphs. See the next section.

Paragraph Indentation Madness

Paragraphs fill the page's margin from side to side, as dictated by the justification or alignment. Exceptions to this rule can be made. A paragraph's first line can be indented, the rest of the lines can be indented, and the left and right sides can be indented. It's paragraph indentation madness!

- ✔ Adjusting a paragraph's indentation doesn't affect the paragraph's alignment.

- ✔ Paragraphs are indented relative to the page's margins. Refer to Chapter 13 for information on page margins.

Indenting the first line of a paragraph

Back in the old days, it was common to start each paragraph with a tab. The tab would indent the first line, helping the reader identify the new paragraph. Word can save you tab-typing energy by automatically formatting each paragraph with an indent on the first line. Here's how:

1. **Click the Home tab.**

2. **In the Paragraph group, click the dialog box launcher.**

   The Paragraph dialog box appears.

3. **Click the Special drop-down list and choose First Line.**

4. Confirm that the By box lists the value 0.5".

The By box shows half an inch, which is the standard tab stop and a goodly distance to indent the first line of text.

5. Click OK.

The first line of the current paragraph or all paragraphs in a selected block are indented per the amount specified in the By box.

To remove the first-line indent from a paragraph, repeat these steps but select (none) from the drop-down list in Step 3.

Word's AutoCorrect feature can automatically indent the first line of a paragraph, which is handy but also annoying. What AutoCorrect does is to convert the tab character into the first-line indent format, which may not be what you want. If so, click the AutoCorrect icon (shown in the margin), and choose the command Convert Back to Tab. I recommend using the steps in this section and not AutoCorrect to format first-line indents.

If you choose to indent the first line of your paragraphs, you don't really need to add space after your paragraphs. See the earlier section, "Making space between paragraphs."

Making a hanging indent (an outdent)

A *hanging indent* isn't in imminent peril. No, it's a paragraph in which the first line breaks the left margin or, from another perspective, in which all lines but the first are indented. Here's an example:

```
Angry Hydrant: Keep the dogs off your lawn with this faux
     firefighting fixture. It looks like the real thing, but
     should rover wander too close, he's met with an annoy-
     ing but legally safe electric shock. Also available in
     mailman shape.
```

The simple way to create such a beast is to press Ctrl+T, the Hanging Indent keyboard shortcut. The command affects the current paragraph or all selected paragraphs.

The not-so-simple way to hang an indent is to use the Paragraph dialog box: In the Indentation area, click the Special menu and choose Hanging. Use the By text box to set the indent depth.

✔ Every time you press Ctrl+T, the paragraph is indented by another half inch.

✔ To undo a hanging indent, press Ctrl+Shift+T. That's the unhang key combination, and it puts the paragraph's neck back in shape.

Indenting a whole paragraph

To draw attention to a paragraph, its left side can be sucked in a notch. This presentation is often used for quoted material in a longer expanse of text.

To indent a paragraph, heed these steps:

1. Click the Home tab.

2. In the Paragraph group, click the Increase Indent command button.

The paragraph's left edge hops over one tab stop (half an inch).

To unindent an indented paragraph, click the Decrease Indent command button in Step 2.

When you want to get specific with indents, as well as indent the paragraph's right side, click the Layout tab and use the Indent Left and Indent Right controls to set specific indentation values. Set both controls to the same value to set off a block quote or a nested paragraph.

✔ The keyboard shortcut to indent a paragraph is Ctrl+M. The shortcut to un-indent a paragraph is Shift+Ctrl+M.

✔ To undo any paragraph indenting, click the Layout tab and in the Paragraph group set both Left and Right indent values to 0.

✔ Indent only one paragraph or a small group of paragraphs. This format isn't intended for long stretches of text.

✔ Do not try to mix left and right indenting with a first-line indent or a hanging indent while drowsy or while operating heavy equipment.

Using the ruler to adjust indents

The most visual way to adjust a paragraph's indents is to use the ruler. That tip is helpful only when the ruler is visible, which it normally isn't in Word. To unhide the ruler, follow these steps:

1. Click the View tab.

2. In the Show area, ensure that the Ruler option is active.

Click to place a check mark by the Ruler option if it isn't active.

The ruler appears above the document text. In Print Layout view, a vertical ruler also appears on the left side of the window.

On the ruler, you see the page margins left and right, and to the far left is something I call the tab gizmo (covered in Chapter 12). Figure 11-4 illustrates the important parts of the ruler with regards to paragraph formatting.

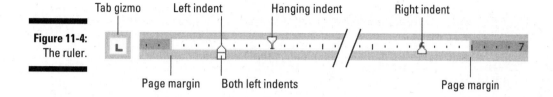

Figure 11-4:
The ruler.

Four doojobbies on the ruler reflect the current paragraph indents. Use these controls to adjust the paragraph indents in a visual manner.

Drag the Left Indent control left or right to adjust a paragraph's left margin. Moving this gizmo does not affect the hanging indent.

Drag the Hanging Indent control left or right to set the first-line indent independently of the left margin.

Drag the Both control to adjust both the left indent and hanging indent together.

Drag the Right Indent control right or left to adjust the paragraph's right margin.

As you drag controls on the ruler, a vertical guide drops down into the document. Use that guide to help adjust indents for the current paragraph or any selected paragraphs.

✔ The ruler doesn't appear in Read Mode or Outline view. In Draft and Web Layout view, the vertical ruler (on the left side of the window) does not appear.

✔ The ruler measures from the page's left margin, not from the left edge of the page. The page's left margin is set when you format a page of text. See Chapter 13.

✔ For more precise setting of indents, use the Paragraph dialog box.

Paragraph-formatting survival guide

This table contains all the paragraph-formatting commands you can summon by holding down the Ctrl key and pressing a letter or number. By no means should you memorize this list.

Format	Key Combination	Command Button
Center	Ctrl+E	
Fully justify	Ctrl+J	
Left align (flush left)	Ctrl+L	
Right align (flush right)	Ctrl+R	
Indent	Ctrl+M	
Unindent	Ctrl+Shift+M	
Hanging indent	Ctrl+T	n/a
Unhanging indent	Ctrl+Shift+T	n/a
Line spacing	Alt+H, K	n/a
Single-space lines	Ctrl+1	n/a
1.15 line spacing	Ctrl+0	n/a
Double-space lines	Ctrl+2	n/a
1.5-space lines	Ctrl+5	n/a

Chapter 12

Tab Formatting

- -

In This Chapter

▶ Revealing tab stops and characters

▶ Viewing the ruler

▶ Working in the Tabs dialog box

▶ Setting left tab stops

▶ Using right, center, and decimal tabs

▶ Decorating with the bar tab

▶ Setting leader tabs

▶ Removing tabs and tab stops

- -

On my ancient Underwood typewriter, the Tab key is located on the right side of the keyboard. It's named Tabular Key. On other old typewriters, I've seen it named Tabulator. The root for these words is the same as the root for table, which is the Latin word *tabula*, meaning list.

In Word, tabs are used to make lists or indent text. That sounds simple, but for some reason tabs remain one of the most complex formatting topics.

Once Upon a Tab

Like other keys on the keyboard, pressing the Tab key inserts a tab *character* into your document. The tab character works like the spacebar, although the character inserted has a variable width. The width is set at a predefined location marked across a page. That location is called the *tab stop*.

It's the tab stop that makes the tab character work: Press the Tab key, and the insertion pointer hops over to the next tab stop. That way, you can precisely line up text on multiple lines. Using a tab is definitely neater than whacking the spacebar multiple times to line up columns of text.

- ✓ Word presets tab stops at every half-inch position across the page. And, of course, you can create your own.

- ✓ Anytime you press the spacebar more than once, you *need* a tab. Believe me, your documents will look prettier and you'll be happier once you understand and use tabs instead of spaces to line up your text.

- ✓ The tab character's behavior is determined by the type of tab stop. In Word, multiple tab stop types help you format a line of text in many ways.

- ✓ As with any other characters, you use the Backspace or Delete keys to remove a tab character.

- ✓ Tabs work best for a single line of text or for only the first line of a paragraph. For more complex lists, use Word's Table command. See Chapter 19.

- ✓ The diet beverage Tab was named for people who like to keep a tab on how much they consume.

Seeing tab characters

Tab characters are normally hidden; they look like blank spaces, which is probably why too many Word users use spaces to create those blanks.

It's not necessary to see tab characters to use them, although if you're having trouble setting tab stops and using tabs, viewing the tab characters is helpful.

Use the Show/Hide command to quickly view tabs in a document. When Show/Hide is active, tab characters appear in your text as a left-pointing arrow, similar to what's shown in the margin.

To activate the Show/Hide command, click the Home tab and in the Paragraph group, click the Show/Hide command button, which looks like the paragraph symbol (¶). Click the button again to deactivate the command.

To direct Word to show tab characters at all times, whether or not the Show/Hide command is active, follow these steps:

1. **Click the File tab.**

2. **Choose Options.**

   The Word Options window appears.

3. Click the Display item on the left side of the window.

4. Put a check mark by the Tab Characters option.

5. Click OK.

With the Tab Characters option set, tabs always appear in a document. They don't print that way, but viewing them in your text may help you solve some formatting puzzles.

Seeing tab stops

Tab stops are invisible; you can't see them in your document, but they exist. The best way to view the tab stops, as well as to set new ones, is to summon the ruler. Follow these steps:

1. Click the View tab.

2. In the Show area, ensure that the check box by the Ruler item has a check in it.

If not, click to set the check mark.

The ruler appears just above the document. Figure 12-1 illustrates how the ruler might look when various tab stops are set. It also shows the location of the Tab gizmo, which is a handy tool you can use to access different tab stop types.

Figure 12-1:
Tab stops
on the ruler.

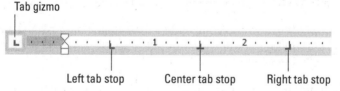

Tab gizmo

Left tab stop   Center tab stop   Right tab stop

If tab stops are not visible on the ruler, Word is using its default setting of one tab stop every half inch. Those tab stops don't appear on the ruler.

✔ When several paragraphs are selected, you may spot a light gray, or *phantom,* tab stop on the ruler. The ghostly appearance indicates that a tab stop is set in one paragraph but not in all. To apply the tab stop to all selected paragraphs, click the phantom tab stop once.

✔ See the later section, "Tab Stop, Be Gone!" for information on using the ruler to remove, or unset, a tab stop.

Using the ruler to set tab stops

The visual and quick way to set a tab stop is to use the ruler. Assuming that the ruler is visible (see the preceding section), the process involves two steps:

1. **Click the Tab gizmo until the desired tab stop type appears.**

   Later sections in this chapter discuss when and how to set each of the five types of tab stops.

   The Tab gizmo also shows paragraph indent controls. These items are covered in Chapter 11 and don't relate to setting tabs.

2. **Click the ruler at the exact spot where you want the tab stop set.**

   For example, click the number 2 to set a tab stop at the 2-inch mark, which is 2 inches in from the page's left margin.

The tab stop icon appears on the ruler, marking the tab stop position. You can further adjust the tab by dragging left or right with the mouse. If a tab character already sits in the current paragraph, its format updates as you drag the top stop hither and thither.

Tab stops are a paragraph-level format. The tab stop you set applies to the current paragraph or any selected paragraphs. Refer to Chapter 6 for information on selected text.

Using the Tabs dialog box to set tabs

For precisely setting tabs, bring up the Tabs dialog box. It's also the only way to get at certain types of tabs, such as dot leader tabs, which are covered elsewhere in this chapter.

Keep in mind that the Tabs dialog box doesn't work like a typical Word dialog box: You must set the tab position and type first and then click the Set button. Click the OK button only when you're done setting tabs. Generally speaking, the process works like this:

1. **Click the Home tab.**

2. **In the lower-right corner of the Paragraph group, click the dialog box launcher.**

   The Paragraph dialog box appears. Tabs are, after all, a paragraph-level format.

3. Click the Tabs button.

The Tabs dialog box appears, as shown in Figure 12-2.

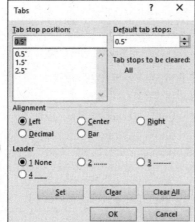

Figure 12-2:
The Tabs
(tab stop)
dialog box.

4. Enter the tab stop position in the Tab Stop Position box.

You can be precise, if you like.

5. Choose the type of tab stop from the Alignment area.

Word's five tab stop types are covered elsewhere in this chapter.

6. Click the Set button.

The tab stop is added to the Tab Stop Position list.

7. Continue setting tab stops.

Repeat Steps 2 through 6 for as many tab stops as you need to set.

8. Click OK.

You must click the Set button to set a tab stop! I don't know how many times I click OK instead, thinking that the tab stop is set when it isn't.

The tab stops you set affect the current paragraph or a selected group of paragraphs.

If the ruler is visible, you can quickly summon the Tabs dialog box: Double-click any existing tab stop.

Reset Word's default tab stops

When you don't set tab stops, Word does it for you. They're called default tab stops, and Word places one every half-inch all across the page. When you press the Tab key, it dutifully hops to the next preset tab stop.

To remove the default tab stops, simply set your own tab stop. All the default tab stops to the left of that new stop are gone.

You can't undo all the default tab stops, but you can change their spacing. In the Tabs dialog box, type a new interval value in the Default Tab Stops box. For example, to set default tab stops to one-inch intervals, type 1 in the box and then click the OK button.

The Standard Left Tab Stop

The left tab stop is the traditional type of tab stop. When you press the Tab key, the insertion pointer advances to the left tab stop position, where you can continue to type text. This type of tab stop works best for typing lists, organizing information in single-line paragraphs, or indenting the first line of a multiline paragraph.

Creating a basic tabbed list

A common use for the left tab stop is to create a simple two-column list, as shown in Figure 12-3.

Tab gizmo   Left tab stop   Left tab stop

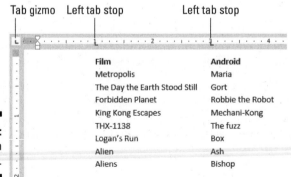

Figure 12-3:
Two-column
list.

Film	Android
Metropolis	Maria
The Day the Earth Stood Still	Gort
Forbidden Planet	Robbie the Robot
King Kong Escapes	Mechani-Kong
THX-1138	The fuzz
Logan's Run	Box
Alien	Ash
Aliens	Bishop

Follow these steps to create this type of list:

1. **On a new line, press Tab.**

2. **Type the item for the first column.**

   This item should be short — two or three words, max.

3. **Press Tab.**

4. **Type the item for the second column.**

   Again, make it short.

5. **Press Enter to end that line and start a new line.**

   Yes, your list looks horrible! Don't worry. Type first, then format.

6. **Repeat Steps 2 through 5 for each line in the list.**

   After the list is finished, use the ruler to visually set the tab stops.

   Refer to the previous section "Using the ruler to set tab stops" for information on summoning the ruler, if it's not currently visible.

7. **Select all lines of text that you want to organize in a two-column tabbed list.**

8. **Choose a left tab stop from the Tab gizmo on the ruler.**

   If necessary, click the Tab gizmo until the Left Tab Stop icon shows up, as shown in the margin.

9. **Click the ruler to set the first tab stop.**

   If the text doesn't line up right, drag the tab stop left or right.

10. **Click to set the second tab stop.**

    Drag the tab stop left or right, if necessary, to help line up text.

Although you could add a third column to the list, things start to get crowded. In fact, any time you need more than a single word or two in a tabbed list, consider cobbling a table instead. See Chapter 19.

You need only one tab between items in a column list. That's because the *tab stop* lines up your text, not the tab character.

Creating a two-tab paragraph thing

You can create a descriptive list by using the power of tabs coupled with a paragraph's hanging indent format. Such a thing is difficult to describe, so refer to Figure 12-4 to see what's up.

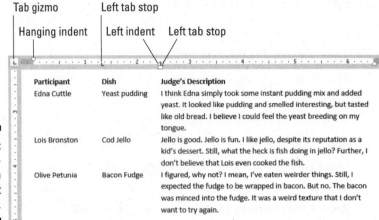

Tab gizmo   Left tab stop

Hanging indent   Left indent   Left tab stop

Participant	Dish	Judge's Description
Edna Cuttle	Yeast pudding	I think Edna simply took some instant pudding mix and added yeast. It looked like pudding and smelled interesting, but tasted like old bread. I believe I could feel the yeast breeding on my tongue.
Lois Bronston	Cod Jello	Jello is good. Jello is fun. I like jello, despite its reputation as a kid's dessert. Still, what the heck is fish doing in jello? Further, I don't believe that Lois even cooked the fish.
Olive Petunia	Bacon Fudge	I figured, why not? I mean, I've eaten weirder things. Still, I expected the fudge to be wrapped in bacon. But no. The bacon was minced into the fudge. It was a weird texture that I don't want to try again.

Figure 12-4:
A tab-tab-paragraph format for text.

Follow these steps to create a list similar to the one shown in Figure 12-4:

1. **On a new line, type the first item.**

   The shorter, the better. This item sits at the left margin, so don't type a tab to start the line.

2. **Press Tab.**

3. **Type the second item and press Tab.**

   This step is optional; you can create a simpler tab-paragraph list, which looks just like the one shown in Figure 12-4, but without the Dish column (and spaced accordingly).

4. **Type the paragraph text.**

   Unlike with the first two items, you're free to type more text here. That's because this final paragraph column wraps, as shown in Figure 12-4.

5. **Press Enter to end the line.**

   Don't let the ugly look of your text deceive you at this point. The text beautifies itself when you add the tab stops.

6. **Repeat Steps 1 through 5 for each item in the tab-tab-paragraph list thing.**

   When you're done, you can set the tab stops.

7. **Select all the lines of text you want to organize into a tab-tab-paragraph list.**

8. **Bid the ruler appear, if need be.**

   Directions for beckoning forth the ruler are found earlier in this chapter.

9. **Ensure that the left tab stop is chosen on the Tab gizmo.**

The margin shows the Left Tab Stop symbol.

10. **Set a left tab stop to mark the first item in the list.**

The second column snaps into place.

11. **Slide the paragraph's left margin to the start of the text item.**

The Left Indent triangle is shown in the margin. It sets the left margin for all text in a paragraph, save the first line. (See Chapter 11 for details.) Slide the triangle to the right until it's past items in the second column, as shown in Figure 12-4.

12. **Adjust the tab stop and left margin as necessary.**

Make the adjustments while text is selected, which provides visual feedback for the paragraphs.

As with formatting any complex list, it's perfectly okay to give up. See Chapter 19 for information on adding a table to your document. You might find a table better to work with than all this paragraph-formatting nonsense.

The Center Tab Stop

The *center tab* is a unique critter with a special purpose: Text placed at a center tab is centered on a line. Unlike centering a paragraph, only text placed at the center tab stop is centered. This feature is ideal for centering text in a header or footer, which is about the only time you need the center tab stop.

Figure 12-5 shows an example of a center tab. The text on the left is at the start of the paragraph, which is left-justified. But the text typed after the tab is centered on the line.

Figure 12-5:
Center tab
in action.

Center tab stop

A Trip To Uranus   Chapter 9: Exploring the curious crevasse

Here's how to make that happen:

1. **Start a new paragraph, one containing text that you want to center.**

Center tabs inhabit one-line paragraphs.

2. **Click the Tab gizmo on the ruler until the center tab stop shows up.**

   The Center Tab Stop icon is shown in the margin.

   Refer to the section, "Using the ruler to set tab stops," earlier in this chapter, for information on displaying the ruler and using the Tab gizmo.

3. **Click the ruler to set the center tab stop's position.**

   Generally speaking, the center tab stop dwells in the middle of the page. That location could be the 3-inch mark or the 3¼-inch mark.

4. **Type any text to start the line.**

   In Figure 12-5, the text *A Trip to Uranus* appears at the start of the line. Typing such text is optional, depending on what you're formatting.

5. **Press the Tab key.**

   The insertion pointer hops over to the center tab stop.

6. **Type the text you want to center.**

   As you type, the text is centered on the line. Don't type too much; the center tab is a single-line thing.

7. **Press Enter to end the line of text.**

Center tab stops are used primarily in a document header or footer, or when typing a title. See Chapter 14 for information on headers and footers.

When you need only centered text on a line, use the center paragraph format instead of a center tab stop. See Chapter 11.

The Right Tab Stop

A right tab stop isn't the opposite of the left tab stop. Instead, it's a special creature that right-justifies text on a single line. You've probably seen such a thing in action many times, but never thought you could easily create such formatted text.

As with the other unusual tab stop types, the right tab stop works best on a single line of text. It's also commonly used in a document header or footer, as described in Chapter 14.

Making a right-stop, left-stop list

A clever way to format a two-column list is to employ both a right tab stop and a left tab stop. The list lines up on a centerline, as shown in Figure 12-6.

Right tab stop   Left tab stop

Dorothy	Taylor Swift
Scarecrow	Michael Cera
Tin Man	Jude Law
Cowardly Lion	Seth Rogan
Wizard	Lewis Black
Wicked Witch of the West	Lady Gaga

To build such a list, follow these steps:

1. **Start out on a blank line, the line you want to format.**

2. **Click the Tab gizmo until the right tab stop shows up.**

   The Right Tab Stop icon appears in the margin.

   See the section, "Using the ruler to set tab stops" for information on displaying the ruler.

3. **Click near the center of the ruler to place the right tab stop.**

4. **Click the Tab gizmo until the left tab stop appears.**

   Click, click, click until you see the Left Tab Stop icon, as shown in the margin.

5. **Click to place the left tab stop just to the right side of the right tab stop on the ruler.**

   Use Figure 12-6 as your guide.

   Now it's time to type the text. Don't worry about getting the tab stops correct at this point in the process; you can adjust them later.

6. **Press the Tab key.**

   The insertion pointer hops over to the right tab stop's position.

7. **Type text for the first, right-justified column.**

8. **Press the Tab key.**

9. **Type your text for the second, left-justified column.**

10. **Press Enter to end the line of text.**

11. **Repeat Steps 6 through 10 for each line in the list.**

If further adjustments are necessary after you're finished, select all the lines and use the mouse to adjust the tab stops' positions on the ruler as necessary.

Building a two-column right-stop list

The right tab stop can be used on the second column of a two-column list. The presentation appears commonly in programs, similar to what's shown in Figure 12-7.

Tab gizmo   Right tab stop

Introductions	Rev. Carlisle
Sunday School Report	Marcia Marsh
Finance Committee	Roger Hannover
Events Committee	Dawn Rogers
Apology for the Bake Sale	Eunice McCarthy

Here's how to concoct such a thing:

1. **Start on a blank line of text.**

2. **Click the Tab gizmo until the right tab stop appears.**

   The Right Tab Stop icon is shown in the margin.

   Refer to the earlier section, "Using the ruler to set tab stops," for information on displaying the ruler and finding the Tab gizmo.

3. **Place the right tab stop on the far right side of the ruler.**

   The position is just a guess at this point. Later, you can adjust the right tab stop position to something more visually appealing.

4. **Type the first column text.**

   The text is left-justified, as it is normally.

5. **Press the Tab key.**

   The insertion pointer hops to the right tab stop.

6. **Type the second column text.**

   The text you type is right-justified, pushing to the left as you type.

7. **Press Enter to end the line of text.**

8. **Repeat Steps 4 through 7 for every line in the list.**

Afterward, you can adjust the list's appearance: Select all the text as a block and then drag the right tab stop back and forth on the ruler.

The Decimal Tab

Use the decimal tab to line up columns of numbers. Although you can use a right tab for this job, the decimal tab is a better choice. Rather than right-align text, as the right tab does (see the preceding section), the decimal tab aligns numbers by their decimal — the period in the number, as shown in Figure 12-8.

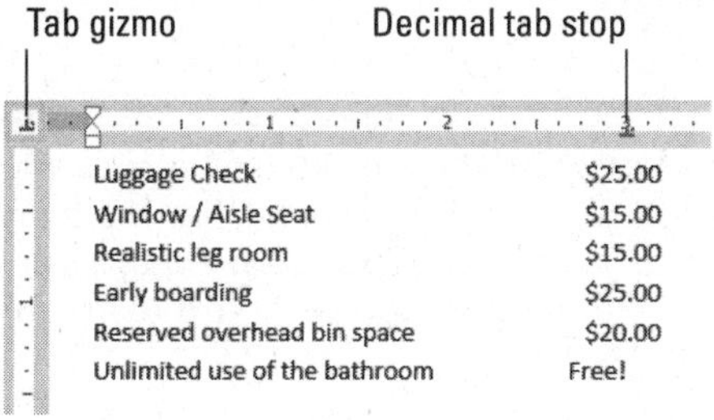

Tab gizmo   Decimal tab stop

Figure 12-8:
Using the
decimal tab
to line up
numbers.

Luggage Check	$25.00
Window / Aisle Seat	$15.00
Realistic leg room	$15.00
Early boarding	$25.00
Reserved overhead bin space	$20.00
Unlimited use of the bathroom	Free!

Here's how to work with such a beast:

1. **Start a blank line of text.**

2. **On the ruler, click the Tab gizmo until the decimal tab stop appears.**

   The Decimal Tab Stop icon is shown in the margin.

3. **Click the ruler to set the decimal tab stop.**

   You can adjust the position later.

4. **Type the first column text.**

   This step is optional, although in Figure 12-8 you see the first column as a list of items.

5. **Press the Tab key.**

6. **Type the number.**

   The number is right-justified until you press the period key. After that, the rest of the number is left-justified.

7. **End that line of text by pressing Enter.**

8. **Repeat Steps 4 through 7 for each line in the list.**

You can make adjustments after the list is complete: Select all the lines in the list and then drag the decimal tab stop left or right.

✔ When a line doesn't feature a period, text typed at a decimal tab stop is right-justified, as shown by the word *Free* in Figure 12-8.

✔ This tab stop is used inside a table cell or column to align values. See Chapter 19 for information on Word's table commands.

The Bar Tab

Aside from being a most excellent pun, the bar tab isn't a true tab stop in Word. Instead, consider it a text decoration. Setting a bar tab merely inserts a vertical bar in a line of text, as shown in Figure 12-9. Using a bar tab is much better than using the pipe (|) character on the keyboard to create a vertical line in a multicolumn list.

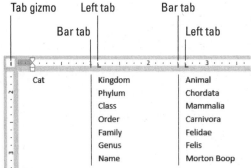

Figure 12-9: The mysterious bar tab.

To set a bar tab stop, follow these steps:

1. Click the Tab gizmo until the bar tab stop appears.

The Bar Tab Stop icon is shown in the margin.

2. Click the ruler to place the bar tab stop.

At each position, a vertical bar appears in the text. The bar appears whether or not the current line contains any tab characters.

To best use the bar tab stop, mix in a few other tab stops. For example, in Figure 12-9, left tab stops are set to the side of each bar tab stop. The effect is that text is organized into columns, but the bar tab serves only to decorate the text. It has no effect otherwise.

Fearless Leader Tabs

Press the Tab key and the insertion pointer hops over to the next tab stop. The space added is empty, but it doesn't have to be. Word lets you apply different styles to the empty space, which help create something called a leader tab.

A *leader tab* shows a series of dots or other characters where the tab appears on the page. Three styles are available: dot, dash, and underline, as illustrated in Figure 12-10.

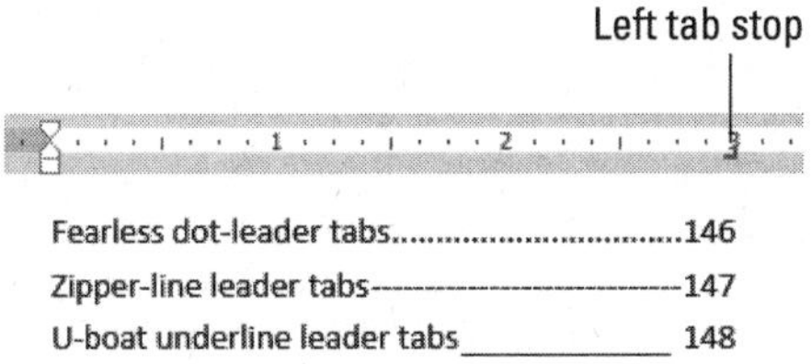

Left tab stop

Figure 12-10:
Leader tab
styles.

You can apply a leader to any tab stop in Word other than the bar tab. To do so, follow these steps:

1. **Create the tab-formatted list.**

   Refer to sections elsewhere in this chapter for information on creating a list of items.

2. **Select the text as a block.**

3. **Bring forth the Tabs dialog box.**

   The quick shortcut is to double-click a tab on the ruler. Also see the section, "Using the Tabs dialog box to set tabs."

4. **Select the tab stop from the Tab Stop Position list.**

5. **In the Leader area, choose the leader style.**

6. **Click the Set button.**

   Don't click OK before you set the tab stop to add the leader. This step is the one you'll screw up most often.

7. **Click OK.**

   The leader is applied.

Use the underline leader tab to create fill-in-the-blank forms. In the Tabs dialog box, set a left tab stop at the far right margin (usually, 6.0 inches). Choose the underline leader style (number 4). Click Set and then click OK. Back in your document, type a tab to create a fill-in-the-blank line, such a:

```
Your name: _____
```

This format is far better than typing a zillion underlines.

Tab Stop, Be Gone!

To unset or clear a tab stop, follow these steps:

1. Select the paragraph(s) with the offending tab stop.

2. Drag the tab stop from the ruler.

Drag downward. The tab stop is removed from the paragraph(s).

Even though you've removed the tab stop, the tab character may still lurk in the paragraph. Remember that Word places automatic tab stops on every line of text.

For complex tab stop removal, such as when tab stops are close to each other or to the paragraph indent controls on the ruler, use the Tabs dialog box: Click to select the tab in the Tab Stop Position list, and then click the Clear button. Click OK to exit the Tabs dialog box.

- ✔ Clicking the Clear All button in the Tabs dialog box removes all tab stops from the current paragraph or selected paragraphs in one drastic sweep.

- ✔ To delete a tab character, use the Backspace key.

Chapter 13

Page Formatting

. . . .

. . . .

Word is only mildly interested in the concept of a page. Unlike the real world, where a page is a physical sheet of paper, Word conjures new pages when needed, pulling them in from the electronic ether. That makes the concept of a page ethereal. To root things in reality, Word lets you define the page format, which includes the page size, orientation, margins, as well as other page formats and attributes.

Describe That Page

Word begins its page-formatting adventure by defining exactly what a page looks like. That includes the page's physical dimensions and which portion of the page contains text.

Setting page size

You probably assume that each new document starts with a page size reflecting a typical sheet of paper.

Such foolishness.

Word's Normal template does specify a page size equivalent to a standard sheet of paper. In the US, that's 8½-by-11 inches. In Europe, the A4 size is used. You're not stuck with either size, because the page size is part of the page format, and you can change it. Follow these steps:

1. **Click the Layout tab on the Ribbon.**

Size

2. **In the Page Setup group, click the Size button.**

   The Size button icon is shown in the margin.

3. **Choose a page size from the list.**

   For example, if you want to print on that tall, legal-size paper, choose Legal from the list.

Your entire document is updated to reflect the new page size, from first page to last.

✔ To select a size not shown on the menu (refer to Step 3), choose the More Paper Sizes menu item. The Page Setup dialog box appears. Use the controls on the Paper tab to manually specify the paper size.

✔ Page size can be changed at any time, whether the document is empty or full of text. Obviously page size affects layout, so such a major change is probably something you don't want to do at the last minute.

✔ Your document can sport multiple page sizes. To do so, split the document into sections and apply the page size to one section at a time. See Chapter 14 for information on sections. Applying page formats one section at a time is done in the Page Setup dialog box, as described later in this chapter.

✔ Page size definitely plays a role when a document is printed. Despite your zeal to choose an oddball page size, unless the printer can handle that size paper, the document can't be printed. It can, however, be published electronically. That process is covered in Chapter 9.

Changing orientation (landscape or portrait)

An aspect of page size is whether the page is oriented vertically or horizontally. (I'm assuming it's no longer the fashion to print on square paper.) Page orientation could be set by adjusting the page size, but it's much easier to change the page orientation. Follow these steps:

1. **Click the Layout tab.**

Orientation

2. **Click the Orientation button.**

   The Orientation button is illustrated in the margin. It has two items on its menu: Portrait and Landscape.

3. Choose Portrait to set the page vertically or Landscape to set the page horizontally.

Word shifts the orientation for every page in your document. This doesn't mean that the text is sideways, but rather that the text prints wide on a page (though I suppose you could look at it as printing sideways).

 ✔ Make the decision to have your document in landscape orientation before you do any extensive formatting. This orientation affects paragraph formatting, which may require you to adjust the document's margins; see the next section.

 ✔ Page-orientation changes affect the entire document unless you split your document into sections. In this case, the change applies to only the current section. Read Chapter 14 for details on sections, including directions on how to stick a single landscape page into a document that's otherwise portrait oriented.

 ✔ Scientists who study such things have determined that human reading speed slows drastically when people must scan a long line of text, which happens when you use landscape orientation. Reserve landscape orientation for printing lists, graphics, and tables for which portrait page orientation is too narrow.

 ✔ Landscape printing is ideal for using multiple columns of text. See Chapter 20.

 ✔ If you just want sideways text without turning the page, use a text box. See Chapter 23 for information on text boxes.

Setting the page margins

Margins create the text area on a page, left, right, top, and bottom. They provide room between the text and the page's edge, which keeps the text from leaking out of a document and all over the computer.

Word automatically sets page margins at 1 inch from every page edge. Most English teachers and book editors want margins of this size because these people love to scribble in margins. (They even write that way on blank paper.)

To adjust page margins in Word, obey these steps:

1. Click the Layout tab.

2. Click the Margins button.

Margins

It's found in the Page Setup group and shown in the margin.

Clicking the Margins button displays a menu full of common margin options.

3. **Pluck a proper margin setting from the menu.**

The new margins affect all pages in your document — unless you split your document into sections, in which case the changes apply to only the current section. See Chapter 14 for information on sections.

The choices available on the Margins menu list settings for the top, left, bottom, and right margins. Yes, all four margins are set at one time. When you want to set specific margins, choose the Custom Margins item from the bottom of the menu, and then use the Margins tab in the Page Setup dialog box to set each margin. Refer to the next section for more information.

✔ The Layout tab's Margins button sets page margins. To set margins for one or more paragraphs, refer to Chapter 11.

✔ The orange stars appearing on the Margins menu's icons represent popular or recent margin choices you've made.

✔ Many printers cannot print on the outside half inch of a piece of paper, usually on one side — top, bottom, left, or right. This space is an *absolute* margin; although you can tell Word to set a margin of 0 inches, text may not print there. Instead, choose a minimum of 0.5 inches for all margins.

Using the Page Setup dialog box

When you want more control over page formatting, you must beckon forth the Page Setup dialog box, as shown in Figure 13-1. Specifically, you use the Margins tab in that dialog box, which is shown in the figure.

To use the Page Setup dialog box to specifically set page margins, obey these steps:

1. **Click the Layout tab.**

2. **Click the dialog box launcher in the lower-right corner of the Page Setup group.**

The Page Setup dialog box appears, Margins tab forward.

3. **Type the margin offsets in the Top, Bottom, Left, and Right boxes.**

Or you can use the spinner gizmo to set the values.

Use the Preview to check the margins as they relate to page size.

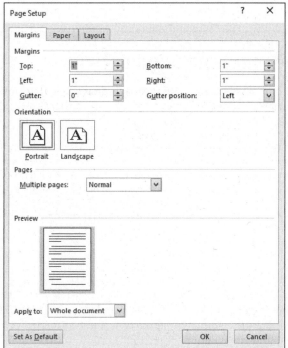

Figure 13-1:
The Margins
tab in the
Page Setup
dialog box.

4. **Ensure that Whole Document is chosen from the Apply To menu button.**

   You can reset margins for only a section or selected text if you instead choose those options from the menu. See Chapter 14 for information on sections.

5. **Click the OK button to confirm your new settings and close the Page Setup dialog box.**

The Gutter settings help set margins when you need extra space on one edge of the page for binding. For example, if you plan on using a 3-hole punch on the left side of a page, choose Left from the Gutter Position menu. Then increase the Gutter margin to accommodate for the three holes in the page without affecting the left margin setting.

✔ The keyboard shortcut to summon the Page Setup dialog box is Alt+P, S, P.

✔ The Page Setup dialog box sports three tabs: Margins, for setting margins, Paper, for selecting the page size, and Layout, for dealing with other page-formatting issues.

Nutty multiple page options

In the Page Setup dialog box, nestled on the Margins tab, is the Pages area (refer to Figure 13-1). The Multiple Pages drop-down list tells Word how to use a single sheet of paper for printing complex documents. This is something you can avoid at all costs, yet I'm compelled by the Computer Book Writers Union to describe the various settings:

Normal means one page per sheet of paper. You can't get more normal than that.

Mirror Margins is used when the printer is smart enough to print on both sides of a sheet of paper. That way, every other page is flip-flopped so that their margins always line up. For example, the gutter may be on the left side of one page but on the right for the page's back side.

2 Pages per Sheet splits the paper right down the center and forces Word to print two "pages" per sheet of paper. Note that this option works best when the pages are in landscape orientation.

Book Fold is Word's attempt to create a multiple-page booklet by printing the proper pages on both sides of a sheet of paper. The Sheets Per Booklet option that appears tells Word how long your booklet is.

Despite these options, Word is a poor bookbinding program. If you're into document publishing, consider getting a desktop-publishing program, such as Adobe InDesign or Microsoft Publisher, which are far better equipped to deal with this topic.

Page Numbering

I remain puzzled by people who manually number their pages in Word. Such a thing is silly beyond belief. That's because

Your word processor numbers your pages for you!

Memorize it. Live it. Be it.

Adding an automatic page number

Word can not only automatically number your pages, but it also lets you place the page number just about anywhere on the page and in a variety of fun and useful formats. Heed these directions:

1. Click the Insert tab.

2. In the Header & Footer area, click the Page Number command button.

A menu drops down, showing various page-numbering options. The first three are locations: Top of Page, Bottom of Page, and Page Margins (the sides of the page).

3. Choose where to place the page numbers.

I want my page numbers on the bottom of the page, so I regularly choose the Bottom of Page option.

4. Pluck a page-numbering style from the list.

You see oodles of samples, so don't cut yourself short by not scrolling through the menu. You can even choose those famous *page X of Y* formats.

Dutifully, Word numbers each page in your document, starting with 1 on the first page, up to however many pages long the thing grows.

Here's the good part: If you delete a page, Word renumbers everything for you. Insert a page? Word renumbers everything for you again, automatically. As long as you insert the page number as described in this section, Word handles everything.

✔ To change the page number format, simply choose a new one from the Page Number menu.

✔ If you merely need to reference the current page number in your document's text, choose the Current Position item in Step 3. Word inserts the current page number at the insertion pointer's location.

✔ The page numbers are placed in the document's header or footer. See Chapter 14 for information on headers and footers.

✔ Page numbers can be removed just as easily: See the section "Removing page numbers," later in this chapter.

✔ See Chapter 23 for information on inserting a page number in your document's text, as opposed to in a header or footer.

Starting with a different page number

You and I know that the first page of a document is page 1, but Word doesn't care. It lets you start numbering your document at whichever page number you want. If you want to start numbering your document at page 42, you can do so, if you follow these instructions:

1. Click the Insert tab.

2. In the Header & Footer area, choose Page Number ⇨ Format Page Numbers.

The Page Number Format dialog box materializes, as shown in Figure 13-2.

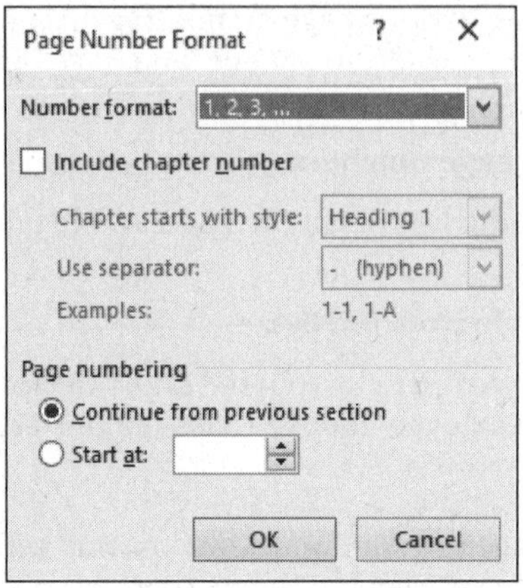

Page Number Format ? ✕

Number format: 1, 2, 3, ... ▾

☐ Include chapter number

Chapter starts with style: Heading 1 ▾

Use separator: - (hyphen) ▾

Examples: 1-1, 1-A

Page numbering

● Continue from previous section
○ Start at: [   ] ⬍

OK   Cancel

Figure 13-2: Gain more control over page numbers.

3. Click the Start At radio button.

4. Type the starting page number in the box.

5. Click OK.

Word starts numbering your document at the specified page number. So if you enter 42 in Step 4, the first page of the document is now page 42, the next page is 43, and so on.

Of course, this trick works best when page numbers are already set for your document, as described in the preceding section.

✔ For more page number control, split your document into sections. Different page-numbering styles or sequences can be set for individual sections. You can even suppress page numbers for a section, such as not numbering the first (cover) page of a document. See Chapter 14 for more information on sections.

✔ If you are working on a novel, don't worry about setting page numbers for each chapter. That's insane. Instead, use Word's Master Document feature to set page numbering when you're finished. See Chapter 25.

Numbering with Roman numerals

When the urge hits you to regress a few centuries and use Roman numerals to tally a document's pages, Word is happy to oblige. *Sic facite*:

1. Set the location for page numbers in your document.

Refer to the section "Adding an automatic page number." Once page numbers are established, you can set a different format.

2. **Click the Insert tab.**

3. **Click the Page Number command button and choose Format Page Numbers.**

   The Page Number Format dialog box appears.

4. **Choose a style from the Number Format menu.**

   Two Roman numeral styles are available, lowercase and uppercase.

5. **Click OK.**

Hail Caesar!

Removing page numbers

To banish automatic page numbers from above, below, or anywhere around your text, follow these steps:

1. **Click the Insert tab.**

2. **Click the Page Number command button.**

3. **Choose Remove Page Numbers.**

   And they're gone.

These steps remove only the page numbers set by using the Page Number command button, as described earlier in this chapter. Page numbers you've inserted in the text are unaffected, as are any page numbers you've manually added to a document's header or footer.

To remove a manually inserted page number, use the Backspace key. Such page numbers are actually document fields. See Chapter 23 for information on fields.

New Pages from Nowhere

With Word, you'll never have the excuse "I need more pages" when writing text. That's because Word adds new, blank pages as needed. These pages are appended to the end of the document, so even if you're typing in the midst of a chapter, the extra pages keep appearing so that no text is lost and nothing falls off the edge. That's refreshing, but it's not the end of Word's capability to add new pages into your document.

Starting text on a new page

You have two choices when it comes to starting text at the top of a page in the middle of a document.

The first choice is to keep whacking the Enter key until that new page shows up. This approach is horribly wrong. It works, but it leads to trouble later as you edit your document.

The second, and preferred, choice is to insert a hard page break:

1. **Position the insertion pointer where you want one page to end and the next page to start.**

   I recommend splitting the page at the start of a new paragraph.

2. **Click the Insert tab.**

3. **In the Pages group, click the Page Break command button.**

   Text before the insertion pointer is on the previous page, and text after the insertion pointer is on the next page.

The hard page break stays with your text. No matter how you edit or add text, the split between pages remains.

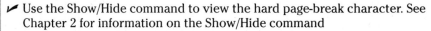

- ✔ The keyboard shortcut to split pages is Ctrl+Enter.

- ✔ To remove a hard page break, position the insertion pointer at the top of the page just after the break. Press the Backspace key. If you goof up, use Ctrl+Z to undo.

- ✔ Use the Show/Hide command to view the hard page-break character. See Chapter 2 for information on the Show/Hide command

- ✔ The hard page break is easier to see in Draft view.

Inserting a blank page

Suddenly, you need a blank page in the middle of a document. Follow these steps:

1. **Click the Insert tab.**

2. **In the Pages group, click the Blank Page command button.**

   A new blank page appears at the insertion pointer's position.

Any text before the insertion pointer appears before the blank page. Any text after the insertion pointer appears after the new page.

  ✔ The Blank Page command inserts *two* hard page breaks in the document.

  ✔ Be mindful of the material you place on the new, blank page. Because two hard page breaks produce the page, its best suited for single-page items, such as graphics or a table. Anything longer than a page makes the rest of the document formatting look funky.

  ✔ You don't need to use this command to add a new page at the end of your document. Just keep typing.

Page Background Froufrou

A page is also a canvas, a background upon which your document rests. That background sports a few formatting options of its own, items that dwell outside a document but remain part of the page formatting.

Coloring pages

The simple way to print colored pages is to choose color paper. When the price of printer ink isn't an option, you can direct Word to format each page in a document with a different background color. Follow these steps:

1. **Click the Design tab.**

2. **In the Page Background group, click the Page color button.**

   You see a menu full of colors.

3. **Choose a color from the palette.**

   Or choose the More Colors menu item to pluck out your own favorite page background color.

The color chosen in Step 3 is applied to the document's pages.

To remove the color, choose the item No Color in Step 3.

  ✔ The colors displayed in the Page Color menu are based on the document theme. See Chapter 16 for information on document themes.

  ✔ Page color is independent of text foreground and background color. See Chapter 10.

✔ Unlike page size, orientation, and numbering, page background color is unaffected by document sections. The color is applied to every page in every section. See Chapter 14 for more information on document sections.

✔ Choose the Fill Effects menu item in Step 3 to view the Fill Effects dialog box. Click the Gradient tab to set *gradients,* or multiple colors, as the page background. Use the Picture tab to apply an image to each page's background.

Printing colored pages

Viewing a colored page on the screen is one thing. Seeing it printed is another. In Word, you must direct the printer to print page background color by following these steps:

1. **Click the File tab and choose Options.**

   The Word Options dialog box appears.

2. **Choose Display from the left side of the Word Options dialog box.**

3. **In the Printing Options area, put a check mark by the item labeled Print Background Colors and Images.**

4. **Click OK.**

   The page background color now appears when the document is printed — well, assuming that you have a color printer.

Because the color isn't part of the paper, it doesn't cover the entire printed page. That's because your printer cannot mechanically access the outside edge of a page, so a white border (or whatever other color the paper is) appears around your colored page. At this point, ask yourself whether it's easier to use colored paper rather than all that expensive printer ink or toner.

Adding a watermark

When fine paper is held up to the light, it shows a *watermark* — an image embedded into the paper. The image is impressive but faint. Word lets you fake a watermark by inserting faint text or graphics behind every page in your document. Here's how:

1. **Click the Design tab.**

2. **In the Page Background group, click the Watermark button.**

   A menu plops down with a host of predefined watermarks that you can safely duck behind the text on your document's pages.

3. **Choose a watermark from the menu.**

   The watermark is applied to every page in your document.

To rid your document's pages of the watermark, choose the Remove Watermark command in Step 3.

- To customize the watermark, choose the Custom Watermark command from the Watermark menu. Use the Printed Watermark dialog box to create your own watermark text, or import an image, such as your company logo.

- The watermark appears on all pages in a document. It's unaffected by section breaks. See Chapter 14 for information on section breaks.

- If the watermark doesn't show up in the printed document, you may need to enable the Print Background Colors and Images setting. Refer to the preceding section.

Chapter 14

More Page Formatting

. . . .

In This Chapter

▶ Using sections

▶ Placing a cover page on your document

▶ Adding a header or footer

▶ Creating unique headers and footers

▶ Suppressing the header and footer on the first page

▶ Working with headers and footers in sections

▶ Deleting a header or footer

. . . .

*R*are is the Hollywood sequel that's better than the original. Most of them present rehashed material, obviously just to make a buck. More common these days is for a complex storyline to be split between several films. Again, the motive is to make a buck, but at least the plot holds through the sequels.

When it comes to this book, a sequel isn't necessary. No, I just took the complex storyline associated with page formatting and split it between two chapters. This chapter continues the saga of Page Format and his adventures in Documentland. Villains abound and peril lies on every page, but the resolution is solid and satisfying.

Slice Your Document into Sections

Many Word page formats apply to an entire document, from "once upon a time" to "happily ever after." Change a format for one page, and it's reflected on every page. That is, unless the document is sliced into larger format chunks called sections.

Understanding sections

A *section* is a part of a document that contains its own page formatting. It can be a single page or a range of pages. A document can sport one or many sections. Each section can sport its own page format, independent of the other sections.

All Word documents have one section. And if you don't plan on changing the page format for the entire document, one section is all you'll ever need. If you plan on changing page numbers, page orientation, paper size, headers and footers, or similar page formats, the document needs more sections.

Figure 14-1 lists three examples of documents sliced up into sections.

Example 1: Change page number style

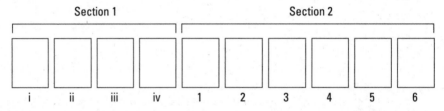

Example 2: No page number on the first page

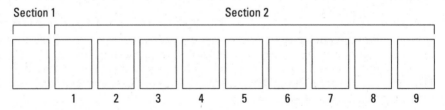

Example 3: Change page orientation

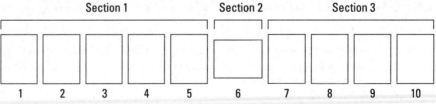

Figure 14-1: How sections control page formatting.

In Example 1, a single document contains two sections. The first section uses Roman numeral page numbers. The second section uses human numerals.

In Example 2, the document also contains two sections. The first section is a cover page that has no page numbering. The second section — all the remaining pages — uses page numbering. Also, see how the second page in the document is numbered as page 1? Again, that's because the page numbering applies only to section 2.

In Example 3, the document has three sections. The first and third sections sport the same formatting; the second section was created so that page 6 could be presented in landscape orientation.

In all three examples, the document's text and paragraph formats remain unaffected by sections. Even page-level formatting can be unaffected: The new page format must be applied specifically to the current section. More information about that process is presented in this chapter as well as in Chapter 13.

Creating a section

If you're new to the concept of sections, think of a new section as similar to a page break. The difference is that the new page starts a new section.

To start a new section in your document, heed these steps:

1. **Position the toothpick cursor where you want the new section to start.**

   Click the mouse where you need to begin a new section, similar to creating a new page break.

2. **Click the Layout tab on the Ribbon.**

3. **In the Page Setup area, click the Breaks button.**

   A menu appears, listing several items. The last four items are various section breaks.

4. **Choose Next Page from the Breaks button menu.**

   A page break is inserted in your document; a new section has started.

When using Print Layout view, the section break looks like a page break. It works like one too: Text stops on the page before the section break and then starts at the top of the next page. Each page, however, is in a different document section.

After the section is created, you can modify the page layout and format of each section in your document.

- ✔ Choose Continuous in Step 4 to place a more flexible form of section break into your document. Depending on which page formats are changed between sections, the Continuous section break may start a new page or it may not.

- ✔ The Even Page and Odd Page section breaks work just like the Next Page section break, but they happen only on even pages or odd pages, respectively. These section breaks are designed for documents that use odd and even headers or sport unique margins for binding purposes.

- ✔ When working with sections, I recommend placing the Section item on the status bar: Right-click the status bar and choose Section from the menu. The Section item lists the current section by number as you work through your document.

Using sections

Sections come into play when using a page-formatting command. You have two options.

The first option is to place the insertion pointer into a specific section and then issue the page-formatting command. For example, in Figure 14-1, Example 1, with the insertion pointer in section 2, change the page number format as described in Chapter 13. The change applies only to that section.

In Figure 14-1, example 3, the insertion pointer is placed in section 2, and then the page orientation is changed. That change doesn't affect sections 1 or 3.

The Page Setup dialog box features a special menu for applying changes made to only the current section. Use the Apply To drop-down menu, shown in Figure 14-2, to choose the item titled This Section. Click OK and the changes made in the dialog box apply only to the current section.

Deleting a section break

A section break sits in your document just like any other character, although it's invisible. To best delete it, you need to see it. Follow these steps:

1. **Click the Home tab.**

2. **In the Paragraph group, click the Show/Hide command button.**

    Hidden codes and characters are revealed in the document.

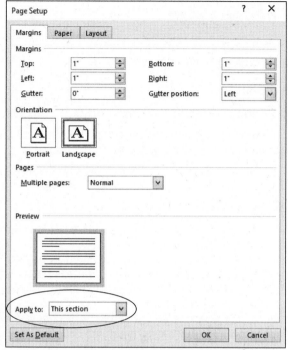

Figure 14-2:
Applying
page for-
matting to
one section
only.

3. **Position the insertion pointer to the start (left end) of the double-dashed lines that say Section Break.**

4. **Press the Delete key.**

   The section break is gone.

5. **Click the Show/Hide command button again to hide the codes.**

After the section break vanishes, the page formatting may change, adopting the format from the previous section. That's to be expected, but it may alter things you can't see, such as page numbering and headers and footers.

If you regret your decision to remove the page number, press Ctrl+Z to undo.

That First Page

Even when you're blessed with a superior knowledge of paragraph formatting and you fully understand the magic of the section break, formatting that first page can be a bother. The kids at Microsoft are aware of your frustration, so they concocted some special first-page formatting features for Word.

Adding a cover page

The sneakiest way to slap down a cover page on your document is to use Word's Cover Page command. Here's how it works:

1. **Click the Insert tab.**

2. **In the Pages group, click the Cover Page button.**

   If you don't see the Pages group or Cover Page button, click the Pages button and then click the Cover Page icon.

   The Cover Page button displays a fat, fun menu full of various cover-page layouts.

3. **Choose a cover-page layout that titillates you.**

   The cover page is immediately inserted as the first page in your document.

Many preset cover pages feature replaceable text, such as [COMPANY NAME]. Click that text and type something appropriate, such as your actual company name. Do so for all bracketed text on the inserted cover page.

- ✔ You can change a cover page at any time by choosing a new one from the Cover Page menu. The new cover page retains any replacement text you typed.

- ✔ To remove a cover page, summon the Cover Page menu and choose the item Remove Current Cover Page.

- ✔ The cover page you add is followed by a hard page break. It is not a section break. Even so, it's treated differently from certain page-formatting commands applied to the rest of the document. That means if you add page numbers or a header or footer to your document, the formatting applies to only the second and later pages, not to the cover page.

Inserting a cover page manually

When you're unsatisfied with Word's Cover Page designs, you can craft your own document cover page. All the formatting tools and document tricks presented in this book are at your disposal. You just need to insert the page at the start of the document.

Here are the general steps to take:

1. **Before writing the cover page, position the toothpick cursor at the tippy-top of the document.**

This step applies whether you've written the document or not. If you've already written the cover page, position the toothpick cursor at the end of the page. And if you've put in a hard page break after the cover page, delete it.

2. **Click the Layout tab.**

3. **Choose Breaks ⇨ Next Page.**

    A section break splits the first page from the rest of the document as its own section.

4. **Create the cover page.**

    Add a title, additional text, graphics, and various document froufrou.

As the first (cover) page is now its own section, the page formatting it sports can be separated from the rest of the document. If you apply page numbering, do so on the second page (in section 2), and ensure that the numbering applies only to that section. The end result is shown in Figure 14-1, Example 2.

Headers and Footers

To best understand headers and footers, it helps to know the difference between a header and a heading and between a footer and a footnote. Specifically, what's a header and what's a footer?

A *header* is text that appears at the top of every page in a document. A *heading* is a text style used to break up a long document, to introduce new concepts, and to help organize the text.

A *footer* is text that appears at the bottom of every page in a document. A *footnote* is a tiny bit of text that appears at the bottom of a page, usually a reference to some text on that page.

- ✔ Typical headers and footers contain page numbers, your name, the document name, the date, and other information that's handy to have on every page.

- ✔ Headers and footers dwell in special, exclusive areas outside the realm of regular text. These areas are found in all Word documents, but unless you place some text or other items inside those areas, they remain invisible.

- ✔ See Chapter 15 for more information on headings.

- ✔ For details on footnotes, see Chapter 21.

- ✔ Headers can also be called *eyebrows*. Weird, huh?

Using a preset header or footer

Most documents use typical headers and footers, placing common information into one or both areas. To accommodate your hurried desires, you can quickly shove such a preset header or footer into your document. Heed these steps:

1. **Click the Insert tab.**

2. **From the Header & Footer group, choose the Header button.**

   The Header menu shows a list of preformatted headers.

3. **Choose a template.**

   The header is added to the document, saved as part of the page format. Also, the Header & Footers Tools Design tab appears on the Ribbon.

4. **Change any [Type here] text in the header.**

   Click the bracketed text and type to personalize your header.

5. **Use the commands on the Header & Footer Tools Design tab, Insert group to add specific items in the header.**

   Examples are offered in the sections that follow.

Close Header
and Footer

6. **When you're done working on the header, click the Close Header and Footer button.**

   The button is found on the far-right end of the Header & Footer Tools Design tab.

To add a footer, choose the Footer button in Step 2 and think of the word *footer* whenever you see the word *header* in the preceding steps.

After you exit from the header or footer, you can see its text at the top or bottom of your document. It appears ghostly, to let you know that it's there but not part of the document. To edit the header or footer, double-click that ghostly text.

Creating a custom header or footer

When one of the preset header/footer designs doesn't cut it, consider creating your own. The secret is to double-click the space at the top or bottom of the page. The header or footer area, respectively, becomes active.

You can place text or any other item, including graphics, in a header or footer. Common and useful commands appear on the Header & Footer Tools

Design tab, but you can use any tab on the Ribbon to create and customize a header or footer.

To switch between the header and footer when editing, click the Go to Footer button. To switch back, click Go to Header. These buttons are found on the Header & Footer Tools Design tab in the Navigation group.

Type text

Any text you type in a header or footer becomes part of the header or footer. It doesn't have to be fancy text, just whatever text you want appearing at the top or bottom of every page in the document.

The standard format for lines in a header or footer includes two tab stops: A center tab stop in the middle of the page and a right tab stop aligned with the right margin. Use these tab stops, as illustrated in Figure 14-3, to create useful header text.

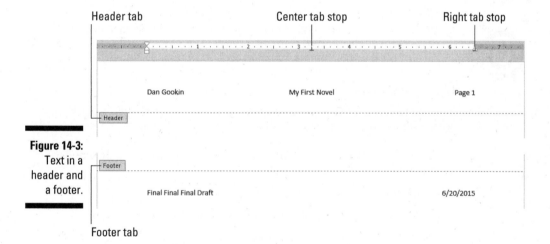

Header tab   Center tab stop   Right tab stop

Dan Gookin   My First Novel   Page 1

Final Final Final Draft   6/20/2015

Figure 14-3: Text in a header and a footer.

Footer tab

Add a page number

It's tempting, and it seems like the obvious choice, but don't use the Page Number command on the Header & Footer Tools Design toolbar. If you need a page number in a header or footer, add a document page-number field. Follow these steps.

1. **Position the insertion pointer where you want the page number to appear.**

2. **Click the Header & Footer Tools Design tab.**

3. **In the Insert group, click the Document Info button and choose Field.**

   The Field dialog box appears. It's a busy place, covered in full detail in Chapter 23.

4. **From the Categories menu, choose Numbering.**

5. **In the Field names list, click to select Page.**

6. **Choose a Format.**

   For example, choose the item 1, 2, 3, . . . to use that numbering style.

7. **Click the OK button.**

   The Page field is inserted in the header. It reflects the current page number for every page printed in the document.

✔ You don't have to go to page 1 to insert a page number in a header. Word is smart enough to place the proper number on the proper page, no matter where you're editing the header in your document.

✔ If you want one of those "Page 3 of 45" things in a header or footer, you need two fields: The Page field as described in this section and the NumPages field. To add that field, repeat the steps in this section, but in Step 4 choose Document Information and in Step 5 choose NumPages.

Add the date and time

To place the current date or time or an updating time field in a header or footer, follow these steps:

1. **Position the insertion pointer where you want the date or time to appear.**

2. **Click the Header & Footer Tools Design tab.**

3. **In the Insert group, click the Date & Time command button.**

   The Date and Time dialog box appears.

4. **Choose a format for the date, or the time, or both.**

5. **To keep the date and time information current, place a check mark by the option Update Automatically.**

6. **Click OK.**

Also see Chapter 23 for information on the PrintDate field.

Working with multiple headers and footers

As your document grows more complex, so does the need for headers and footers to accommodate it. As an example, this book uses different headers for its odd and even pages. Or maybe you have a document where you don't want the header on the first page. All of that is possible.

Odd and even headers and footers

To spice up your document with a different header and footer on the odd (left) and even (right) pages, obey these steps:

1. **Create a header or footer, as described elsewhere in this chapter.**

   You don't have to create a header — just double-click the header or footer area. As long as you see the Header & Footer Tools Design tab, you're in business.

2. **Click the Header & Footer Tools Design tab.**

3. **Click the Different Odd & Even Pages check box.**

   With this feature active, Word sets up headers and footers for odd and even pages. The Header and Footer tags in the document reflect the change as well, saying Odd Page Footer or Even Page Footer. The tag tells you which header or footer you're editing.

4. **Create the header and footer for the odd pages.**

   Follow the suggestions listed in this chapter.

5. **In the Navigation group, click the Next button.**

   Word displays the even page header or footer, allowing you to create or edit its contents. The Header or Footer tag changes to reflect which header you're editing.

   If clicking the Next button does nothing, your document has only one page. Add a page to enable the even headers and footers.

   To return to the odd header or footer, click the Previous button.

6. **Close the header or footer when you're done.**

To return to using only one header and footer for a document, repeat these steps but in Step 3 remove the check mark. Any even header and footer you've set is removed, leaving only the odd header and footer.

No header or footer on the first page

Most people don't want the header or footer on the first page, which is usually the title page or a cover page. Suppressing the header for that page is easy, if you follow these steps:

1. **Edit the document's header or footer.**

2. **Click the Header & Footer Tools Design tab.**

3. **In the Options group, place a check mark by Different First Page.**

   That's it.

The Header or Footer tag on the first page changes to read First Page Header or First Page Footer. It's your visual clue that the first page of the document sports a different header from the ones in the rest of the document. If you don't want anything to appear there, leave it blank.

Headers, footers, and sections

As a document format, headers and footers can be unique to the different sections in your document. Unless you direct Word otherwise, all sections use the same headers and footers. To break the link between all the sections and set a new header and footer for a specific section, follow these steps:

1. **Edit the document's header or footer.**

   I'm assuming that the document has multiple pages, at least two sections, and that the Header & Footer Tools Design tab is displayed.

2. **Click the Header & Footer Tools Design tab.**

3. **In the Navigation Group, click the Next button to locate the start of the next section's header or footer.**

   The Header or Footer tag is updated to reflect the current section, as shown in Figure 14-4. You also see the text Same as Previous, which is the clue that the header is identical to the header in the previous section. For example, if you change something in the first section's header, the change is reflected in all linked headers.

Figure 14-4:
A header in
Section 2,
linked to
Section 1.

Dan Gookin   My First Novel   Page 2

Header -Section 2-   Same as Previous

Section 2 header   Headers are linked

4. **In the Navigation group, click the button Link to Previous.**

   The link is broken. The tag Same as Previous disappears. The header or footer doesn't change — yet.

5. **Edit the section's header or footer.**

   Changes made apply only to the current section.

The link is what confuses a lot of people. They know about sections, but when they change the header or footer in one section, the text isn't updated. That's because the link hasn't been broken, as described in these steps.

To restore the link, return to the given section's header or footer and repeat the steps in this section. Clicking the Link to Previous button a second time reestablishes the link.

✔ This trick may not work if your document uses different headers and footers on odd and even pages, as described earlier in this chapter.

✔ The Different First Page option, described earlier in this chapter, doesn't link the header or footer between the first page and the rest of the document.

Removing a header or a footer

You can't destroy the header or footer area in a document, but you can remove all text and other stuff: Edit the header or footer, press Ctrl+A to select everything, and press the Delete key. Poof!

The more official way to remove a header or footer is to follow these steps:

1. **Edit the document's header or footer.**

2. **Click the Header & Footer Tools Design tab.**

3. **In the Header & Footer group, click the Header button.**

4. **Choose Remove Header.**

   The header is gone.

5. **Click the Footer button and choose Remove Footer.**

   The footer is gone.

Chapter 15

Style Formatting

If all of Word's formatting commands are ingredients, a style is a recipe. It's a single command that applies a virtual stew of formatting commands, all at once. Even better, when you update or change a style, all text formatting using that style changes as well. In the end, you save time — and your documents look fabulous.

The Big Style Overview

A style is a collection of text and paragraph formats. These formats are saved as a collection, given a name, and applied to text just like any other format. The difference is that when you apply a style, you're applying all the formats stored in that style. For heavy-duty formatting, styles save time.

Styles are available in all documents, whether or not you choose to use them. In fact, any text you type has a style automatically applied; it can't be avoided. All text in a blank document uses the Normal style, Word's primary (or *default*) text style.

The Normal style is defined with the following formats: Calibri font, 11 points tall, left-justified paragraphs, multiple line spacing at 1.08 lines, no indenting, zero margins, and 8 points of space after every paragraph.

Word's Style names give you a clue to how to use the style, such as Heading 1 for the document's top-level heading, or Caption, used for figure and table captions.

Styles are also categorized by which part of the document they affect. Five style types are available:

Paragraph: The paragraph style contains both paragraph- and text-formatting attributes: indents, tabs, font, text size — you name it. It's the most common type of style.

Character: The character style applies to characters, not paragraphs. This type of style uses the character-formatting commands, which are mentioned in Chapter 10.

Linked: The linked style can be applied to both paragraphs and individual characters. The difference depends on which text is selected when the style is applied.

Table: The table style is applied to tables, to add lines and shading to the table cells' contents. Refer to Chapter 19 for more information on tables in Word.

List: The list style is customized for presenting lists of information. The styles can include bullets, numbers, indentation, and other formats typical for the parts of a document that present lists of information. See Chapter 21 for info on lists.

These types come into play when you create your own styles, as well as when you're perusing styles to apply to your text.

Finding the styles

Styles dwell on the Home tab, in the aptly named Styles group, as shown in Figure 15-1. What you see on the Ribbon is the Style Gallery, which can be expanded into a full menu of style choices, as illustrated in the figure.

Click the dialog box launcher in the lower-right corner of the Styles group to view the Styles pane, also shown in Figure 15-1. To dismiss the Styles pane, click the X (Close) button in its upper-right corner.

✔ The Styles pane lists more styles than the Style Gallery, including styles you've created.

✔ To preview the styles in the Styles pane, put a check in the box by the Show Preview option, found at the bottom of the Styles pane.

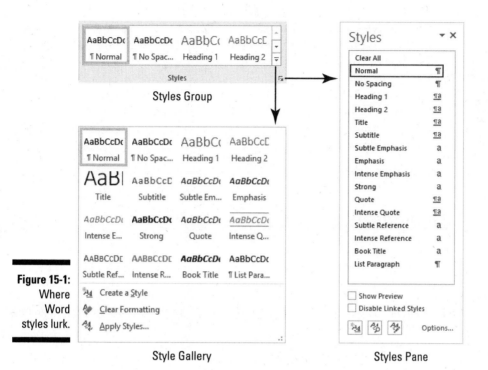

Styles Group

Style Gallery

Styles Pane

Figure 15-1:
Where
Word
styles lurk.

- ✔ You can see more information about a style by simply hovering the mouse pointer over the style's name in the Styles pane.

- ✔ To view all available styles in the Styles pane, click the Options link (in the lower-right corner). In the Styles Pane Options dialog box, choose All Styles from the Select Styles to Show menu. Click OK.

- ✔ Word's predefined styles are specified in the Style Gallery, though you can customize the list to replace Word's styles with your own. See the section "Customizing the Style Gallery," later in this chapter.

Using a style

Styles are applied to text just like any other formatting: Select a block of text and then apply the style or choose the style and start typing. The big difference between a style and an individual format is that the style contains multiple formats, applied all at once.

- ✔ As you hover the mouse pointer over a style in the Style Gallery, text in the document is updated with a style preview.

- Some styles are assigned a keyboard shortcut. For example, the shortcut for the Normal style is Ctrl+Shift+N. Use the keyboard shortcut to apply the style.

- Heading styles play a special role in Word. They're used for document navigation, outlining, as well as creating a table of contents. See the later section "Creating heading styles" for details.

- As with any other formatting, applying a style replaces the text's previously applied style.

- Also see the later section "Removing style formatting."

Discovering the current style

To determine which style is currently in use, refer to the Style Gallery. The style of any selected text, or text where the insertion pointer blinks, appears highlighted. The current style is also highlighted if the Styles pane is visible.

To specifically examine the style for any text, use the Style Inspector. Follow these steps:

1. **Place the insertion pointer in a specific chunk of text.**

2. **Click the Home tab.**

3. **Click the launcher icon in the lower-right corner of the Styles group.**

   The Styles pane appears.

4. **Click the Style Inspector button.**

   The Style Inspector icon is shown in the margin.

Upon success, you see the Style Inspector window, similar to what's shown in Figure 15-2. The Style Inspector discloses the text's formatting based on the style plus any additional formatting applied to the style.

To see even more details, such as the specific formats used, click the Reveal Formatting button, as illustrated in Figure 15-2. Use the Reveal Formatting pane to examine all details for the style.

- The shortcut key to summon the Reveal Formatting pane is Shift+F1.

- The Reveal Formatting pane shows the exact formatting applied to your document's text. Click any jot or tittle to expose the specifics. Choose a link in the pane to summon the proper dialog box to alter or remove a formatting tidbit.

Clear specific attribute

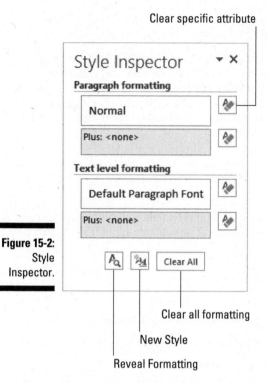

Figure 15-2:
Style
Inspector.

Clear all formatting

New Style

Reveal Formatting

Removing style formatting

You don't remove style formatting from text as much as you reapply another style. The only official way to remove a style is to replace it with the Normal style.

Because many Word users don't understand styles, Word comes with Clear Formatting commands. You can see such commands referenced in Figure 15-2, which illustrates the Style Inspector. Clicking those buttons simply replaces the given style with the Normal style.

- ✔ See the section, "Updating the Normal style," for more details on setting default formatting.

- ✔ Also see Chapter 10 for information on using the Clear Formatting command, which applies to font formats.

Make Your Own Styles

To convince you why styles are important, consider this: You create a custom format for your document's headings. You pick the right font, size, and color, and add just enough space after the heading. Then you decide to change the font. If you'd created a style, you'd make only one change and all the document's headers would be updated. Otherwise, you must change each individual heading. And that sucks.

Creating a style

The easiest way to make up a new style is to format a single paragraph just the way you like. Once you've set text and paragraph formatting, follow these steps to create the new style:

1. **Select the text you've formatted.**

2. **Click the Home tab.**

3. **In the Styles group, display the full Quick Styles Gallery.**

   Click the down-pointing arrow in the lower-right corner of the Gallery.

4. **Choose the command Create a Style.**

   The Create New Style from Formatting dialog box appears.

5. **In the Name box, type a short and descriptive name for your style.**

   For example, *proposal body* for the main text of a proposal or *dialog* for a character's lines in a play.

6. **Click the OK button to create the style.**

   The style is created and applied to the selected text.

The style you create appears on the Ribbon, in the Style Gallery.

- ✔ Styles you create are saved with the document, along with the text and other document info.

- ✔ To make the style available to other documents, build a template, as described in Chapter 16. Styles in a template are available to all documents created by using that template.

- ✔ You may have to tweak some settings in your style. See the section "Modifying a style," later in this chapter.

Using the Create New Style from Formatting dialog box

A more detailed way to build a style is to summon the Create New Style from Formatting dialog box. Beyond having a tediously long name, the Create New Style from Formatting dialog box lists all Word's formatting settings and options in one place. If you're familiar with Word's formatting commands, you can use the dialog box to create new styles. Follow these steps:

1. **Summon the Styles pane.**

   The keyboard shortcut is Ctrl+Shift+Alt+S, If you don't want to tie your fingers in a knot, see the earlier section "Finding the styles" for the long way to bring up the Styles pane.

2. **Click the New Style button.**

   The button is shown in the margin. Click it to see the Create New Style from Formatting dialog box, as shown in Figure 15-3.

Follow-me style

Create New Style from Formatting   ?   ×

Properties

Name:	Document Title
Style type:	Paragraph
Style based on:	¶ª Title
Style for following paragraph:	¶ First Paragraph

Formatting

Calibri Light (Head   28   **B** *I* U   Automatic

Previous Paragraph Previous Paragraph Previous Paragraph Previous Paragraph Previous Paragraph Previous Paragraph Previous Paragraph Previous Paragraph Previous Paragraph Previous Paragraph

Eating Boogers

Following Paragraph Following Paragraph Following Paragraph Following Paragraph Following Paragraph
Following Paragraph Following Paragraph Following Paragraph Following Paragraph Following Paragraph
Following Paragraph Following Paragraph Following Paragraph Following Paragraph Following Paragraph
Following Paragraph Following Paragraph Following Paragraph Following Paragraph Following Paragraph
Following Paragraph Following Paragraph Following Paragraph Following Paragraph Following Paragraph
Following Paragraph Following Paragraph Following Paragraph Following Paragraph Following Paragraph

Style: Show in the Styles gallery
  Based on: Title
  Following style: First Paragraph

☑ Add to the Styles gallery   ☐ Automatically update
◉ Only in this document   ○ New documents based on this template

Format ▾   OK   Cancel

Figure 15-3:
The Create New Style from Formatting dialog box.

Choose specific formatting

The follow-me style

A great shortcut for applying styles is the Style for Following Paragraph menu, found at the top of the Create New Style from Formatting dialog box. When you choose a style from this item's menu, Word switches automatically to that style after using the current style. It's what I call the follow-me style.

For example, suppose your Document Title style is followed by the First Paragraph style. After typing the Document Title text, Word switches to the First Paragraph style for you. That type of formatting control can save you time.

3. **Type a short, descriptive name for the new style.**

4. **Ensure that Paragraph is chosen for the style type.**

   If the format is a character style, choose Character. An example of a character style is blue, bold, Courier, 12-point — the one that I use in my documents for filenames.

5. **Choose an existing style as a base from the Style Based On drop-down list.**

   Use this step to save time. If the style you're creating features a lot of the same formatting as an existing style, choose that style from the list. The formats from that style are copied over, letting you build upon them or reuse them in a different way.

6. **Use the controls in the dialog box to set the style's format.**

   The Create New Style from Formatting dialog box is brimming with style command buttons.

   Use the Format button in the dialog box's lower-left corner to apply specific formatting commands. Choose a category from the button's menu to see a dialog box specific to one of Word's formatting categories.

7. **Click the OK button when you're done.**

The new style is created.

Modifying a style

Styles change. Who knows? Maybe blow-dried hair and wide lapels will creep back into vogue someday.

When you change your mind about a style and want to update some specific element, heed these steps:

1. **Summon the Styles pane.**

   Keyboard shortcut: Ctrl+Shift+Alt+S.

2. **Position the mouse pointer over the style you want to change.**

   Don't click, which selects the style. Instead, hover the pointer in the style's entry and a menu button appears on the right.

3. **Click the menu button.**

   The style's menu appears.

4. **Choose Modify.**

   The Modify Style dialog box appears, although it's the same Create New Style from Formatting dialog box (refer to Figure 15-3), just with a shorter name.

5. **Change the style's formatting.**

   Use the Format button to alter specific styles: font, paragraph, tabs, and so on. You can even add new formatting options or assign a shortcut key (covered in the next section).

6. **Click OK when you're done.**

Modifying the style affects updates text with that style applied. For example, if you change the font for your Figure Caption style, all figure caption text changes at once. That's the power of using styles.

Assigning a shortcut key to your style

With a keyboard-centric program such as Word, it's handy to use shortcut keys. When you find yourself applying the same styles over and over, why not assign them a special shortcut key combination? Follow these steps:

1. **Press the keyboard shortcut Ctrl+Shift+Alt+S to summon the Styles pane.**

2. **In the Styles pane, click a style's menu button.**

   Position the mouse pointer over the style you want to change and the menu button appears.

3. **Choose Modify.**

   The Modify Style dialog box appears.

4. **Click the Format button and choose Shortcut Key from the menu.**

   The Customize Keyboard dialog box appears. The two items you must pay attention to are the Press New Shortcut key box and the area just below the Current Key list.

5. **Press your shortcut key combination.**

   Use at least two of the shift keys — Shift, Alt, or Ctrl — when pressing your shortcut key combination. Most of the Ctrl+Alt key combinations are unassigned in Word.

   The keys you press are named in the Press New Shortcut Key box.

   If you make a mistake, press the Backspace key and then choose another key combination.

6. **Confirm that the key combination you chose isn't already in use.**

   Look below the Current Keys list. The text there explains which Word command uses the key combination you've pressed. When you see [unassigned], it means that your key combination is good to go.

7. **Click the Assign button.**

8. **Click the Close button.**

   The Customize Keyboard dialog box skulks away.

9. **Click the OK button to dismiss the Modify Style dialog box.**

Try out your shortcut: Position the insertion pointer in a block of text and press the key combination. The style is applied instantly.

I'll be honest: All the good shortcut keys are taken. Word uses most of them for its important commands. That leaves you with some Shift+Alt and Ctrl+Alt key combinations. They're better than nothing.

Deleting a style

To peel away any style you've created, follow these steps:

1. **Display the Styles pane.**

   The keyboard shortcut is Ctrl+Shift+Alt+S.

2. **Right-click the style you want to obliterate.**

3. **Choose the Delete item.**

   The Delete item is followed by the style's name.

4. **Click the Yes button to confirm.**

   The style is removed from the document.

You cannot delete the Normal or Heading style or any other standard Word style.

Style Tips and Tricks

Awash in a sea of styles, it's easy to overlook some of the more subtle aspects of Word's styles. For example, the Normal style need not be stuck the way Word presets things. And those heading styles offer more power than you may suspect.

Updating the Normal style

All documents sport the Normal style, which is the standard text and paragraph style and probably the style upon which all your personal styles are based. Like just about anything in Word, the Normal style can be changed — but I urge caution if you do so.

To alter the Normal styles font or paragraph format, summon the Font or Paragraph dialog boxes. Refer to specific steps in Chapters 10 and 11 for details. In both dialog boxes, you find a Set as Default button. To update the Normal style with changes made in either dialog box, click that button.

For example, to reset the Normal style's font to Times New Roman, follow these steps:

1. **Apply the Normal style to the current paragraph.**
2. **Press Ctrl+D to summon the Font dialog box.**
3. **Choose Times New Roman as the font.**
4. **Click the Set as Default button.**

   A dialog box appears.
5. **Choose the All Documents option to update the Normal template and change the Normal style for all documents.**

   If you choose the This Document Only option, the style is updated only for the current document.
6. **Click OK.**

I don't recommend making this choice unless you're determined to alter the Normal style. Mostly, people get into trouble when they accidentally change the Normal style and then want to change it back. If so, follow the steps in this section to restore the Normal style. A description of Word 2016's Normal style can be found in the earlier section, "The Big Style Overview."

Creating heading styles

Word's heading styles are numbered Heading 1, Heading 2, on down to Heading 9. You use them to identify different parts of a document, but they also take advantage of other Word features.

For example, text formatted with a heading style appears whenever you use the vertical scroll bar to skim a document. Headings can be expanded or collapsed, as part of Word's Outline feature, as described in Chapter 25. Headings appear in the Navigation pane when you search for text. They can be used when creating a table of contents.

You're not stuck with using Word's preset heading styles; you can create your own. The key is to set your own heading style's outline level: In the Paragraph dialog box, use the Outline Level menu to set the heading level: Set Level 1 from the Outline Level menu for top-level headings. For the next heading level (subheading), choose Level 2, and so on. These paragraph formats are used by Word's document organization tools, such as the Navigation pane and table of contents command.

Follow the steps in the earlier section "Using the Create New Style from Formatting dialog box" to update your heading styles to reflect the proper Outline Level paragraph format.

- ✔ Heading text is typically only one line long. Larger font sizes are usually selected. The Space After paragraph format is frequently applied.
- ✔ Word's predefined Title style isn't a heading style.

Customizing the Style Gallery

To ensure that the styles you use most appear in the Style Gallery, follow these steps:

1. **Summon the Styles pane.**

   Press the ungainly Ctrl+Shift+Alt+S key combination.

2. **Right-click the style you want to add to the Style Gallery.**

3. **Choose the command Add to Style Gallery.**

To remove a style from the Style Gallery, right-click the style and choose the command Remove from Style Gallery from the shortcut menu that appears.

Although this trick can be useful, the Style Gallery shows only a pittance of the styles available to a document. When you find yourself using more than a half-dozen or so styles (or however many show up on the Ribbon), use the Styles pane instead.

Chapter 16

Template and Themes Formatting

*Y*ou can exert great effort on the formatting task, getting your text to look just so. Given that the computer is supposed to save you time, obviously a better way must exist. That way is to use a template or a theme. These tools format your prose easily and rapidly. You can choose form a preset template or theme, or you can craft your own templates to preserve previous formatting efforts. Either way, the goal is to automate the document-formatting chore.

Instant Documents with Templates

A template is a timesaver. It lets you create documents that use the same styles and formatting without your having to re-create all that work and effort. Basically, the template saves time.

✔ Choosing a specific template for a document is optional.

✔ When you don't choose a template and elect to start a blank document, you're using the Normal template.

✔ Every document in Word is based on a template. Some Word users refer to templates as being attached to documents.

✔ Word's templates are divided into two categories: Featured and Personal. The Featured templates are those supplied by Microsoft and made available over the Internet. The Personal templates are those you create.

✔ Just because you use a template, and formatting and other items might be done for you, you must still save your work.

✔ Word uses three filename extensions for its document templates: dot, dotx, and dotm. Older Word templates use the dot extension. Word 2007 and later uses the dotx extension, with macro-enabled templates using the dotm extension. Filename extensions are not normally visible in Windows, although you may see them referenced when choosing a file type in the Open dialog box.

Starting a new document by using a template

To create a new, blank document in Word, press the Ctrl+N key combination. What you see is a new document based on the Normal template. To choose another template, either one supplied by Microsoft or one you've created, follow these steps:

1. **Click the File tab.**

   The File screen appears.

2. **Choose New from the left side of the File screen.**

   You see a list of template thumbnails. The list is divided into two categories, Featured and Personal, as illustrated in Figure 16-1.

3. **To peruse your own templates, click the Personal heading; otherwise, browse those available in the Featured list.**

   When you choose Personal, the screen shows only the templates that you crafted yourself.

4. **Click a template.**

5. **If prompted, click the Create button.**

   The button appears when you use one of Word's predefined templates.

Word/Office templates   Your templates   Pushpin   Available templates

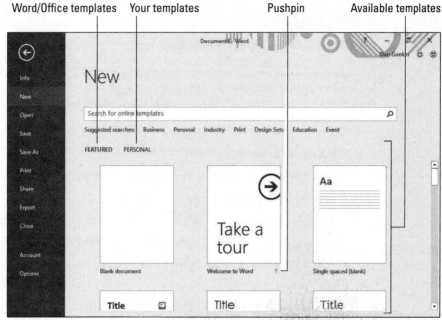

Figure 16-1:
Choosing
a template
from the
New screen.

6. Start working on the new document.

Text, graphics, headers, and footers appear in the document — providing such things were supplied with the template. You also have access to all the styles and formatting preset in the template.

Save your work! Even though you used a template to start the document, you still must save: Use the Save command and give your document a proper name as soon as possible.

✔ Using a template to create a new document doesn't change the template. To change or modify a template, see the section "Modifying a template," later in this chapter.

✔ Refer to the section "Templates of Your Own" for information on making your own templates.

✔ It's possible to pin your personal templates to the Featured screen: Click the pushpin icon, as illustrated in Figure 16-1. That way you can skip Step 3 (in the preceding list) and choose one of your own templates to quickly start a new document.

Changing a document's associated template

Documents, including blank documents that use the Normal template, are associated with a template. If you choose the wrong template or suddenly desire to change or reassign a document's template, follow these steps:

1. **Open the document that needs a new template attached.**

2. **Click the File tab.**

3. **On the File screen, choose the Options command.**

   The Word Options dialog box appears.

4. **Choose Add-Ins from the left side of the Word Options dialog box.**

5. **Choose Templates from the Manage drop-down list.**

   You find the Manage drop-down list near the bottom of the dialog box.

6. **Click the Go button.**

   The Templates and Add-ins dialog box appears. You should see which template is attached to the document, such as Normal.

7. **Click the Attach button.**

   Word displays the Attach Template dialog box, which looks and works like the Open dialog box.

8. **Select the template you want to attach.**

   The templates listed are stored on your computer, so you don't see the full range of templates that you would find on the New screen.

9. **Click the Open button.**

   The template is attached to your document.

10. **Ensure that the option Automatically Update Document Styles is selected.**

    Updating styles means that your document's current styles are changed to reflect those of the new template, which is probably what you want.

11. **Click OK.**

    The styles stored in that template are now available to your document, and the document is now attached to the template.

Note that attaching a template doesn't merge any text or graphics stored in that template. Only the styles (plus custom toolbar and macros) are merged into your document.

You can also follow these steps to un-attach a template. Do that by selecting Normal (normal.dotm) as the template to attach.

Templates of Your Own

If you enjoy the thrill and excitement of templates, you'll eventually have the desire to create your own. Over time, you'll build up a collection. Your own custom templates greatly help expedite your document production duties.

Creating a template based on a document you already have

The easiest way to create a new template, the way I do it about 90 percent of the time, is to base the template on an existing document — for example, a document you've already written and formatted to perfection. The template retains the document's formatting and styles so that you can instantly create a new document with those same settings.

To make a template based on a document you've already created, follow these steps:

1. **Open or create the document, one that has styles or formats or text that you plan to use repeatedly.**

2. **Strip out any text that doesn't need to be in every document.**

   For example, my play-writing template has all my play-writing styles in it, but the text includes only placeholders — just to get me started.

3. **Click the File tab.**

4. **On the File screen, choose the Save As command.**

   Don't worry about choosing the document's location. All Word templates are saved in a predefined folder, and Word automatically chooses that location for you.

5. **Click the Browse button.**

   The Save As dialog box appears. It's the same Save As dialog box that Word uses for saving everything. Refer to Chapter 8 for a refresher.

6. **Type a name for the template.**

   Type the name in the File Name box. Be descriptive.

   You don't need to use the word *template* when naming the file.

7. **From the Save As Type drop-down list, choose Word Template.**

   Ah-ha! This is the secret. The document must be saved in a document template format. That's what makes a template superior over a typical, boring Word document.

8. **Click the Save button.**

    Your efforts are saved as a document template, nestled in the proper storage location where Word keeps all its document templates.

9. **Close the template.**

    The reason for closing it is that any changes you make from now on are saved to the template. If you want to use the template to start a new document, you choose that template from the New window, as described earlier in this chapter.

Refer to the later section, "Modifying a template," for information on updating or changing a template.

Making a new template from scratch

It's okay to create a template from scratch, primarily for very basic templates. Otherwise, I recommend you first build a document to experiment, which is covered in the preceding section.

When you're bold enough to build a template from scratch, start by adding any common text. Then create the styles and any text formatting you plan on using in the template.

Once everything is set, use the Save As dialog box to save the document as a template, as described in the preceding section.

The biggest drawback to this approach is that your template probably isn't complete. As you start creating new documents based on the template, you find that you need to modify existing styles as well as add new ones. That just means more template editing, which is covered in the next section.

Modifying a template

You have two options for changing a template. The first is to start a new document by using the template. Make the changes you want. Then save the document as a template file, overwriting the original file.

The second way is to open the template file directly. This way is more difficult because Word keeps the template files in a special folder that may not be that easy for you to find. The good news is that with Word 2016, the folder is named Custom Office Templates, and it's found in the My Documents folder. Use the Open dialog box to open a template file held in that location.

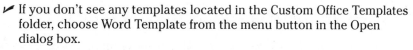

✔ If you don't see any templates located in the Custom Office Templates folder, choose Word Template from the menu button in the Open dialog box.

✔ Changing a template has a widespread effect. When you update or modify a template, you're changing all documents that use the template. Although such a thing can be beneficial, and one of the best reasons for using a template, be mindful of your changes!

The Theme of Things

Themes apply decorative styles, such as fonts and colors, to your document, giving your written efforts a professionally formatted feel with minimal fuss or talent. It's like having a graphics designer assist you but without having to suffer through her lamentable complaints about how her boyfriend pays no attention to her and never takes her anywhere.

A theme consists of three elements:

Colors: A set of colors is chosen to format the text foreground and background, any graphics or design elements in the theme, plus hyperlinks.

Fonts: Two fonts are chosen as part of the theme — one for the heading styles and a second for the body text.

Graphical effects: These effects are applied to any graphics or design elements in your document. The effects can include 3-D, shading, gradation, drop shadows, and other design subtleties.

Each of these elements is organized into a theme, given a name, and placed on the Design tab's Themes menu for easy application in your document.

✔ A professionally licensed, certified mentally stable graphics designer creates a theme's fonts, colors, and design effects so that they look good and work well together.

✔ A theme doesn't overrule styles chosen for a document. Instead, it accents those styles. The theme may add color information, choose different fonts, or present various graphical elements. Beyond that, it doesn't change any styles applied to the text.

✔ The graphical effects of a theme are only applied to any graphics in your document; the theme doesn't insert graphics into your text. See Chapter 22 for information on graphics in Word.

✔ Choosing a theme affects your entire document all at once. To affect individual paragraphs or bits of text, apply a style or format manually. Refer to Chapter 15.

Applying a document theme

You choose a theme by using the Themes button found on the Design tab. Built-in themes are listed along with any custom themes you've created.

Each built-in theme controls all three major theme elements (colors, fonts, graphical effects), changing your document's contents accordingly. Hovering the mouse pointer over a theme changes your document visually, which is a way to preview the themes. Click a theme to choose it.

- ✔ Because a document can use only one theme at a time, choosing a new theme replaces the current theme.

- ✔ To unapply a theme from your document, choose the Office theme or the menu command Reset to Theme from Template.

- ✔ If you would rather change only one part of a theme, such as a document's fonts, use the Colors, Fonts, or Effects command button on the Design tab.

Modifying or creating a theme

You can't create your own themes from scratch, but you can modify existing themes to make your own custom theme. You start by modifying existing theme colors and fonts:

To create a custom color theme, choose Colors ➪ Customize Colors. Use the Create New Theme Colors dialog box to pick and choose which colors apply to text or various graphical elements in your document.

To create a custom font theme, choose Fonts ➪ Customize Fonts. Use the Create New Theme Fonts dialog box to select fonts — one for the headings and another for the body text.

In each case, give the new theme a name and save it. You can then choose that theme from the Custom area of either the Colors or Fonts menu.

When you've added elements to your document and are using a set of theme colors, fonts, and graphics styles — even if you didn't create them yourself but, rather, used them merely to organize your document — you can use those items collectively as a theme. Choose Save Current Theme from the Theme menu, and use the dialog box to give your theme a proper descriptive name and save it. The theme you create then appears in the Custom area of the Themes menu.

To remove a custom theme, right-click it on the Themes menu and choose the Delete command. Click the Yes button to remove the theme.

Chapter 17

Sundry Formatting

Everyone has one, even neat people who proudly profess to be organized. It's the random stuff drawer. Maybe it's in the kitchen, or perhaps you have several such storage locations around the home or office. While everything else is organized neat and tidy, you still need a location for stuff that just doesn't fit anywhere else.

Word features various formatting commands that just don't fit well with other formatting categories. I wouldn't call them "random," although sundry seems to be a good term. It refers to useful items but also those not important enough to be mentioned individually.

Weird and Fun Text Effects

 On the Home tab, in the Font group, you find a button adorned with a fuzzy A, as shown in the margin. It's the Text Effects and Typography button. Click that button to view the Text Effects menu, as shown on the far left in Figure 17-1. This menu lists special text formats, well beyond the standard text decorations shown in Chapter 10. Choose an effect from the menu to apply it to your text.

If the effects on the menu aren't exactly what you want, you can create your own. You can choose custom effects from the submenus on the Text Effects and Typography menu, or you can use the Format Text Effects dialog box, shown on the center and right in Figure 17-1.

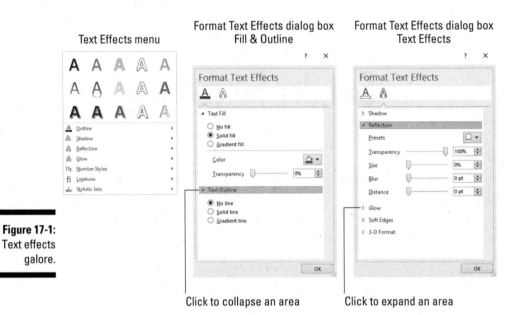

Text Effects menu

Format Text Effects dialog box
Fill & Outline

Format Text Effects dialog box
Text Effects

Figure 17-1:
Text effects
galore.

Click to collapse an area   Click to expand an area

To access the Format Text Effects dialog box, follow these steps:

1. Press Ctrl+D.

This keyboard shortcut brings up the Font dialog box.

2. Click the Text Effects button.

The Format Text Effects dialog box appears. It features two categories:
Text Fill & Outline and Text Effects, shown on the center and right in
Figure 17-1, respectively.

3. Manipulate the controls in the dialog box to customize text effects.

Choose a category, then click a triangle to expand items in a subcat-
egory. Controls appear, as illustrated in Figure 17-1, which let you customize the effect. Sadly, the dialog box lacks a preview window, so you'll
have to make your best guess as to the results.

4. Click the OK button to dismiss the Format Text Effects dialog box.

5. Click the OK button to close the Font dialog box.

The font effects you select affect any selected text in the document or any
text you type from that point onward.

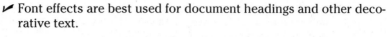

✔ Font effects are best used for document headings and other decorative text.

✔ The Text Effect button appears dimmed (Step 2) on older Word documents or if an older Word template was used to create the document. See Chapter 24 for information on converting older Word documents. If the document is based on an older template, you need to update the template and then re-attach the document to that template. See Chapter 16.

Steal This Format!

It's not a whisk broom, and it's definitely not a shaving brush. No, it's a paintbrush. Not only that, but it's also a *special* paintbrush — one that steals text and paragraph formatting by borrowing it from one place in your document and splashing it down in another. It's the Format Painter, and here's how it's used:

1. **Place the insertion pointer in the midst of the text that has the formatting you want to copy.**

   Think of this step as dipping a brush into a bucket of paint.

2. **Click the Home tab.**

3. **In the Clipboard group, click the Format Painter command button.**

   The mouse pointer changes to a paintbrush/I-beam, as depicted in the margin. It's used to select and reformat text.

4. **Hunt for the text you want to change.**

5. **Select the text.**

   Drag over the text you want to change — to "paint" it.

Voilà! The text is changed.

✔ The Format Painter works with character and paragraph formatting, not with page formatting.

✔ To change the formatting of multiple bits of text, double-click the Format Painter. That way, the Format Painter mouse pointer stays active, ready to paint lots of text. Press the Esc key to cancel your Dutch Boy frenzy.

✔ If you tire of the mouse, you can use the Ctrl+Shift+C key combination to copy the character format from one location to another. Use the Ctrl+Shift+V key combination to paste the character format.

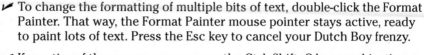

✔ You can sorta kinda remember to use Ctrl+Shift+C to copy character for-matting and use Ctrl+Shift+V to paste, because Ctrl+C and Ctrl+V are the copy-and-paste shortcut keys. Sorta kinda.

✔ Don't confuse the Format Painter with the highlighting tool, found in the Font group. See Chapter 26.

Automatic Formatting

Part of Word's AutoCorrect function (covered in Chapter 7) is a feature named AutoFormat. Whereas AutoCorrect fixes typos and common spelling boo-boos, AutoFormat fixes formatting fumbles.

Enjoying automagical text

AutoFormat controls some minor text formatting as you type. All its settings are visible in the AutoCorrect dialog box's AutoFormat as You Type tab, as shown in Figure 17-2.

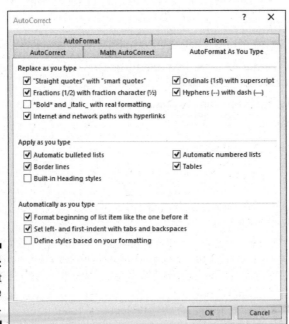

Figure 17-2:
AutoFormat As You Type settings.

To display that dialog box, heed these steps:

1. **Click the File tab.**

2. **Choose Options.**

   The Word Options dialog box appears.

3. **Select Proofing from the left side of the window.**

4. **Click the button labeled AutoCorrect Options.**

   The AutoCorrect dialog box appears.

5. **Click the AutoFormat as You Type tab.**

   The part of the dialog box you see is where all the AutoFormat options dwell. (Well, aside from the AutoFormat tab, which is redundant.) Turning an option off or on is as easy as removing or adding a check mark.

The best way to demonstrate the AutoFormat-as-you-type concept is to have a Word document on the screen and then type the examples in the following sections. Note that these samples demonstrate only a few of the things AutoFormat can do.

Smart quotes

The quote characters on the keyboard are *tick marks:* " and '. AutoFormat converts them into the more stylish open and closed curly quotes. Type hither:

```
He said, "Yes, I'm being honest. I really do love
you, but the monster is coming and you broke your
ankle, so I figured that you'd understand."
```

Both the single and double quotes are converted.

Real fractions

You can format a fraction by typing the first value in superscript, the slash mark, and then the second value in subscript. Or you can let AutoFormat do it for you. Here's an example:

```
I spend twice the time doing ½ the work.
```

The characters *1/2* are converted into the single character ½. This trick works for some, but not all, common fractions. When it doesn't work, use the superscript/subscript trick described in Chapter 31, in the section about building your own fractions.

Hyperlinks

Word can underline *and* activate hyperlinks that are typed in your document, such as

> I've been to http://www.hell.com and back.

The website http://www.hell.com is automatically underlined, colored, and turned into an active web page link for you. (To follow the link, Ctrl+click the text.)

Ordinals

You're guessing wrong if you think that *ordinals* are a baseball team or a group of religious leaders. They're numbers that end in the letters *st, nd,* or *rd,* as this line demonstrates:

> There were two of us in the race; I came in 1st and Oglethorpe came in 3rd.

Word's AutoFormat feature automatically superscripts ordinal numbers, making them look oh-so-spiffy.

Em dashes

An *em dash* is the official typesetting term for a long dash, longer than the hyphen (or its evil twin, the en dash). Most people type two hyphens to emulate the *em dash.* Word fixes that problem:

> A red one is a slug bug—not a punch buggy.

As you type the -- (dash dash), AutoFormat replaces it with the official em dash character.

- ✔ The keyboard shortcut for typing an em dash is Ctrl+Alt+minus sign, where the minus sign is the minus key on the numeric keypad.
- ✔ The keyboard shortcut for typing an en dash is Ctrl+minus sign.
- ✔ The en dash is approximately the width of the letter *N.* Likewise, the em dash is the width of the letter *M.*

Formatting tricks for paragraphs

At the paragraph level, AutoFormat helps you quickly handle some otherwise irksome formatting issues. Some folks enjoy this feature, some despise it. The following sections provide a few examples of what AutoFormat is capable of.

Numbered lists

Anytime you start a paragraph with a number, Word assumes (through AutoFormat) that you need all your paragraphs numbered. Here's the proof:

```
Things to do today:
1. Get new treads for the tank.
```

Immediately after typing 1., you probably saw the infamous AutoFormat lightning bolt icon and noticed your text being reformatted. Darn, this thing is quick! That's AutoFormat guessing that you're about to type a list. Go ahead and finish typing the line; after you press Enter, you see the next line begin with the number 2.

Keep typing until the list ends or you get angry, whichever comes first. To end the list, press the Enter key twice. That erases the final number and restores the paragraph formatting to Normal.

✔ This trick works also for letters (and Roman numerals). Just start something with a letter and a period, and Word picks up on the next line by suggesting the next letter in the alphabet and another period.

✔ Bulleted lists can also be created in this way: Start a line by typing an asterisk (*) and a space to see what happens.

✔ See Chapter 21 for more information on Word's numbering and bulleted list formats.

✔ Although you don't press the Enter key twice to end a typical paragraph in a document, pressing Enter twice to terminate an AutoFormat list is completely acceptable. Doing so doesn't add a blank paragraph to your document.

Borders (lines)

A line above or below a paragraph in Word is a *border*. Most folks call them lines, but they're borders in Word. Here's how to use AutoFormat to whip out a border:

```
- - -
```

Type three hyphens and press the Enter key. Word instantly transmutes the three little hyphens into a solid line that touches the left and right paragraph margins.

✔ To create a double line, type three equal signs and press Enter.

✔ To create a bold line, type three underlines and press Enter.

✔ Refer to Chapter 18 for details on borders and boxes around your text.

Undoing an AutoFormat

You have two quick ways to undo autoformatting. The first, obviously, is to press Ctrl+Z on the keyboard, which is the Undo command. That's easy.

You can also use the Lightning Bolt icon to undo autoformatting. Clicking the icon displays a drop-down menu, shown in Figure 17-3. Use the options displayed to control the AutoFormat options as you type.

Figure 17-3: AutoFormat options.

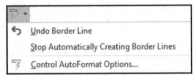

The first option (refer to Figure 17-3) simply undoes what's been done, the same as pressing Ctrl+Z on the keyboard. The second option disables the feature so that it never happens again. Lots of people like that option. The final option displays the AutoCorrect dialog box's AutoFormat as You Type tab, which was shown earlier in Figure 17-2.

Also see Chapter 33 for more details on disabling AutoFormat features.

Center a Page, Top to Bottom

Nothing makes a document title nice and crisp as having it sit squat in the center of a page, as shown in Figure 17-4. The title is centered left to right, which is a paragraph formatting trick, but how can it be centered top to bottom on the page?

If you're thinking about whacking the Enter key 17 times in a row to center a title top to bottom, stop! Let Word do the math to make the title perfectly centered. Here's how:

1. **Press the Ctrl+Home key combination.**

   The insertion pointer moves to the start of the document.

2. **Type and format the document's title.**

   It can be on a single line or on several lines.

   To center the title, apply center paragraph justification: Press Ctrl+E. Apply any additional font or paragraph formatting as necessary.

**A Perfectly
Centered
Title**

By Even Middleston

Avoid the temptation to press the Enter key to add space above or below the title. Such space isn't needed, and would wreck Word's automatic centering powers.

3. **Position the mouse pointer at the end of your title.**

   Press the End on the last line of the title, or the author line (refer to Figure 17-4).

4. **Click the Layout tab.**

5. **In the Page Setup group, choose Breaks ➪ Next Page.**

   A new page section break is inserted into the document. The title now sits on its own page as its own section.

6. **Click the document's first page.**

   You need to be on the page you want to format.

7. **Click the Layout tab.**

8. **Click the dialog box launcher in the lower-right corner of the Page Setup area.**

   The Page Setup dialog box appears.

9. **Click the Layout tab.**

10. **Click the Vertical Alignment drop-down list and choose Center.**

11. Confirm that the Apply To drop-down list shows This Section.

12. Click OK.

The first page of the document is centered from top to bottom. Because that page is its own section, the top-to-bottom centering applies only to that page and not the rest of the document.

Review Chapter 14 for more information on document sections.

Part IV
Spruce Up a Dull Document

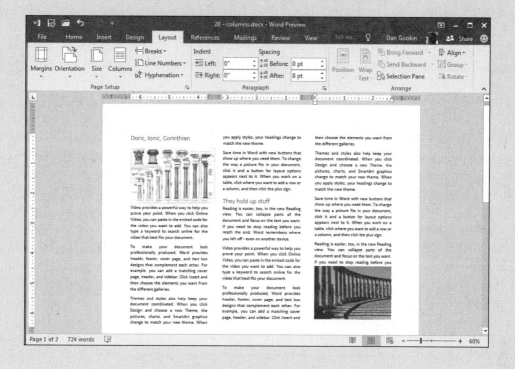

See how to assign a shortcut key to a symbol at www.dummies.com/extras/
word2016.

In this part . . .

- Learn how to use borders, draw lines, and add color to a document's background.
- Use tables in your documents.
- Split your text into multiple columns.
- Discover how to make several types of lists, including bulleted lists, numbered lists, and indexes.
- Learn how you can insert images and captions into a document.

Chapter 18

Borders and Lines

- -

- -

Seriously: Alarms sound at Microsoft headquarters when you attempt to use the hyphen or underline characters to draw a line in your document. It's just wrong.

Despite the array of interesting keys festooning the PC keyboard, avoid the temptation to use those characters to draw boxes, lines, or otherwise decorate your text. To sate that desire, I recommend exploring Word's broad basket of border commands.

The Basics of Borders

When it comes to understanding lines in Word, your topmost goal is to keep from pulling out your hair. To keep your luscious locks (or what's left of them), know two keys:

✔ Borders are a paragraph-level format.

✔ Borders and lines are two different things in Word.

When you apply a border to a paragraph — top, bottom, left, right, or all sides — that format sticks to the paragraph. It's echoed in subsequent paragraphs you type, just like any other paragraph-level format. (See Chapter 11 for paragraph format options.)

Unlike a border, a *line* is a drawing object. To add lines to your document, use the drawing tools described in Chapter 22. These objects are graphics, not text formats.

 To set borders for a paragraph, click the Home tab. In the Paragraph group look for the Borders button.

The Borders button shows the paragraph's current border format, such as Bottom Border, shown in the margin. Click that button to apply the format, or click the triangle next to the button to display the Borders menu to choose another format. The Borders menu is shown in Figure 18-1.

	Bottom Border
	Top Border
	Left Border
	Right Border
	No Border
	All Borders
	Outside Borders
	Inside Borders
	Inside Horizontal Border
	Inside Vertical Border
	Diagonal Down Border
	Diagonal Up Border
	Horizontal Line
	Draw Table
	View Gridlines
	Borders and Shading...

Figure 18-1:
The Border
and Shading
menus.

The last item in the Borders menu displays the Borders and Shading dialog box, covered in the later section, "The Borders and Shading Dialog Box." Use that dialog box to get more flexibility when formatting paragraph borders.

Other sections in this chapter describe how to use the Borders button to apply borders (lines) to paragraphs in a document.

✔ A line around a paragraph is a border. It's a style applied to the paragraph and it sticks to any subsequent paragraphs you type.

✔ Another way to call out text on a page is to create a text box. Unlike a border, which is a paragraph style, a text box is a graphical element. See Chapter 23.

✔ Not all lines in Word are borders. For example, an underline is a character-level format. Red and blue underlines indicate spelling and grammatical errors. A vertical red line in the left margin, as well as solid red underlines, are used by Word's Revision Marks commands.

Putting borders around a paragraph

To apply a border to any or all sides of a paragraph, follow these steps:

1. **Place the insertion pointer in a paragraph.**

2. **Click the Home tab.**

3. **In the Paragraphs group, click the triangle next to the Borders command button.**

   The Borders menu appears.

4. **Choose a border style from the menu.**

   For example, to place a line atop the paragraph, choose Top Border. Its icon is shown in the margin.

The border is applied using the line style, thickness, and color set in the Borders and Shading dialog box. See the later section, "The Borders and Shading Dialog Box," for details.

To apply multiple lines, choose both border styles sequentially. For example, to add rules to a paragraph (a line above and below), first choose the Top Border command, and then click the Borders command again and choose Bottom Border.

✔ Horizontal borders stretch between the paragraph's left and right margins. These margins are different from the page margins. See Chapter 11 for information on setting a paragraph's left and right margins.

✔ A common use of paragraph borders is to set off a document title or heading. See the later section, "Creating a fancy title," for formatting tips.

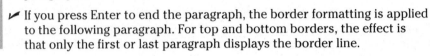

REMEMBER

✔ When multiple paragraphs are selected, the border is applied to all paragraphs as a group. Therefore, a top or bottom border appears on only the first or last paragraph in the selected block.

✔ To place lines between paragraphs, see the section, "Boxing multiple paragraphs."

✔ If you press Enter to end the paragraph, the border formatting is applied to the following paragraph. For top and bottom borders, the effect is that only the first or last paragraph displays the border line.

Drawing a thick line between paragraphs

A handy border tool to break up paragraphs of text is the Horizontal Line. It's not a paragraph format, so unlike a border it doesn't stick to a paragraph. Instead, it works like a quasi-graphical element inserted into the text.

To add a horizontal line between paragraphs, follow these steps:

1. **Position the insertion pointer at the start or end of a paragraph, where you want the horizontal line to appear.**

2. **Click the Home tab.**

3. **In the Paragraph Group, click the Borders button.**

4. **Choose Horizontal Line.**

    Word inserts a line stretching from the left to right margins.

Click the line to adjust its size. Use the mouse to drag one of the six handles (top and bottom and the four corners) to set the line's width or thickness.

To format the horizontal line, double-click it. Use the Format Horizontal Line dialog box to set the width (as a percentage), height, color, and alignment.

To remove the horizontal line, click once to select it and then press the Delete key.

Boxing multiple paragraphs

To stick a box around a paragraph, use the Outside Borders command, found on the Borders menu and shown in the margin. When multiple paragraphs are selected, the box wraps around the group.

If you desire to box several paragraphs in a row and keep lines between the paragraphs, use the All Borders command instead of Outside Borders. The All Borders icon is shown in the margin.

✔ More and fancy options for boxing paragraphs can be found in the Borders and Shading dialog box. See the section, "The Borders and Shading Dialog Box."

✔ Before you go paragraph-boxing crazy, what you might need in your document is really a table. See Chapter 19 for information on tables.

Removing borders

 To peel away the border format from one or more paragraphs of text, apply the No Border format: Select the paragraph(s), click the Borders button, and then choose No Border, as shown in the margin.

 To remove specific parts of a border, use the Borders and Shading dialog box, as covered next in this chapter.

The Borders and Shading Dialog Box

To fully flex Word's border bravado, summon the Borders and Shading dialog box:

1. **Click the Home tab.**

2. **In the Paragraph group, click the triangle by the Borders button to display the Borders menu.**

3. **Choose the Borders and Shading command.**

The Borders and Shading dialog box appears, as shown in Figure 18-2.

Unlike the Border menu, additional and custom border-setting options are available in the Borders and Shading dialog box. Most notably, you can set the border line style, thickness, and color.

✔ The Borders and Shading dialog box also allows you to place a border around a page, which is covered in the section, "Applying a page border."

✔ You can use the commands in the Borders and Shading dialog box to format a table. See Chapter 19 for information on tables in Word.

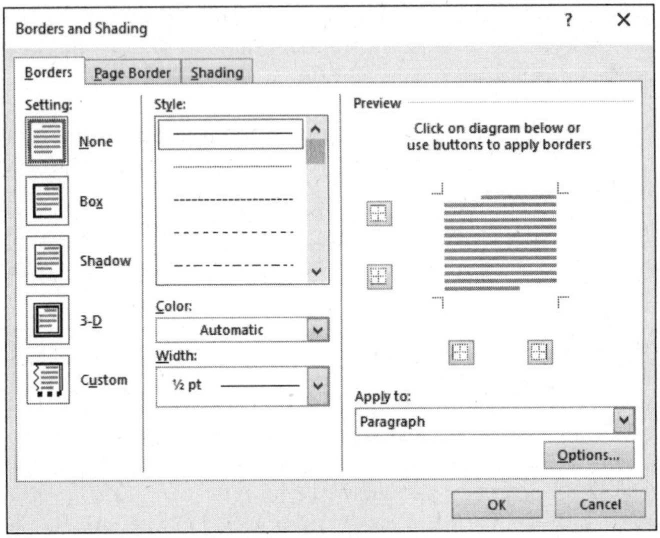

Figure 18-2:
The Borders
and Shading
dialog box.

Creating a fancy title

To create custom titles for newsletters, documents, or anything you want to pretend is super important, click to select a paragraph and then go nuts in the Borders and Shading dialog box. You may end up with results similar to what's shown in Figure 18-3.

Figure 18-3:
Fancy
borders.

Sterling, Worbletyme, & Grockmeister

869 Van Horn Road, Culpepper, MO, 63054 ~ (636) 555-6797

Attorneys at Law, weekdays   Children's Parties, weekends

To properly apply a special border, follow these general steps in the Borders and Shading dialog box:

1. Choose a line style in the Style list.

Scroll the list to view the full variety of styles (refer to Figure 18-2).

2. **Set the color in the Color list.**

   The Automatic color uses black, or the standard color as set by the document's theme (usually black).

3. **Choose a width in the Width list.**

4. **Click in the Preview part of the dialog box to place the line: top, bottom, right, or left.**

To remove a line, click it in the Preview window.

To start out quickly, select a preset design from the list of icons on the right side of the dialog box (refer to Figure 18-2).

Click the OK button to apply the customized border to your document's text.

Boxing text

Although applying a border is a paragraph-level format, you can also wrap borders around tiny tidbits of text. To do so, follow these steps:

1. **Select the text.**

2. **Summon the Borders and Shading dialog box.**

   Directions are found earlier in this chapter.

3. **Set the border style you desire.**

   Only the Box and Shadow options are available, although you can set the color and line thickness.

4. **Ensure that the Apply To menu shows Text and not Paragraph.**

5. **Click OK.**

Also see Chapter 10 for information on shading text. From a design point of view, I believe shading text is a better option than wrapping it in a box.

Applying a page border

One gem hidden in the Borders and Shading dialog box is the tool required to place a border around an entire page of text. The border sits at the page's margins, and is in addition to any paragraph borders you might apply.

Here's how to set a page border:

1. **Put the insertion pointer on the page you want to border.**

   For example, you might put it on the first page in your document.

2. **Summon the Borders and Shading dialog box.**

3. **Click the Page Border tab.**

4. **Set the border style.**

   Choose a preset style, line style, color, thickness.

   Use the Art drop-down list to choose a funky pattern for the border.

5. **Click the Apply To menu button to select which pages you want bordered.**

   Choose Whole Document to put borders on every page. To select the first page, choose the This Section–First Page Only item. Other options let you choose other pages and groups, as shown in the drop-down list.

   And now, the secret:

6. **Click the Options button.**

   The Border and Shading Options dialog box appears.

7. **In the Measure From drop-down list, choose the Text option.**

   The Edge of Page option just doesn't work with most printers. Text does.

   To add more "air" between your text and the border, increase the values in the Margin area.

8. **Click OK.**

9. **Click OK to close the Borders and Shading dialog box.**

To remove the page border, choose None under Settings in Step 4 and then click OK.

A page border is a page-level format. If you desire borders to sit on only certain pages, split your document into sections. Use the Apply To drop-down menu (Step 5) to select the current section for your page borders. See Chapter 14 for more information on section formatting.

Chapter 19

Able Tables

*W*riting is a linear task. Characters flow into words, which flow into sentences, which form paragraphs. You start reading here and end up there. That's how it works, up until the information you're trying to organize is best presented in a grid. That's when you need to summon a table.

Put a Table in Your Document

A table presents information organized into rows and columns — a grid. You can use the Tab key to build such a thing, setting various and clever tab stops and formatting your text accordingly. That works, but it's not the best solution.

The best way to add a table in your document is to use one of Word's table creation commands. The commands build a custom grid of rows and columns. Within the gird are cells, into which you can place text or graphics. You can format each cell with its own margins, spacing, or paragraph style. Lines and background colors format the table itself. These feats are beyond the capabilities of the silly old Tab key.

The Tab key gets its name from the same root as the word *table*. Its original purpose was to format tabular data. In fact, on some early typewriters, the Tab key was named *Tabulator*.

Working with tables in Word

To begin your table-making journey, click the Ribbon's Insert tab. In the Tablets group, the only item is the Table button. Click that button to see the Table menu, as illustrated in Figure 19-1.

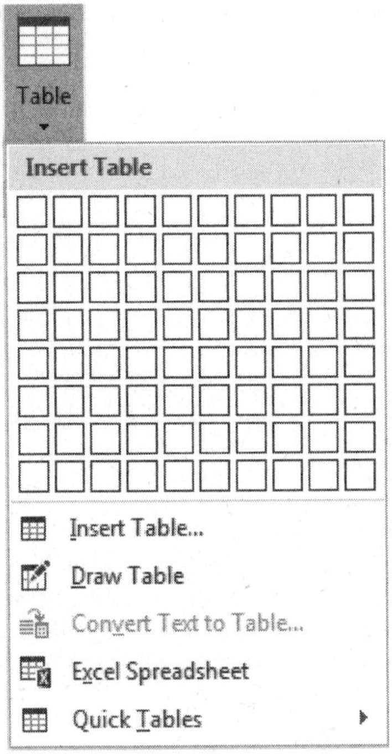

Figure 19-1:
The Table
menu.

The Table menu features multiple ways to slap down a table in your document, each of which is illustrated in the following sections.

Once the table is created, start filling it in. See the later section, "Typing text in a table" for details. Or, if you already used the Tab key to create the text, see the section, "Convert tab-formatted text into a table."

When a table is selected, or the toothpick cursor blinks inside the table, two new tabs appear on the Ribbon: Table Tools Design and Table Tools Layout. These tabs contain the specific commands to format and modify the table. Details are offered later in this chapter.

Creating a table

Word offers multiple ways to create a table, from right brain to left brain to options between. The choices allow for more flexibility, but also make this chapter longer than it would be otherwise.

> ✔ I recommend placing the table on a blank line by itself. Furthermore, add a second blank line *after* the table. That makes it easier to continue typing text below the table.

> ✔ Don't fret if you've already used tab stops to create a table. Word deftly converts tab-formatted text into a table, which is described in the section "Convert tab-formatted text into a table," later in this chapter.

> ✔ Don't worry about getting the table dimensions wrong. You can easily add rows or columns to or remove them from a table. See the later section, "Adding or removing rows or columns."

The quick way to create a table

The best way to make a table in Word is to use the grid on the Table button's menu, as shown in Figure 19-1. Follow these steps:

1. **Click where you want the table in your document.**

2. **Click the Insert tab.**

3. **Click the Table button.**

4. **Drag through the grid to set the desired number of rows and columns.**

   You don't need to be precise; you can always add or remove rows or columns later; see the later section, "Adding or removing rows or columns."

   In Figure 19-2, a four-column-by-three-row table is created. As you drag the mouse pointer on the menu, the table's grid magically appears in the document.

5. **Release the mouse button to begin working on the table.**

See the later section, "Text in Tables," to continue your table task.

The right-brain way to create a table

When dialog boxes make more sense than using menus and graphical goobers, follow these steps:

1. **On the Insert tab, click the Table button.**

2. **From the Table menu, choose the Insert Table command.**

   The Insert Table dialog box appears.

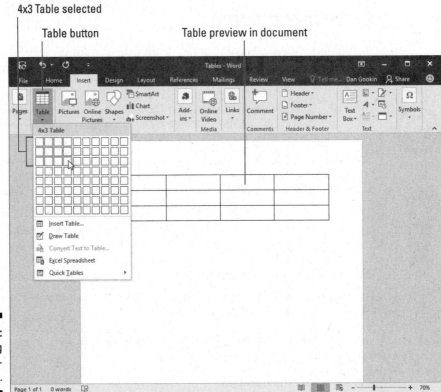

4x3 Table selected

Table button

Table preview in document

Figure 19-2:
Creating
a four-by-
three table.

3. **Enter the number of rows and columns.**

4. **Click the OK button to plop down your table.**

The left-brain way to create a table

Free your mind from the constraints of conventionalism, clutch a crystal, and use the mouse to draw a table inside your document:

1. **Click the Table button and choose Draw Table.**

   The mouse pointer changes to a pencil, as shown in the margin.

2. **Drag to draw the table's outline in your document.**

   Start in the upper-left corner and drag to the lower-right corner, which tells Word where to insert the table. You see an outline of the table as you drag down and to the right, as shown in Figure 19-3.

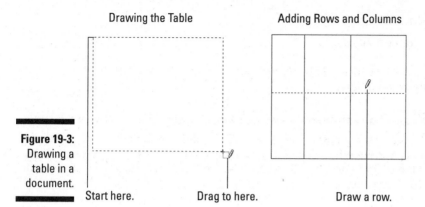

Drawing the Table   Adding Rows and Columns

Figure 19-3:
Drawing a
table in a
document.

Start here.   Drag to here.   Draw a row.

3. **Draw horizontal lines to create rows; draw vertical lines to create columns.**

   Refer to Figure 19-3 (on the right) for an example of drawing a row.

   As long as the mouse pointer looks like a pencil, you can use it to draw the rows and columns in your table.

4. **Press the Esc key when you've finished drawing the table.**

Convert tab-formatted text into a table

If you've used the Tab key to create rows and columns of text, you can quickly snap that part of your document into an official Word table. Follow these steps:

1. **Select the tab-formatted text.**

   If columns are separated by tabs, great. If not, each paragraph you select becomes a row in a single-column table.

2. **Click the Insert tab.**

3. **Choose Table ⇨ Convert Text to Table.**

4. **Confirm the guesses made in the Convert Text to Table dialog box.**

   Ensure that the values for columns and rows are correct. If the columns are separated by tabs, ensure that Tabs is chosen at the bottom of the dialog box. Generally speaking, Word does a good job of guessing the conversion settings.

   Drag around the Convert Text to Table dialog box so that you can better see the text in your document.

5. Click OK.

A table is born.

See the later section, "Table Modification" for information on fixing the freshly-created table.

The "I can't do anything — please help" approach to creating a table

Word comes with an assortment of spiffy predefined tables. Plopping one down in your document is as easy as using the Quick Tables submenu: Click the Table button and from the menu choose Quick Tables. Select a table type from the submenu.

Once the table is inserted, you can add or edit the existing text, add more rows or columns, or otherwise modify the table. Refer to directions elsewhere in this Chapter for specifics.

Un-creating a table

At some point, you may surrender the notion of needing a table, and desire the text to be freed from the table's confines. To perform such a jailbreak, you convert the table back into plain text or even tab-formatted text. Obey these steps:

1. Click inside the table you want to convert.

Don't select anything — just click the mouse.

2. Click the Table Tools Layout tab.

3. From the Table group, choose Select ⇨ Select Table.

4. From the Data group, choose Convert to Text.

The Convert to Text dialog box appears. It guesses how you want the table converted, such as using tabs or paragraphs.

5. Click OK.

Bye-bye, table. Hello, ugly text.

Some post-table-destruction cleanup might be necessary, but generally the conversion goes well. The only issue you may have is when a cell contains multiple paragraphs of text. In that case, undo the operation (press Ctrl+Z) and choose Paragraph Marks from the Convert to Text dialog box (before Step 5).

Deleting a table

To utterly remove the table from your document, text and all, heed these destruction directions:

1. **Click inside the table.**

2. **Click the Table Tools Layout tab.**

3. **In the Rows & Columns group, choose Delete ⇨ Delete Table.**

    The table is blown to smithereens.

Deleting the table deletes its contents as well. If you need to save the contents, I recommend converting the table instead of deleting it. See the preceding section.

Text in Tables

Text fills a table on a cell-by-cell basis. A cell can be empty or contain anything from a single letter to multiple paragraphs. The cell changes size to accommodate larger quantities of text.

- Within a cell, text is formatted just as it is elsewhere in Word, including margins and tabs.

- Although a single cell can deftly handle vast quantities of text, graphic artists don't put a lot of text into a single cell. Consider another way to present such information.

- I don't recommend formatting text inside a cell with first-line indents. Although it's possible, such formatting can be a pain to manipulate.

- Show the ruler when you work with formatting text in a table: Click the View tab, and in the Show group, place a check mark by the Ruler item.

Typing text in a table

Text appears in whichever cell the insertion pointer is blinking. Type your text and it wraps to fill the cell. Don't worry if it doesn't look right; you can adjust the cell size after you type the text, as described in the later section, "Adjusting row and column size."

- To move to the next cell, press the Tab key.
- To move back one cell, press Shift+Tab.

- Pressing Tab at the end of a row moves the insertion pointer to the first cell in the next row.

- Pressing the Tab key while the insertion pointer is in the table's bottom-right cell adds a new row to the table.

- To produce a tab character within a cell, press Ctrl+Tab. Even so:

- I don't recommend putting tabs into table cells. It makes the cell formatting all funky.

- When you press the Enter key in a cell, you create a new paragraph in the cell, which probably isn't what you want.

- The Shift+Enter key combination (a soft return) can be used break up long lines of text in a cell.

Selecting in a table

Two things you can select in a table are the text inside the cells or the cells themselves. You can also select rows, columns, or the entire table. Here are my suggestions:

- Triple-click in a cell to select all text in that cell.

- Select a single cell by positioning the mouse pointer in the cell's lower-left corner. The pointer changes to a northeastward-pointing arrow, as shown in the margin. Click to select the cell, which includes the cell's text but primarily the cell itself.

- Move the mouse pointer into the left margin and click to select a row of cells.

- Move the mouse pointer above a column, and click to select that column. When the pointer is in the sweet spot, it changes to a downward-pointing arrow (shown in the margin).

- Clicking the table's handle selects the entire table. The handle is visible whenever the mouse points at the table or when the insertion pointer is placed inside the table.

If you have trouble selecting any part of a cell, click the Table Tools Layout tab. In the Table group, the Select button's menu provides commands to select the entire table, a row, a column, or a single cell.

Aligning text in a cell

Text in a cell sports some special, table-specific alignment options. To adjust the position of text in a cell, follow these steps:

Doing math in a table

Just to keep the Excel program on its toes, Word lets you insert formulas into a table cell. These formulas aren't as sophisticated as those used in Excel, which some would consider a blessing.

To insert a formula into a table, click in a given cell. Click the Table Tools Layout tab. In the Data group, click the Formula button. (You may have to choose Data ➪ Formula, depending on the size of Word's window.) You see the Formula dialog box, along with a suggested calculation in the Formula text box.

The problem at this point is that Word offers no help on how to use the functions, what they do, or how to reference cells in a table. My advice is to use Excel to create such complex tables, and then copy and paste that part of the Excel worksheet into your Word document.

---

1. **Click in the cell's text.**

2. **Click the Table Tools Layout tab.**

3. **In the Alignment group, click an icon representing the desired alignment.**

The nine icons represent all alignment combinations: left, center, and right, with top, middle, and bottom.

 Click the Alignment group's Text Direction button (shown in the margin) to change the way text reads in a cell. Keep clicking the button to reset the orientation.

Table Modification

No table is perfect. You may need to add or remove a row or column, adjust the width or height, or otherwise fine tune and format the table. The tools to help you are found on two special tabs on the Ribbon: Table Tools Design and Table Tools Layout. To summon these tabs, click anywhere in a table. Then start making your adjustments.

The best time to format and fix a table is *after* you've added its text.

Adding or removing rows or columns

Not only can you add rows and columns to any of a table's four sides, you can squeeze new rows and columns inside a table. The secret is to click the Table Tools Layout tab. In the Rows & Columns group, use the Insert buttons to add new rows and columns.

To remove a row or column, click to position the mouse, and then click the Table Tools Layout tab. In the Rows & Columns group, choose the proper command from the Delete button menu.

- Rows and columns are added relative to the insertion pointer's position: First click to select a cell, and then choose the proper Insert command to add a row or column relative to that cell.

- Refer to the earlier section, "Selecting in a table," for information on selecting a row or column. Make that selection before choosing a Delete command to ensure that the proper row or column is removed.

- When you choose the Delete ⇨ Delete Cells command, you see a dialog box asking what to do with the other cells in the row or column: Move them up or to the left. Also see the later sections, "Merging cells" and "Splitting cells."

- A mousey way to add a new row is to position the mouse pointer outside the table's left edge. A + (plus) button appears, as shown in the margin. Click that button to insert a new row.

- Likewise, if you position the mouse pointer at the table's top edge, click the + (plus) button, shown in the margin, to insert a new column.

Adjusting row and column size

After text is in the table, you should adjust row height and column width to best present the information. This process works best *after* you've added text.

To automatically adjust the column width, position the mouse pointer at the left side of the column, just on the vertical border. The mouse pointer changes to the icon shown in the margin. Double-click and the column width is adjusted.

To adjust all column widths, put the mouse pointer at the far left vertical border in the table. Double-click.

To evenly distribute row and column sizes, click the Table Tools Layout tab. In the Cell Size group, click the Distribute Rows and Distribute Columns command buttons.

To oddly distribute row and column sizes, click the Auto Fit button, also found in the Cell Size group on the Table Tools Layout tab. Use the commands on the Auto Fit menu to choose how to adjust a table's row and column size.

The most common way to adjust rows and columns in a table is to use the mouse: Position the mouse pointer at the vertical or horizontal border within a table. When the pointer changes to a left-right or up-down pointy thing, drag left, right, up, or down to change the border's position.

Merging cells

The completely rational way to combine two cells into one or to split one cell into two is to use the table drawing tools. Heaven have mercy on you should you decide to merge or split cells in any other fashion.

To combine two cells, erase the line that separates them. Follow these steps:

1. **Click the Table Tools Layout tab.**

2. **In the Draw group, click the Eraser tool.**

    The mouse pointer changes to a bar of soap, shown in the margin, but it's supposed to be an eraser.

3. **Click the line between the two cells.**

   The line is gone.

4. **Click the Eraser tool again to quit merging.**

   Or you can tap the Esc key.

 To merge a clutch of cells, select them and click the Merge Cells button. That button is found on the Table Tools Layout tab, in the Merge group.

Splitting cells

The easy way to turn one cell into two is to draw a line separating the cell. Follow these steps:

1. **Click the Table Tools Layout tab.**

2. **In the Draw group, click the Draw Table button.**

    The mouse pointer changes to the pencil pointer.

3. Draw a line in the table to split a cell.

You can draw horizontally or vertically.

4. Click the Draw Table button again when you're done.

Any text in the cell you split goes to one side of the drawn line.

You can split cells also by selecting a single cell, and then choosing the Split Cells command from the Table Tools Layout tab's Merge group. Use the Split Cells dialog box to determine how to best mince up the cell.

Making the table pretty

Unless you want your table to look like it was designed using hog wire, I recommend applying some table formatting. You can set the line's thickness, color, and style, and apply color to the various rows and columns. The commands necessary are found on the Table Tools Design tab; click anywhere with a table to summon that tab on the Ribbon.

Rather than get bogged down with details, you should know that the spiffiest way to spruce up a table is to choose a preset format from the Table Styles gallery: Click inside the table, and then position the mouse pointer at a thumbnail in the gallery to see a preview. Click the thumbnail to apply that format to your table.

✔ More thumbnails are available in the Table Styles gallery than are shown on the Ribbon: Scroll through the list or click the down-pointing arrow (below the scroll bar on the left) to view the lot.

✔ If you'd rather format your table in a more painful manner, use the Shading button as well as the commands located in the Borders group.

✔ To remove the table's gridlines, select the table and choose No Border from the Borders menu. If you choose that format, I recommend that you still show the tablet's gridlines, which aren't printed. To do that, select the table and choose the View Gridlines command from the Borders menu.

Adding a table caption

The best way to stick a title or caption on your table is to use Word's Insert Caption command. Don't bother trying to find that command on any of the Table Tools tabs. Instead, follow these steps:

1. **Click in the table you want to caption.**

2. **Click the References tab.**

3. **Click the Insert Caption button.**

   The Caption dialog box appears.

4. **Type the table's caption in the Caption text box.**

   Don't worry about the text *Figure 1*, not yet.

5. **Click the Label menu and choose Table.**

   The text in the Caption box changes from *Figure 1* (or whatever number) to *Table 1*. You might need to edit the caption to add some space between the number and your text.

6. **Click the Position menu and choose whether to place the caption above or below the table.**

7. **If you prefer a reference other than Table 1, click the new Label button and type the desired format.**

   Word supplies a sequential caption number after whatever text you type. The change is reflected in the Caption text box.

8. **Click OK to set the caption.**

An advantage of using Word's Insert Caption command is that you can easily create a list of tables for your document. See Chapter 21 for details on building such a list.

Chapter 20

Columns of Text

. . . .

. . . .

*I*f someone asks about columns and you immediately think of something written in a magazine or newspaper, you're a writer. If you think Doric, Ionic, and Corinthian, you're a history nerd. And if you think of rows of marching soldiers or rolling tanks, you're a military buff. What you probably don't think of are columns of text in a document, despite Word sporting such a clever formatting tool.

All about Columns

You probably don't think of a document's text as a column. No, it's just text on a page, margin to margin. Secretly, however, Word looks at such text as a single column. So whether you use columns or not, Word has already formatted your document that way.

To set the number of text columns on a page, you use Word's Columns command: Click the Layout tab, and in the Page Setup group, click the Columns button. A menu appears, listing common column-formatting options, as shown on the left in Figure 20-1.

To be more specific with column layout, choose the More Columns command, at the bottom of the Columns menu. The Columns dialog box appears, as shown on the right in Figure 20-1.

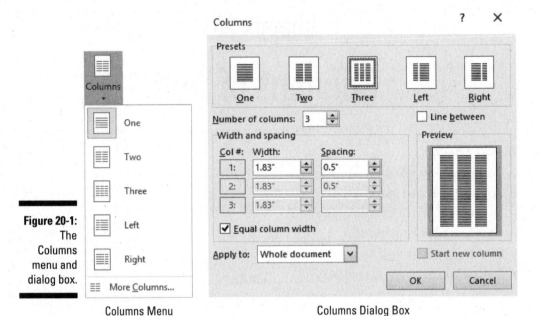

Figure 20-1:
The
Columns
menu and
dialog box.

Columns Menu   Columns Dialog Box

The Columns dialog box helps you to create and design multiple columns not available on the Columns menu: Use the Number of Columns box to set the quantity of columns desired. Use the Preview window to determine how the page is formatted. Click the OK button to apply the column format to the text.

- ✔ Click the mouse to best position the insertion pointer on a page when working with multiple text columns. That's because the keyboard's cursor-movement keys don't operate in a predictable manner when a document uses more than one column of text.

- ✔ Columns are a document-level format. Choosing a column format from the Columns button menu affects the entire document, reformatting every page to the number of columns specified.

- ✔ If you need to set different column formats on different pages, split the document into sections. In that case, the column type you chose affects only the current section. See Chapter 14 for more information on sections in Word.

- ✔ When you're working with columns and notice that Word starts acting slow and fussy, *save your work!*

- ✔ Maximum number of columns per page? That depends on the size of the page. Word's minimum column width is half an inch, so a typical sheet of paper can have up to 12 columns — not that such a layout would be appealing or anything.

Making two-column text

When you desire to impress someone with your text, I suggest putting two columns on your page. Any more columns, and the text width would be too skinny and difficult to read. Two columns, however, is a great way to get fancy and remain legible.

1. **Start up a new document.**

   Or if you have an existing document, move the toothpick cursor to the document's tippy-top by pressing Ctrl+Home.

2. **Click the Layout tab.**

3. **Click the Columns button and choose Two.**

   You're done.

The entire document flows into two columns. As you type, you'll see text flow down the left side of the page, and then hop up to the top right to start a new column.

✔ To restore the document to one column, repeat the steps in this section, but in Step 3, choose One.

✔ Columns look best when full justification is applied to all paragraphs. The keyboard shortcut is Ctrl+J. See Chapter 11 for more information on paragraph alignment.

✔ You can make specific column adjustments in the Width and Spacing area of the Columns dialog box (refer to Figure 20-1).

✔ If you want an attractive line to appear between the columns of text, visit the Columns dialog box and put a check mark in the Line Between box.

✔ The space between columns is the *gutter*. Word sets the width of the gutter at 0.5" (half an inch). This amount of white space is pleasing to the eye without being too much of a good thing.

Building a trifold brochure

The three-column text format works nicely on paper in landscape mode. This method is how most trifold brochures are created. Obey these steps:

1. **Start a new document, or work with an existing document — if you're so bold.**

2. **Click the Layout tab.**

3. Choose Orientation ⇨ Landscape.

The document's pages appear in landscape orientation, which is best for three columns of text and traditional for trifold brochures, programs, and documents.

4. Click the Columns button and choose Three.

Your trifold brochure is effectively formatted. Three columns are evenly spaced across the page, as illustrated in Figure 20-2.

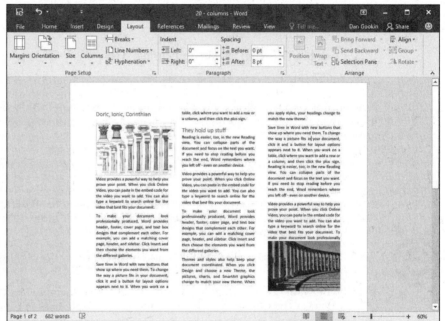

Figure 20-2:
A trifold brochure in Word.

For more sprucing up, summon the Columns dialog box; click the Columns button and choose More Columns. That way, you can adjust the spacing between columns, add a line between, and perform other magic.

See Chapter 22 for information on sticking graphics into a document, like those in Figure 20-2.

Giving up on columns

Converting a multicolumn document into a "normal" document merely involves switching the format back to one column:

1. **Click the Layout tab.**

2. **Click the Columns button and choose One.**

   The document is restored.

When these steps don't work, summon the Columns dialog box (refer to Figure 20-1) and choose One from the list of presets. Ensure that Whole Document is chosen from the Apply To menu and then click the OK button. The columns are gone.

- ✔ In Word, you don't remove column formatting as much as you choose the standard column format, One.

- ✔ Removing columns from a document doesn't remove sections or section breaks. See Chapter 14 for information on deleting section breaks.

Column Termination

You can stop the multicolumn format in one of several ways. For a newspaper column, the newspaper can go bankrupt. For Doric, Ionic, and Corinthian columns, civilization can collapse. For a military column, use a nuke. For a column of text, however, Word offers a number of tricks, none of which involves bankruptcy, revolution, or radiation.

Changing column formats

Your whole document doesn't have to sport just one column format. You can split things up so that part of the document is in one column and another part is in two columns and then maybe another part goes back to only one column.

To change column formats at a specific spot in the text, follow these steps:

1. **Click to place the insertion pointer at the spot where you need the columns to change.**

2. **Click the Layout tab.**

3. **Click the Columns button and choose More Columns.**

   The Columns dialog box appears.

4. **Choose the new column format.**

   Click one of the presets or use the clicker thing to set a specific number of columns.

5. **From the Apply To drop-down list, choose This Point Forward.**

6. **Click OK.**

The text is broken at a specific point in your document (set in Step 1). Above that point, one column format is used; after that point, the format chosen in Step 4 is used.

- ✔ To pull off this feat, Word inserts a continuous section break in your document.

- ✔ If you really know section breaks, it's easier to add the section break first, and then switch column formats. In the Columns dialog box, choose This Section from the Apply To drop-down list to apply the column format to the document's current section.

- ✔ Refer to Chapter 14 for more information on section breaks.

Placing a column break

To help lay out more than two columns on a page, it helps to use a column break. Like a page break, the column break ends a column. Text after the break starts at the top of the next column, either on the same page or the next page, depending on where you place the column break.

In Figure 20-3, you see an example of a column break. The column break is inserted in the column on the left. That column break stops the left side column and continues the text at the top of the right column.

To break a column, heed these steps:

1. **Click to place the insertion pointer in your document.**

   The insertion pointer's location becomes the start of the next column.

2. **Click the Layout tab.**

3. **In the Page Setup group, click the Breaks button.**

   A menu appears.

4. **Choose Column.**

   The text hops to the top of the next column.

Column breaks don't end columns; they merely split a column, ending text at a certain point on a page and starting the rest of the text at the top of the next column.

Text continues here

Doric, Ionic, Corinthian

Video provides a powerful way to help you prove your point. When you click Online Video, you can paste in the embed code for the video you want to add. You can also type a keyword to search online for the video that best fits your document.

To make your document look professionally produced, Word provides header, footer, cover page, and text box designs that complement each other. For example, you can add a matching cover page, header, and sidebar. Click Insert and then choose the elements you want from the different galleries.

Save time in Word with new buttons that show up where you need them. To change the way a picture fits in your document, click it and a button for layout options appears next to it. When you work on a table, click where you want to add a row or a column, and then click the plus sign.

They hold up stuff

Reading is easier, too, in the new Reading view. You can collapse parts of the document and focus on the text you want. If you need to stop reading before you reach the end, Word remembers where you left off - even on another device.

Video provides a powerful way to help you prove your point. When you click Online Video, you can paste in the embed code for the video you want to add. You can also type a keyword to search online for the video that best fits your document.

To make your document look professionally produced, Word provides header, footer, cover page, and text box designs that complement each other. For example, you can add a matching cover page, header, and sidebar. Click Insert and then choose the elements you want from the different galleries.

Themes and styles also help keep your document coordinated. When you click Design and choose a new Theme, the pictures, charts, and SmartArt graphics change to match your new theme. When you apply styles, your headings change to match the new theme.

Save time in Word with new buttons that show up where you need them. To change the way a picture fits in your document, click it and a button for layout options appears next to it. When you work on a table, click where you want to add a row or a column, and then click the plus sign. Reading is easier, too, in the new Reading view. You can collapse parts of the document and focus on the text you want. If you need to stop reading before you reach the end, Word remembers where you left off - even on another device.

Video provides a powerful way to help you prove your point. When you click Online Video, you can paste in the embed code for the video you want

Figure 20-3:
A column
break.

Column break inserted here

TIP

Use the Show/Hide command in the Home group (the Paragraph Mark button) to know where exactly to place the column break. You might want to insert the column break *after* a paragraph mark (¶) to have the columns line up at the top of the page.

To remove a column break, switch to Draft view: Click the View tab and choose Draft. The column break appears in the text as a line by itself. Delete that line. Switch back to Print Layout view to examine your document's columns.

Chapter 21

Lots of Lists

*L*ists can be simple, such as a list of the various diets you've tried over the past years. Lists can be complex, such as a table of contents, an index, and other more professional listy things. In Word, you can type such lists manually, but it's better to use the proper tools. That way, a list of anything can be formatted automatically and updated as necessary. Add that tip to your list of timesavers.

Lists with Bullets and Numbers

Whenever you have more than two items to describe in your document, consider using one of Word's automatic list-formatting commands. These tools format the list in a way that draws attention, calling it out from the rest of your text.

✔ Word's list commands are found on the Home tab, in the Paragraph group.

✔ You might find Word overly eager to format a list for you. The feature is called AutoFormat. See Chapter 33 for information on disabling this potentially annoying feature.

Making a bulleted list

In typesetting, a *bullet* is a graphical element, such as a ball or a dot, which highlights items in a list. The word *bullet* comes from the French word *boulette,* which has more to do with food than with round pieces of lead quickly exiting a firearm, like this:

- Bang!
- Bang!
- Bang!

To apply bullets to your text, highlight the paragraphs you want to shoot and click the Bullets button, shown in the margin. Instantly, your text is not only formatted with bullets but also indented and made all neat and tidy.

✔ To choose a different bullet style, click the menu triangle next to the Bullets command. Select a new bullet graphic from the list, or use the Define New Bullet command to concoct a unique bullet style.

✔ Bullets are a paragraph format. As such, the bullets *stick* to the paragraphs you type until you remove that format. To do so, click the Bullet command button again and the bullets are removed from the paragraph format.

Numbering a list

For a list of numbered items, just write the text. Don't write the numbers at the start of each paragraph. Then, after the list is complete, select the paragraphs as a block and click the Numbering command button, shown in the margin. The Numbering command assigns a number to each paragraph, plus it formats the paragraphs with a hanging indent, which looks nice.

The paragraph numbering continues (it's a format) until you turn it off. To do so, either press the Enter key twice or click the Numbering command button again.

As a bonus, if you insert or rearrange paragraphs in the list, Word automatically renumbers everything. That makes this feature better than trying to manually number and format the paragraphs.

✔ To choose another numbering format, click the menu triangle next to the Numbering command button. You can choose letters or Roman numerals, or you can concoct a numbering scheme by choosing the command Define New Number Format.

- ✔ The None number format removes numbering from a paragraph.

- ✔ You can break and resume paragraph numbering: First, apply the numbering to all paragraphs. To un-number a paragraph, click at the start of the first word and press the Backspace key. The numbering for that paragraph is removed, and the remaining paragraphs are renumbered.

Creating a multilevel numbered list

A multilevel list consists of items and subitems all properly indented, similar to those presented in Figure 21-1. Word automatically formats such a list, but it's a tricky thing to do. Pay attention!

Figure 21-1:
A multilevel
list.

> **North Diamond Mosquito Abatement Board By-Laws**
> 1. Purpose.
>   a. We exist to abate mosquitos.
> 2. Board composition.
>   a. The board shall consist of seven (7) members.
>   i. Two members shall be at large.
>   ii. Five members shall be elected by district.
>   b. Members shall be elected every year.
>   c. The term of each member shall be 3 years.
>   d. No mosquitoes are allowed to be members.
> 3. Duties

To format a multilevel list, click the Multilevel List button, shown in the margin. Start typing the list. Press the Tab key to indent and create a sublevel. Press Shift+Tab to unindent and promote an item to a higher level.

You can also write the entire list in advance, select it, and then click the Multilevel List button to format it. As long as you use Tab and Shfit+Tab to organize the topics, you won't break the format and the list stays intact.

If you're creating a complex, hierarchical list, use Word's Outline view instead of the multilevel list format. See Chapter 25.

Numbering lines on a page

Word lets you slap down numbers for every line on a page, a popular feature with those in the legal profession. Here's how it goes:

1. **Click the Layout tab.**

2. **In the Page Setup group, click the Line Numbers command button to display its menu.**

3. **Choose a numbering format.**

   For example, to number lines on each page 1 through whatever, chose the Restart Each Page option. Or to number all lines on all pages cumulatively, choose Continuous.

   To remove the line numbers, choose None from the Line Numbers command button. Or choose Suppress for Current Paragraph if you don't want the selected paragraph numbered.

Line numbering is a page-level formatting command. It sticks to each page in your document. If you prefer to number only one page, set aside that page as its own section. See Chapter 14 for more information on sections.

Document Content Lists

Word helps you build lists of items in your document, lists that would otherwise be brutally cumbersome to create and monstrous to maintain. These lists include a table of contents and an index.

Creating a table of contents

The trick to creating a tablet of contents, or TOC, for your document is to use Word's Heading styles. Use Heading 1 for main heads, Heading 2 for subheads, and Heading 3 for lower-level heads and titles. Word's Table of Contents command uses those formats to build a table of contents field, which reflects the heading names and their page numbers.

Providing that you've used the Heading (or equivalent) styles in your document, follow these steps to create a table of contents:

1. **Create a separate page for the TOC.**

   Word places the TOC field at the insertion pointer's location, though I prefer to have the thing on its own page. Refer to Chapter 13 for information on creating pages; a blank page near the start of your document is ideal for a TOC.

2. **Click the mouse to place the insertion pointer on the blank page.**

   The TOC field is inserted at that point.

3. **Click the References tab.**

4. **In the Table of Contents group, click the Table of Contents button.**

   The Table of Contents menu appears.

5. Choose a format.

The TOC is created and placed in your document, page numbers and all.

Above the TOC, you may also want to add a title — something clever, such as *Table of Contents*. Do not format that title as a heading unless you want it included in the table of contents.

✔ When the steps in this section don't produce the effect you intended, it usually means that your document doesn't use the Heading styles.

✔ If your document uses your own heading styles, ensure that the paragraph format specifies the proper outline level. See Chapter 15 for more information.

✔ The TOC field is static, so it won't reflect further edits in your document. To update the field, click once to select it. On the References tab, click the Update Table button. Use the Update Table of Contents dialog box to choose what to update. Click OK.

✔ Cool people in publishing refer to a table of contents as a *TOC,* pronounced "tee-o-see" or "tock.")

✔ See Chapter 23 for more information about fields in your document.

Building an index

An index is yet another document reference or list Word can build and format, providing that you know the trick: You must mark text in a document for inclusion in the index. Once the words are marked, an index field is inserted, which displays the index.

Select index entries

To flag a bit of text for inclusion in an index, follow these steps:

1. Select the text you want to reference.

The text can be a word or a phrase or any old bit of text.

2. On the References tab in the Index group, click the Mark Entry button.

The selected text appears in the Mark Entry dialog box.

3. If the entry needs a subentry, type that text in the Mark Index Entry dialog box.

The subentry further clarifies the main entry. For example, the word you select (the main entry) might be *boredom* and you type **In a waiting room** as the subentry.

4. **Click one of the buttons, *either* Mark or Mark All.**

Click the Mark button to mark only the selected text. Click the Mark All button to direct Word to include all matching instances of the text in your document.

When you mark an index entry, Word activates the Show/Hide command, where characters such as spaces, paragraph marks, and tabs appear in your document. Don't let it freak you out.

Because Show/Hide is on, the Index code appears in the document. It looks something like this: {@@dmsXE@@dms"boredom"@@dms}.

5. **Continue scrolling your document and looking for items to place in the index.**

The Mark Index Entry dialog box remains open as you continue to build the index.

6. **Click the Close button when you're done, or just tired, to banish the Mark Index Entry dialog box.**

7. **Press Ctrl+Shift+8 to cancel the Show/Hide command.**

Use the 8 key on the keyboard, not on the numeric keypad.

Place the index in the document

After marking bits and pieces of text for inclusion in the index, the next step is to build and place the index. Do this:

1. **Position the insertion pointer where you want the index to appear.**

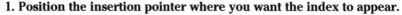

If you want the index to start on a new page, create a new page in Word (see Chapter 13). I also recommend putting the index at the *end* of your document, which is what the reader expects.

2. **Click the References tab.**

3. **In the Index group, click the Insert Index button.**

The Index dialog box appears. Here are my recommendations:

- The Print Preview window is misleading. It shows how your index might look but doesn't use your actual index contents.

- Use the Formats drop-down list to select a style for your index. Just about any choice from this list is better than the From Template example.

- The Columns setting tells Word how many columns wide to make the index. The standard is two columns. I usually choose one column, which looks better on the page, especially for shorter documents.

- I prefer to use the Right Align Page Numbers option.

4. Click the OK button to insert the index into your document.

What you see is an index field, displayed using the information culled from the document. See Chapter 23 for more information on fields.

Review your index. Do it now. If you dislike the layout, press Ctrl+Z to undo and start over. Otherwise, you're done.

If you modify your document, update the index: Click the index field. Then choose the Update Index command button from the Index group. Word updates the index to reference any new page numbers and includes freshly marked index entries.

✔ Feel free to add a heading for the index because Word doesn't do it for you.

✔ Use a Heading style for the index header so that it's included in your document's table of contents. See the section, "Creating a table of contents."

✔ Word uses continuous section breaks to place the index field in its own document section. Refer to Chapter 14 for more information on sections.

Adding a list of figures

The References tab's groups help you insert other document lists, but only if you've created the list appropriately.

For example, you can create a table of figures, providing you've used the References tab's Caption button. (See Chapter 22 for details.) To build the table of figures, click the Insert Table of Figures button. The process works similarly to inserting a table of contents or an index, but it works only when you've properly inserted the captions.

Footnotes and Endnotes

Both footnotes and endnotes contain bonus information, a clarification, or an aside to supplement text on a page. Each is marked by a superscripted number or letter in the text[1].

The difference between a footnote and an endnote is in the placement: A footnote appears on the bottom of the page and an endnote appears at the end of a document. Otherwise, both references are created in a similar way:

---

[1] See? It works!

1. **Click the mouse so that the insertion pointer is to the immediate right of a word or text that you want the footnote or endnote to reference.**

   There's no need to type the note's number; it's done automatically.

2. **Click the References tab.**

3. **From the Footnotes group, choose either the Insert Footnote or Insert Endnote command button.**

   A superscripted number is inserted into the text, and you're instantly whisked to the bottom of the page (footnote) or the end of the document (endnote).

4. **Type the footnote or endnote.**

5. **To return to where you were in the document, press Shift+F5.**

   The Shift+F5 keyboard shortcut returns to the previous spot in your document where you were editing.

Here are some footnote endnote notes:

- The keyboard shortcut for inserting a footnote is Alt+Ctrl+F.

- The keyboard shortcut for inserting an endnote is Atl+Ctrl+D.

- If you're curious, you'll want to know that the keyboard shortcut Alt+Ctrl+E enables and disables Word's Revision Marks feature, covered in Chapter 26.

- The footnote and endnote numbers are updated automatically so that all footnotes and endnotes are sequential in your document.

- To browse footnotes and endnotes, click the References tab. In the Footnotes group, use the Next Footnote button's menu to browse between footnote and endnote references.

- You can preview a footnote's or endnote's contents by hovering the mouse pointer at the superscripted number in the document's text.

- Use the Show Notes button (References tab, Footnotes group) to examine footnotes or endnotes as they appear on the page.

- To delete a footnote or an endnote, highlight its reference number in the text and press the Delete key. Word magically renumbers any remaining footnotes or endnotes.

- To convert a footnote to an endnote, right-click the footnote's text at the bottom of the page. Choose the command Convert to Endnote. Likewise, you can convert endnotes to footnotes by right-clicking the endnote text and choosing the command Convert to Footnote.

- For additional control over footnotes and endnotes, click the dialog box launcher button in the Footnotes group. Use the Footnote and Endnote dialog box to customize the reference text location, format, starting number, and other options.

Chapter 22

Here Come the Graphics

*I*t's sacrilege, of course. Word processing is about words. Images and words mix and mingle in the software realm of desktop publishing. Regardless, the mighty Microsoft Word allows you to slap down a picture, insert an object, edit images, and otherwise pretend it's some sort of graphics program. This trick might just save you 1,000 words, providing that you know how it works.

Graphical Goobers in Your Text

The door to Word's graphical closet is found on the Insert tab. The command buttons nestled in the Illustrations group place various graphical goobers into your text. Here's how the process works for pictures in the text:

1. **Click the mouse at the spot in your text where you desire the image to appear.**

   You don't need to be precise because you can always move the image later.

2. **Click the Insert tab.**

3. **Use one of the command buttons to choose which type of image to add.**

   You can also paste a previously copied image, as described in the next section.

Figure 22-1 illustrates how a freshly added image looks, highlighting some of its features.

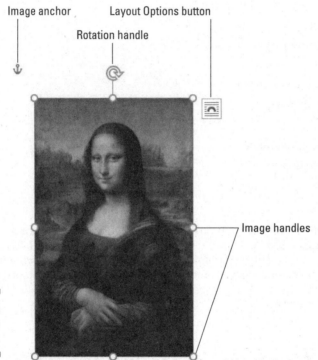

Image anchor   Layout Options button

Rotation handle

Image handles

Figure 22-1:
An image in
a document.

While the image is selected, a new tab appears on the Ribbon. For pictures, it's the Picture Tools Format tab; for other types of graphics, the Drawing Tools Format tab appears. Both tabs offer tools that help you perfect the recently inserted graphic. Later sections in this chapter cover using those tools, as well as the controls illustrated in Figure 22-1.

Some images, specifically shapes, are drawn on the page. In that case, they appear in front of or behind your text. Refer to the "Image Layout" section for information on precise image placement.

- ✔ To remove an image, click to select it and then tap the Delete key. If the graphical object, such as a shape, contains text, ensure that you've clicked the object's border before you tap the Delete key.

- ✔ The more graphics you add in Word, the more sluggish it becomes. My advice: Write first. Add graphics last. Save frequently.

Copying and pasting an image

One of the simplest ways to stick an image into your document is to copy an image from elsewhere: Select the image, press Ctrl+C to copy it, and then switch to Word and press Ctrl+V to paste the image into your document.

- ✔ The image you copy can come from any other program in Windows.

- ✔ Some image formats might not be allowed in Word. If you're unable to use the Paste button (found on the Home tab in the Clipboard group), or pressing Ctrl+V doesn't work, the image format is incompatible.

- ✔ Images found on web pages are the easiest type of image to copy and paste into your document. While dutifully remaining aware of various copyright laws around the world, right-click the image and choose the Copy Image (or similar) command from the pop-up menu. Switch to your document's window and press Ctrl+V to paste.

Plopping down a picture

Your computer is most likely littered with picture files. No matter how the image was created, as long as it's found somewhere on your PC, you can stick it into your document. Follow these steps:

1. **Click the mouse in your text where you want the image to appear.**

2. **Click the Insert tab; in the Illustrations group, click the Pictures button.**

   The Insert Picture dialog box appears.

3. **Locate the image file on your PC's storage system.**

4. **Click to select the image.**

5. **Click the Insert button.**

   The image is slapped down in your document.

A nifty picture to stick at the end of a letter is your signature. Use a desktop scanner to digitize your John Hancock. Save your signature as an image file on your computer, and then follow the steps in this section to insert that signature picture in the proper place in your document.

Stealing images from the Internet

It's easy to obtain an image from the web by copying and pasting that image, as covered in the earlier section, "Copying and pasting an image." To perform a web image search from Word, click the Insert tab and then click the Online Pictures button in the Illustrations group. The Insert Pictures window appears.

Use options in the Insert Pictures window to help locate an online image. For example, click the text box next to Bing Image Search and type a description of the image you want. Press the Enter key and then choose an image. Click the Insert button to download the image from the Internet and thrust it into your document.

Refer to the later section "Image Layout" for information on properly positioning the image. If the image needed to be adjusted, see the "Image Editing" section.

Slapping down a shape

Word comes with a library of common shapes ready to insert in your document. These include basic shapes, such as squares, circles, geometric figures, lines, and arrows, plus popular symbols. Graphics professionals call these types of images *line art*.

To place some line art into your document, follow these steps:

1. **Click the Insert tab.**

2. **In the Illustrations group, click the Shapes button.**

   The button is a menu, which lists shapes organized by type.

3. **Choose a predefined shape.**

   The mouse pointer changes to a plus sign (+).

4. **Drag to create the shape.**

   The shape is placed into the document, floating on top of the text.

At this point you can adjust the shape: Change its size, location, or colors. Use the Drawing Tools Format tab, conveniently shown on the Ribbon while the shape is selected, to affect those changes.

- ✔ Drag the image to another location. See the "Image Layout" section for specifics on image placement and text-wrapping options.

- ✔ Instantly change the image by using the Shape Styles group on the Ribbon's Drawing Tools Format tab. Choose a new style from the Shape Gallery. Styles are related to the document's theme; see Chapter 16 for information on themes.

- ✔ To set the shape's color style, click the Shape Fill button.

- ✔ Use the Shape Outline button to set the shape's outline color.

- ✔ To set the shape's outline thickness, click the Shape Outline button and choose a thickness from the Weight submenu.

- ✔ The Shape Effects button lets you quickly apply 3D effects, shadows, and other fancy formatting to the shape.

- ✔ To more effectively format a shape, click the Launcher in the lower-right corner of the Shape Styles group. Use the Format Shape pane to manipulate settings for any selected shape in your document.

Sticking things into a shape

Shapes need not be clunky, colorful distractions. You can use a shape to hold text or a picture, which makes them one of the more flexible items to add to a document.

To add to a shape a smidgen of text, which the graphic layout artists refer to as a *callout*, right-click the shape and choose Add Text. The blinking toothpick cursor appears in the shape. Type and format the text.

To stick a picture into a shape, click to select the shape. Click the Drawing Tools Format tab. Click the Shape Fill button and choose the Picture menu item. Use the Insert Pictures window to hunt down an image to place in the shape.

- ✔ Yes, it's possible to have both a picture and text inside a shape.

- ✔ To further deal with text in a shape, click the shape, and then click the Drawing Tools Format tab on the Ribbon. The Text group contains buttons that manipulate the text.

- ✔ To remove text from a shape, select and delete the text.

> ✐ To remove a picture, select a solid color from the Shape Fill menu.
>
> ✐ Also see Chapter 23 for information on text boxes, which are similar to shapes with text inserted.

Using WordArt

Perhaps the most overused graphic that's stuck into any Word document is WordArt. This feature is almost too popular. If you haven't used it yourself, you've probably seen it in a thousand documents, fliers, and international treaties. Here's how it works:

1. **Click the Insert tab.**

2. **In the Text group, click the WordArt button to display the WordArt menu.**

   The Word Art button is shown in the margin.

3. **Choose a style from the WordArt gallery.**

   A WordArt graphic placeholder appears in your document.

4. **Type the (short and sweet) text that you want WordArt-ified.**

Use the Word Art Styles group on the Drawing Tools Format tab to customize the WordArt appearance. If you don't see the Drawing Tools Format tab, first click the WordArt graphic.

Adding a caption

Some images work best when they have a caption. For example, that picture of the exploding watermelon is far more significant with the caption, "Never buy fruit from a guy who also sells ammunition."

In Word, captions aren't attached to an image. Instead, the caption is its own image, a separate graphical element on the page. As such, it helps to align and group the image with its caption. Follow these steps:

1. **Click to select the graphic.**

   The graphic you want to caption must already be in the document. It's also best to choose an image layout for the graphic, as described in the later section, "Wrapping text around an image."

2. **Click the References tab.**

3. **In the Captions group, click the Insert Caption button.**

   The Captions dialog box appears.

4. Type the caption's text in the Caption text box.

Windows supplies the figure number as a suggestion. You cannot remove that preset text, but you can place a check mark in the Exclude Label from Caption box to reduce the text to just a number.

5. Choose a position for the caption from the Position drop-down list.

The caption position is relative to the figure. Most commonly, captions appear below the selected item.

6. Click the OK button.

The caption is applied to the figure. The caption uses the same text wrapping and horizontal dimensions as the figure.

7. Press and hold down the Shift key and click the image.

The caption is already selected. When you Shift+Click its image, both the image and caption are selected.

8. Click the Drawing Tools Format tab.

9. In the Arrange group, click the Group button and choose Group.

The Group icon is shown in the margin. Refer to the later section, "Grouping images," for more information on what the icon does.

Both the image and its caption are now placed in your document. Because you grouped them, they will work as a single unit.

✔ To change the caption, click the caption text. Type or edit something new.

✔ To remove the caption, ungroup it from its image. Refer to the later section, "Grouping images," for details. Once ungrouped, click the caption to select it. Press the Delete key.

✔ An advantage to applying captions this way is that you can create a list of captions or figures for your document, summarizing them along with their page references. To do so, click the References tab and then click the Insert Table of Figures button in the Captions group. Also see Chapter 21 for information on automatic lists and references.

Image Layout

Graphics in a Word document must cohabit well with the text. To keep both happy, you must understand Word's image layout options. These options fall into three general categories:

✔ **Inline:** The image is inserted directly into the text, just like a large, single character. It stays with the text, so you can press Enter to place it on a line by itself or press Tab to indent the image, for example.

✔ **Wrapped:** Text flows around the graphic, avoiding the image like all the girls at a high school dance avoid the guys from the chess club.

✔ **Floating:** The image appears in front of or behind the text. Shapes (or line art) inserted in the document originally appear floating in front of the text.

When set properly, these layout options allow you to place images into your document in a clean, professional manner.

 To set image layout options, click to select an image and then click the Layout Options button, as shown in the margin. The Layout Options menu lists various layout settings, as illustrated in Table 22-1.

Table 22-1		Image Layout Options
Icon	**Setting**	**What It Does**
	Inline	The image acts like a character in the text, moving with other text on the page.
	Square	Text flows around the image in a square pattern, regardless of the image's shape.
	Tight	Text flows around the image and hugs its shape.
	Through	Text flows around the image but also inside the image (depending on the image's shape).
	Top and Bottom	Text stops at the top of the image and continues below the image.
	Behind Text	The image floats behind the text, looking almost like the image is part of the paper.
	In Front of Text	The image floats on top of your text, like a photograph dropped on the paper.

Wrapping text around an image

For smaller images, or images that otherwise break up a document in an inelegant manner, choose one of the text-wrapping layout options. Heed these steps:

1. **Click to select the image.**

   A selected image appears with eight handles, as shown earlier, in Figure 22-1.

2. **Click the Layout Options button.**

   Word features four text-wrapping options, found in the With Text Wrapping area of the Layout Options menu. These options are Square, Tight, Through, and Top and Bottom, described in Table 22-1.

3. **Choose a text-wrapping option.**

Examine your image and the text to see whether it wraps the way you like. If it doesn't, repeat these steps and choose another setting in Step 3.

To remove text wrapping, choose the Inline option from Step 3.

Floating an image

When you want an image to be placed in your document independently of the text, you float the image. The image can be in front of the text, like some little kid pasted a sticker on the page, or behind the text, as if the image were part of the paper.

To float an image, select it and then click the Layout Options button, as shown in the margin. Choose Behind Text or In Front of Text. Refer to Table 22-1 for the appropriate icons.

After choosing either Behind Text or In Front of Text, you see the image released from the confines of the text. The image floats freely, either behind or in front of your text.

  ✔ See the next section for information on moving a floating image.

  ✔ Also see the later section, "Keeping an image with text," if you want the floating picture to stay close to a specific paragraph in the document.

Keeping an image with text

Inline images always stay with the text that surrounds them. For images with other layout options, you can choose where the image attaches to the text or whether it attaches at all.

To keep an image associated with a specific paragraph of text, use the Anchor icon, as shown in the margin. Drag that icon to the paragraph that references the image. That way, if the paragraph moves to another page, the image moves with it.

To keep an image pasted to the same spot on a page, select the image and then click the Layout Options button. Choose the setting Fix Position on Page. The image becomes stuck on the page at a specific location regardless of how the text flows around it.

Image Editing

Word is not an image-editing program. It does feature a handful of commands that let you manipulate pictures and images in a document but only in a simple way. For anything else, you need an image-editing program, such as Photoshop or one of its less-expensive relatives.

✔ Use Word's Undo command, Ctrl+Z, to undo any image editing boo-boos.

✔ When you're using a document theme, theme effects are automatically applied to any graphic inserted into your document. Refer to Chapter 16 for more information on themes.

Resizing an image

To make an image larger or smaller, heed these steps:

1. **Select the image.**

   The image grows handles, as shown earlier in Figure 22-1.

2. **Drag one of the image's four corner handles inward or outward to make the image smaller or larger, respectively.**

   If you hold down the Shift key as you drag, the image is proportionally resized.

You can use the buttons in the Picture Tools Format tab's Size area to nudge the image size vertically or horizontally or to type specific values for the image's size.

Cropping an image

In graphics lingo, *cropping* works like taking a pair of scissors to the image: You make the image smaller, but by doing so, you eliminate some content, just as an angry, sullen teen would use shears to remove his cheating scumbag former girlfriend from a prom picture. Figure 22-2 shows an example.

Figure 22-2: Cropping an image.

To crop, click the image once to select it. Click the Picture Tools Format tab, and then click the Crop button in the Size group. Adjust the image by dragging one of the crop handles in or out. Press the Enter key to crop the image.

I use the edge (left, right, top, or bottom) handles to crop. The corner handles never crop quite the way I want them to.

Rotating an image

You have two handy ways to rotate an image, neither of which involves turning the computer's monitor or craning your neck to the point of chiropractic necessity.

To freely rotate an image, use the mouse to grab the rotation handle at the top of the image. (Refer to Figure 22-1.) Drag the mouse to orient the image to any angle.

For more precise rotation, click the Picture Tools Format tab and in the Arrange group use the Rotate command button. From its menu, you can choose to rotate the image 90 degrees to the left or right or to flip the image horizontally or vertically.

Changing an image's appearance

To manipulate an image, click the Picture Tools Format tab, and use the tools in the Adjust group. Specifically, use the tools Corrections, Color, and Artistic Effects. As a bonus, each tool's button shows a menu full of options previewing how the image will be affected. To make the change, simply choose an option from the appropriate button's menu. Here are some suggestions:

- ✔ Brightness and contrast settings are made from the Corrections button menu.

- ✔ To wash out a picture you placed behind your text, click the Color button and choose the Washout color from the Recolor area.

- ✔ To convert a color image to monochrome (black and white), click the Color button and choose the first item in the menu, Saturation 0%.

- ✔ A slew of interesting, artistic brushstrokes and other effects are found on the aptly named Artistic Effects button menu.

Image Arrangement

Word's image arrangement commands help you manage multiple images on a page. Using these commands, you can group similar shapes or an image and its caption. You can also line up shapes to keep them even, or place one image in front of or behind another.

- ✔ To arrange images, click a graphic to summon the Picture Tools or Drawing Tools Format tab. For either tab, the tools you need are located in the Arrange group.

- ✔ To select multiple images, press and hold down the Shift key as you click each one.

Moving an image hither and thither

To relocate an image to a better spot, point the mouse at the image. The mouse pointer changes to a four-way arrow, similar to what's shown in the margin. Now you can drag the image nigh and yon.

- ✔ Point the mouse at the center of the image to drag. If you accidentally point at one of the image's handles, you resize the image.

✔ How the graphic sits with your text (covered elsewhere in this chapter) determines where and how you can move it. When an image floats behind your text, you may need to open up a spot so that you can grab the image. To do so, position the mouse pointer by or on the same line as the image, and then whack the Enter key a few times. After moving the image, delete the extra blank paragraphs you created when you pressed the Enter key.

Aligning graphics

Image alignment is necessary to keep two or more graphical objects looking neat and tidy on the page. Especially when the images use a floating or wrapped layout, you want to ensure that they line up by the top edges, side-to-side, or centered.

To align graphics, follow these steps:

1. **Click the first image to select it.**
2. **Hold down the Shift key and click the rest of the images.**

3. **On the Picture Tools Format tab, in the Arrange group, click the Align Object button.**

   The button is shown in the margin. Click that button to display a menu of alignment choices.

4. **Choose an alignment command.**

   For example, choose Align Top to ensure that the top edge of both pictures will be aligned on the page.

If you'd rather eyeball the arrangement, activate Grid: Click the Align Object button, and choose View Gridlines from the menu. Instantly, the page looks like it's a sheet of graph paper. Use the grid to help you position multiple images. Choose the View Gridlines command again to hide the grid.

The Distribute commands on the Align Object menu help you organize multiple images evenly across a page. For example, if you have three images left-to-right and want to space them evenly, first align the images by choosing Align Middle. Then choose Distribute Horizontally to evenly space the images.

Shuffling images front or back

Graphics are plunked down on a page one atop the other. This arrangement is difficult to notice unless two images overlap, as shown in Figure 22-3. To change the order, and shuffle images in front of or behind each other, click the Picture Tools Format tab, and in the Arrange group, use the Bring Forward or Send Backward commands.

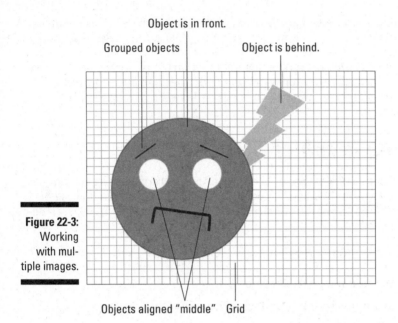

Object is in front.

Grouped objects   Object is behind.

Figure 22-3:
Working
with mul-
tiple images.

Objects aligned "middle"   Grid

To move one image in front of another, first click that image. Choose Bring Forward ➪ Bring Forward to shuffle that image forward one position. To bring the image in front of all other images, choose Bring Forward ➪ Bring to Front.

Likewise, use the Send Backward ➪ Send Backward or Send Backward ➪ Send to Back commands to shuffle an image to the background.

Grouping images

When you cobble together a complex image using smaller shapes, or when you arrange an image and its caption, use the Group command to keep those items together. That way, you can move them as a single unit, copy and paste them, and apply image effects to the entire group.

To group two or more graphical objects in your document, select the images. Click the Picture Tools Format tab, and in the Arrange Group, click the Group button and choose the Group command. The images are then treated as a unit, such as the face shown in Figure 22-3, which is a collection of individual shapes.

To ungroup, click the grouped images and then choose the Ungroup command from the Group menu.

Chapter 23

Insert Tab Insanity

Aside from formatting, pretty much anything you put into a Word document is inserted. That makes me curious as to why the magicians at Microsoft sought to dedicate a tab on the Ribbon to the topic of Insert. What weird, wonderful, and wanted buttons could crowd that tab's various groups — especially those items not covered elsewhere in this book.

Characters Foreign and Funky

The computer's keyboard lets you type all 26 letters of the alphabet — plus numbers, a smattering of symbols, and punctuation thingies. That's a lot to type, and some authors spend their entire lives weaving those characters into a tapestry of text heretofore unseen in literary history. As if that weren't enough, you can sprinkle even more characters into your document, spicing it up like garlic in a salad. Foreign language letters, symbols — all sorts of fun stuff is covered in this section.

Nonbreaking spaces and hyphens

The space and the hyphen characters are special because Word uses either of them to wrap a line of text: The space splits a line between two words, and the hyphen (using hyphenation) splits a line between a word's syllables.

Sometimes, however, you don't want a line to be split by a space or a hyphen. For example, splitting a phone number is bad because you want the number to stay intact. And you may desire to have two words that are separated by a space to be stuck together like glue. For those times, you need *unbreakable* characters.

- ✔ To prevent the hyphen character from breaking a line, press Ctrl+Shift+- (hyphen).
- ✔ To prevent the space character from breaking a line, press Ctrl+Shift+spacebar.

Both commands insert a nonbreaking character into the text. Word utterly refuses to use an unbreakable hyphen or space to split a line of text.

Typing characters such as Ü, Ç, and Ñ

You can be boring and type *deja vu* or be all fancy and type *déjà vu* or *café* or *résumé*. Such tricks make your readers think that you know your stuff, but what you really know is how to use Word's diacritical mark keys.

Diacritical is not an urgent medical situation involving elimination. Instead, it's a term that refers to symbols appearing over certain letters. Foreign languages and words use diacritical marks, such as the examples used in the preceding paragraph.

To create a diacritical mark in Word, you press a special Control-key combination. The key combination you press somewhat represents the diacritical mark you need, such as Ctrl+' to produce the ' diacritical mark. The Ctrl-key combination is followed by the character that needs the new "hat," as shown in Table 23-1.

Table 23-1	Those Pesky Foreign Language Characters
Prefix Key	**Characters Produced**
Ctrl+'	á é í ó ú
Ctrl+`	à è ì ò ù
Ctrl+,	ç
Ctrl+@	å
Ctrl+:	ä ë ï ö ü
Ctrl+^	â ê î ô û
Ctrl+~	ã õ ñ
Ctrl+/	ø

For example, to insert an é into your document, press Ctrl+' and then type the letter *E*. Uppercase *E* gives you É, and lowercase *e* gives you é. It makes sense because the' (apostrophe) is essentially the diacritical mark you're adding to the vowel.

Be sure to note the difference between the apostrophe (or *tick*) and the accent grave (or back tick). The apostrophe (') is next to your keyboard's Enter key. The accent grave (`) is below the Esc key.

For the Ctrl+@, Ctrl+:, Ctrl+^, and Ctrl+~ key combinations, you also need to press the Shift key, which is required anyway to produce the @, :, ^, or ~ symbols on the keyboard. Therefore, Ctrl+~ is really Ctrl+Shift+`. Keep that in mind.

Word's AutoCorrect feature has been trained to know some special characters. For example, when you're typing *café,* Word automatically sticks that whoopty-doop over the *e.*

Inserting special characters and symbols

On the far right of the Insert tab dwells the Symbols group. Two items are found in that group: Equation and Symbol. (If the window is too narrow, you see the Symbols button, from which you can choose Equation or Symbol.) Click the Symbol button see some popular or recently used symbols. Choose a symbol from the menu to insert the special symbol directly into your text.

To see a hoard of symbols and characters, click the Symbol button and choose the More Symbols command. The Symbol dialog box appears, as shown in Figure 23-1. Choose a decorative font, such as Wingdings, from the Font menu to see strange and unusual characters. To see the gamut of what's possible with normal text, choose (normal text) from the Font drop-down list. Use the Subset drop-down list to see specific symbols and such.

To stick a character into your document from the Symbol dialog box, select the symbol and click the Insert button.

You need to click the Cancel button when you're done using the Symbol dialog box.

✔ Click the Insert button once for each symbol you want to insert. For example, when you're putting three Σ (sigma) symbols into your document, you must locate that symbol on the grid and then click the Insert button three times.

Highlighted symbol   Symbol character code

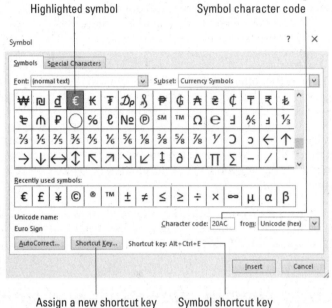

Figure 23-1:
The Symbol
dialog box.

Assign a new shortcut key   Symbol shortcut key

✔ Some symbols have shortcut keys. They appear at the bottom of the
  Symbol dialog box (refer to Figure 23-1). For example, the shortcut for
  the degree symbol (°) is Ctrl+@, spacebar — press Ctrl+@ (actually,
  Ctrl+Shift+2) and then type a space.

✔ You can insert symbols by typing the symbol's character code and then
  pressing the Alt+X key combination. For example, the character code
  for Σ (sigma) is 2211: Type **2211** in your document and then press Alt+X.
  The number 2211 is magically transformed into the Σ character.

Spice Up Your Document with a Text Box

A *text box* is a graphical element that contains — hold your breath, wait for it,
wait — *text.* The text is used as a decorative element (commonly called a *pull
quote* or *callout*) to highlight a passage of text on the page, or it can be simply
an information box or an aside, such as those elements that litter the pages
of *USA Today.* The primary purpose of the text box is to prevent your document from becoming what graphic designers refer to as the dreaded Great
Wall of Text.

To shove a text box into a document, follow these steps:

1. **Click the Insert tab.**

2. **In the Text group, choose Text Box.**

3. **Choose a preformatted text box from the list.**

   The text box is splashed onto the current page in your document.

4. **Rewrite the text in the box.**

   La-di-da.

Even though it contains text, a text box is a graphical element. As such, when it first appears in your document, or any time it's selected, the Drawing Tools Format tab appears on the Ribbon. This tab hosts a garrison of text box formatting and style commands.

Other text in your document wraps around the text box. As such, you can drag the text box (by its edge) to any position on the page. You can set the layout options for the text box just as you would for any picture or graphical goober in your document. These options are covered in Chapter 22, which also covers formatting commands available on the Drawing Tools Format tab.

✔ It's common to copy and paste text from the document into the box, which is how pull quotes work.

✔ To change text orientation within the text box, click the box, and then click the Drawing Tools Format tab. In the Text group, click the Text Direction button to peruse orientation options.

✔ To delete a text box, click its edge and press the Delete key.

Fun with Fields

The phrase "carved in stone" refers to text that doesn't change. What you write in Word isn't carved in stone — well, unless you have a cool printer I've not heard of. Still, the text you scribble remains static until you change it or until the computer screws up.

To liven things up a tad, Word lets you add *dynamic* elements to a document. Unlike the text you normally compose, dynamic text changes to reflect a number of factors. To add these dynamic elements to a document, you use a Word feature called *fields*.

Understanding fields

Word's dynamic field feature is part of the Quick Parts tools. To add a field to a document, click the Insert tab and in the Text group, click the Quick Parts button, shown in the margin. Choose the Field command from the Quick Parts menu to behold the Field dialog box, shown in Figure 23-2.

Narrow down things by choosing a category   Even more options!

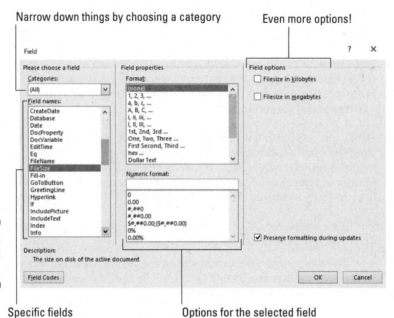

Figure 23-2:
The Field
dialog box.

Specific fields   Options for the selected field

The scrolling list on the left side of the Field dialog box shows field categories. These represent various dynamic nuggets you can insert in a document. Choose a specific category to narrow the list of Field Names.

The center and right part of the dialog box contain formats, options, and other details for a selected field.

To insert the field, click the OK button. The field appears just like other text, complete with formatting and such, but the information displayed changes to reflect whatever the field represents. For example, a page number field always shows the current page.

When the insertion pointer is placed inside a field, the text is highlighted with a dark gray background. That's your clue that the text is a field and not plain text. Also see the later section, "Deleting fields."

Adding some useful fields

Word offers an abundance of fields you can thrust into a document. Of the lot, you might use only a smattering. My favorites are listed in this section.

These subsections assume that the Fields dialog box is open, as described in the preceding section.

Page numbers

To ensure that the document accurately reflects the current page number, insert a current page number field:

1. **In the Field dialog box, select Numbering from the Categories drop-down list.**

2. **Select Page from the Field Names list.**

3. **In the Field Properties section of the Field dialog box, select a format for the page number.**

4. **Click OK.**

The current page number dynamically appears in your document. No matter how you edit or modify the document, that number reflects the current page number.

Total number of pages

To insert the total number of pages in your document, heed these directions:

1. **Select Document Information from the Categories drop-down list.**

2. **Select NumPages from the Field Names list.**

3. **Select a format.**

4. **Click OK.**

Word count

Getting paid by the word? Stick an automatic word count at the end of your document:

1. **From the Categories list, select Document Information.**

2. **Select NumWords from the Field Names list.**

3. **Click OK.**

Document filename

Many organizations place the document's filename into a document header or footer. Rather than guess, why not use a field that contains the document's exact name? Do this:

1. **From the Categories list, select Document Information.**

2. **Select FileName from the Field Names list.**

3. **In the field properties list, choose a text case format.**

4. **Optionally (though recommended), put a check mark by the option Add Path to Filename.**

5. **Click OK.**

The FileName field always reflects the name of the file, even when you change it.

Updating a field

Just because a field contains dynamic text doesn't mean that the field is always accurate. Occasionally, fields need updating.

Many fields are updated automatically when you open a document. Printing fields update when you print the document. For fields that don't update, right-click the field in your document and choose the Update Field command. The field's text is refreshed.

Changing a field

Although you can't edit a file, you can modify the way it displays information. To do so, right-click the field and choose Edit Field from the pop-up menu. The Field dialog box is displayed, allowing you to make whatever modifications you deem necessary.

Just as those mutants at the end of *Beneath the Planet of the Apes* removed their human masks, you can remove a field's mask by right-clicking it and choosing the Toggle Field Codes command. For example, the FileSize field looks like this:

```
{ FILESIZE \* MERGEFORMAT }
```

To restore the field to human-readable form, right-click it again and choose the Toggle Field Codes command. All praise be to the bomb.

The mystery of content controls

Word's fields aren't the only dynamic text gizmos you can stick into a document. Another changing goober is the content control. It's not really a field, though it can be inserted and updated in a similar manner. The primary difference is how a content control looks, which is something like this:

$$A = \pi r^2$$

Content controls are usually inserted by Word commands, such as those that automatically create headers or footers or insert page numbers. On the Insert tab, in the Text group, you can choose Quick Parts ⇨ Document Property to insert a property control. The Equation menu, found in the Insert tab's Symbols group, also inserts content controls.

As with a field, you might not be able to edit text in a content control, although some controls are designed that way.

To update a time-sensitive content control, press the F9 key. Some Date content controls have a pick-the-date button, displaying a tiny calendar from which you can set the property's date.

Deleting fields

Removing a field works almost like deleting text. Almost. The main difference is that you have to press the Delete or Backspace key twice.

For example, when you press Backspace to erase a field, the entire field is highlighted. That's your clue that you're about to erase a field, not regular text. Press Backspace again to remove the field.

The Date and Time

With few exceptions, time travelers are the only ones who bother asking for the current year. Otherwise, people merely want to know the month and day or just the day of the week. Word understands those people (but not time travelers), so it offers a slate of tools and tricks to insert date and time information into a document.

Adding the current date or time

Instead of looking at a calendar and typing a date, follow these steps:

1. **Click the Insert tab.**

2. **In the Text group, click the Date and Time button.**

   The button may say Date & Time or you may see only the icon, shown in the margin.

3. **Use the Date and Time dialog box to choose a format.**

4. **If desired, click the Update Automatically option so that the date-and-time text remains current with the document.**

   Setting the Update Automatically option inserts a content control into the text, which is updated when you open or print the document.

5. **Click the OK button to insert the current date or time into your document.**

The keyboard shortcut to insert the current date is Alt+Shift+D. To insert the current time, press Alt+Shift+T. The date is inserted as a content control; the time is inserted as a field.

See the nearby sidebar "The mystery of content controls" for information on content controls.

Using the PrintDate field

The date field I use most often is PrintDate. This field reflects the current date (and time, if you like) that a document is printed. It's marvelous for including in a letterhead template or other document you reuse or print frequently. Here's how it's done:

1. **Click the Insert tab.**

2. **In the Text group, click Quick Parts ⇨ Field.**

   The Field dialog box, which is covered earlier in this chapter, appears.

3. **Select Date and Time from the Categories drop-down list.**

4. **Select PrintDate from the Field Names list.**

5. **Choose a date-and-time format from the Field Properties area.**

6. **Click OK.**

The field looks gross until you print the document, which makes sense. Also, the field reflects the last day you printed the document. It's updated once you print again.

Part V
The Rest of Word

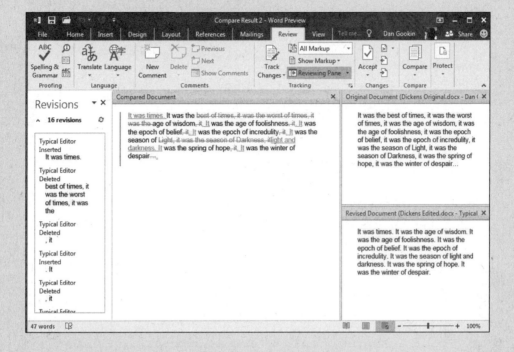

Discover how to create labels that include graphics at www.dummies.com/extras/word2016.

In this part . . .

- Find out how to work with multiple documents at one time.
- Use writing tools such as Outline view and the master document feature.
- Insert comments in your documents and exchange ideas with others.
- Find out how to use mail merge.
- Learn about how to use and print labels.

Chapter 24

Multiple Documents, Windows, and File Formats

. . . .

In This Chapter

▶ Working with more than one document at a time

▶ Comparing documents side by side

▶ Seeing one document in two windows

▶ Splitting the screen

▶ Opening a non-Word document

▶ Converting older Word documents

. . . .

*Y*ou need not limit your word processor usage to toiling with one document in a single window. Oh, no! You can open multiple documents, working on the lot and moving from window to window at your whim. You could even split a single document into two views in a single window, or open one document in two windows. Word does it all, plus it lets you work with documents in strange and alien non-Word formats.

Multiple Document Mania

It's not a question of whether Word can work on more than one document at a time. No, it's a question of how you open those documents. Let me count the ways:

> ✔ **Just keep using the Open command to open documents.** (See Chapter 8.) No official limit exists on the number of documents Word can have open, though I would avoid having more than nine or so open because they slow down your computer.

✔ **In the Open dialog box, select multiple documents to open.** Press and hold down the Ctrl key as you click to select documents. Click the Open button, and all the documents open, each in its own window.

✔ **From any folder window, select multiple Word document icons.** Lasso them with the mouse, or Ctrl+click to select multiple documents. Press the Enter key to open the lot.

Each document dwells in its own Word program window. To switch between them, click a window or choose a window by clicking the Word icon on the Windows taskbar.

To switch windows in Word, follow these steps:

1. **Click the View tab.**

2. **In the Window group, click the Switch Windows button.**

3. **Choose a document from the menu.**

If you're insane enough to have more than nine documents open at a time, the last command on the Switch Windows menu is More Windows. Choose this item to view the Activate dialog box, which lists *all* open document windows. Select a document from the window and click OK to switch to it.

Should you spy any document in the list named Document1, Document2, or similar, immediate switch to that window! Save the document before it's too late! Refer to Chapter 8.

Arranging open document windows

To see two or more documents displayed on the screen at the same time, select the View tab and click the Arrange All button. Immediately, Word organizes all its windows. They're arranged like the pieces of fabric in a quilt.

✔ The Arrange All command works best when only a few documents are open. Otherwise, the document windows are too small to be useful.

✔ Word doesn't arrange minimized windows.

✔ Although you can see more than one document at a time, you can *work* on only one at a time. The document with the highlighted title bar is the one "on top."

Comparing two documents side by side

A quick and handy way to review two documents is to arrange them side by side. Both documents are visible on the screen and their scrolling is locked so that you can peruse both in parallel. Here's how to accomplish this trick:

1. **Open both documents.**

2. **On the View tab, in the Window group, click the View Side by Side button.**

    Word instantly arranges both documents in vertical windows, with the current document on the left and the other on the right.

3. **Scroll either document.**

    Scrolling one document also scrolls the other. In this mode, you can compare two different or similar documents.

     You can disable synchronous scrolling by clicking the Synchronous Scrolling button, found in the Window group.

4. **When you're done, choose View Side by Side again.**

Also see Chapter 26, which covers reviewing changes made to a document.

Viewing one document in multiple windows

A handy document-viewing trick — especially for long documents — is to open a single document in two windows. This trick makes writing and editing easier than hopping back and forth within the same document window and potentially losing your place.

To open a second window on a single document, obey these steps:

1. **Click the View tab.**

2. **In the Window group, click the New Window button.**

    A second window opens, showing the current document.

To confirm that the same document is open in two windows, check the title bar: The first window's filename is followed by :1, and the second window's filename is followed by :2.

When you no longer need the second window, simply close it. You can close either window :1 or :2; it doesn't matter. Closing the second window merely removes that view. The document is still open and available for editing in the other window.

 ✔ Even though two windows are open, you're still working on only one document. The changes you make in one window are updated in the second.

 ✔ This feature is useful for cutting and pasting text or graphics between sections of a long document.

 ✔ You can even open a third window by choosing the New Window command again, but that's just nuts.

Using the old split-screen trick

Splitting the screen allows you to view two parts of your document in the same window. No need to bother with extra windows here: The top part of the window shows one part of the document; the bottom part, another. Each half of the screen scrolls individually, so you can peruse different parts of the same document without switching windows.

To split a window, heed these directions:

1. Click the View tab.

2. In the Window group, click the Split Window button.

   A line bisects the document, splitting it from side to side, as shown in Figure 24-1. If the ruler is visible, a second copy appears below the line, as shown in the figure.

You can scroll the top or bottom part of your document independently. That way, you can peruse or edit different parts of the document in the same window.

To undo the split, choose the Remote Split command from the Window group. Or you can double-click the line separating the document.

The line splitting your document is adjustable. To change the size of the top or bottom part of the split, drag the line up or down.

Drag up or down   Word's window trick commands   Double-click to close

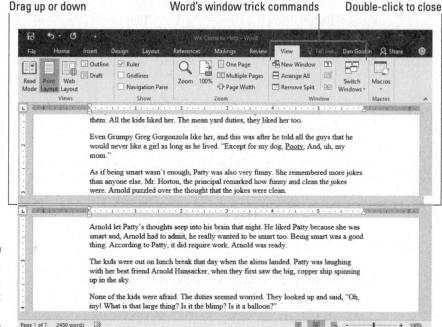

Figure 24-1:
Splitting a
document
window.

Many, Many Document Types

Word begrudgingly recognizes that it's not the only word processor and that
its documents are not the only type of document file. As such, the program
condescends to allow for the accommodation of lesser, mortal document
formats. This feature allows you to read and edit non-Word documents as
well as share your documents with non-Word users, who will be blessed with
Word's beneficence.

Understanding document formats

When you save a document, Word places the document's text, formatting,
and other information in a file. To keep the information organized, Word
uses a specific *file format*. The file format makes a Word document unique
and different from other types of files languishing on your computer's
storage system.

Although Word's document format is popular, it's not the only word-processing document format available. Other word processors, as well as document utilities such as Adobe Acrobat, use their own formats. Word permits you to open documents saved in those formats as well as save your Word documents in the alien formats. I'm not certain whether the software is pleased to do so, but it's capable.

- ✔ Basic document opening and saving information is found in Chapter 8.

- ✔ The best way to save a file in another format is to use the Export command, discussed in Chapter 9.

- ✔ The standard Word document format uses the docx filename extension. This extension is applied automatically to all Word documents you save, although it may not be visible when viewing files in a folder. The older Word document format used the doc filename extension. See the section, "Updating an older Word document."

Opening a non-Word document

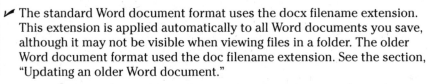

Word can magically open and display a host of weird, non-Word documents. Here's how it works:

1. **Press Ctrl+F12 to summon the traditional Open dialog box.**

   It's possible, but not simple, to display the Open dialog box by using the Open screen. When you must open a non-Word document, it makes more sense to use the weirdo Ctrl+F12 keyboard shortcut and call it good.

2. **Choose a file format from the menu button.**

   The menu button has no label, though it might say *All Word Documents,* as shown in Figure 24-2.

   When you choose a specific file format, Word narrows the number of files displayed in the Open dialog box; only files matching the specific file format are shown.

   If you don't know the format, choose All Files from the drop-down list. Word then makes its best guess.

3. **Click to select the file.**

   Or work the controls in the dialog box to find another storage media or folder that contains the file.

4. **Click the Open button.**

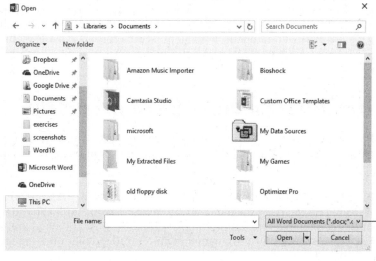

Figure 24-2:
Change
file types in
the Open
dialog box.

File type menu

The alien file appears onscreen, ready for editing, just like any other Word document — or not. Word tries its best to open other file formats, but it may not get everything 100 percent okeydoke.

- ✔ For some document types, Word displays a file-conversion dialog box. Use the controls to preview the document, although clicking the OK button is usually your best bet.

- ✔ The Recover Text from Any File option is useful for peering into unknown files, especially from antique and obscure word-processing file formats.

- ✔ Word *remembers* the file type! When you use the Open dialog box again, the same file type is already chosen from the Files of Type drop-down list. That means your regular Word document may be opened as a plain text document, which looks truly ugly. Remember to check the Files of Type drop-down list if such a thing happens to you.

- ✔ Accordingly, when you want to open a Word document after opening an HTML document, or especially when using the Recover Text from Any File option, you *must* choose Word Documents from the list. Otherwise, Word may open documents in a manner that seems strange to you.

- ✔ You may see a warning when opening a document downloaded from the Internet. Word is just being safe; the document is placed into Protected View. You can preview the document, but to edit it, you need to click the Enable Editing button.

✔ Don't blame yourself when Word is unable to open a document. Many, many file formats are unknown to Word. When someone is sending you this type of document, ask the person to resend it using a common file format, such as HTML or RTF.

Updating an older Word document

Microsoft Word has been around for ages. It's used the same doc file format since the early days, back when Word ran on steam-powered computers that took three people to hoist onto a table.

In 2007, Word changed its document file format. Gone was the doc format, replaced by the docx format. Because a lot of people still use older versions of Word, and given the abundance of older doc files still used and available, it became necessary to work with and convert those older documents.

Working with an older Word document is cinchy: Simply open the document. You see the text *[Compatibility Mode]* after the filename at the top of the window. This text is a big clue that you're using an older Word document. Another clue is that a lot of Word's features, such as the capability to preview format changes and document themes, don't work when you edit an older document.

To update an older document, follow these steps:

1. **Click the File tab.**

2. **On the Info screen, click the Convert button.**

   A descriptive dialog box appears. If not, skip to Step 5.

3. **In the Microsoft Word dialog box, click to place a check mark by the item Do Not Ask Me Again about Converting Documents.**

4. **Click the OK button.**

5. **Click the Save button to save your document.**

   Use the Save As dialog box as covered in Chapter 8. If you're paying attention, you'll see that the chosen file format is Word Document (*.docx).

   The document is updated.

The older document isn't removed when you follow these steps. It lingers, although you can freely delete it.

See Chapter 8 if you desire to save a current document in the older Word file format.

Chapter 25

Word for Writers

• •

In This Chapter

▶ Creating an outline in Word

▶ Adding topics, subtopics, and text topics

▶ Rearranging topics in an outline

▶ Demoting and promoting topics

▶ Printing an outline

▶ Making a master document

▶ Using the thesaurus

▶ Pulling a word count

• •

The word processor is the best tool for writers since the ghostwriter. Of course, cobbling together words in a word processor doesn't make you a writer any more than working with numbers in a spreadsheet makes you an accountant. Even so, beyond its basic word-processing capabilities, Word comes with an armada of tools for making a writer's job easier. Whether you're writing your first guest piece for the church newsletter or crafting your 74th horror-thriller, you'll enjoy Word's features for writers.

Organize Your Thoughts

Good writers use an outline to organize their thoughts. Back in the old days, an outline would dwell on a stack of 3-by-5 cards. Today, an outline is a Word document. That makes it easier not to confuse your outline with grandma's recipes.

Word's Outline view presents your document in a unique way. By using Word's header styles, you can group and organize thoughts, ideas, or a plotline in a hierarchical fashion. Outline view makes it easy to shuffle around topics, make subtopics, and mix in text to help get your thoughts organized. Even if you're not a writer, you can use Word's Outline mode to create lists, work on projects, or look busy when the boss comes around.

Entering Outline view

To enter Outline view, click the View tab, and in the Views group, click the Outline button. The document's presentation changes to show Outline view, and the Outlining tab appears on the Ribbon, as shown in Figure 25-1.

No subtopics

Open/close topic

Move topic

Set topic level

Outlining tab   Set which levels appear   Exit Outline View

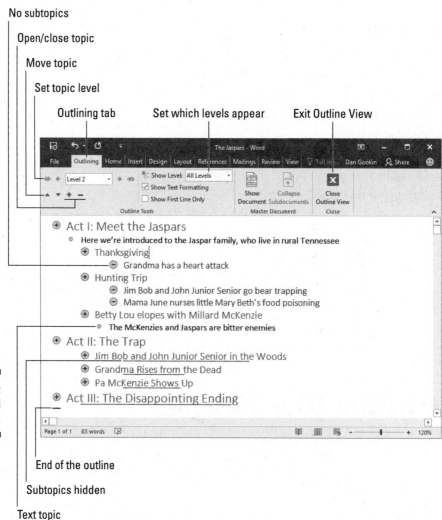

Figure 25-1:
A typical
outline.

End of the outline

Subtopics hidden

Text topic

To exit Outline view, click the View tab and choose another document view. You can also click the big, honkin' Close Outline View button (labeled in Figure 25-1).

- ✔ A squat, horizontal bar marks the end of your outline. You cannot delete that bar.

- ✔ All basic Word commands work in Outline view. You can use the cursor keys, delete text, check spelling, save, insert oddball characters, print, and so on.

- ✔ Don't worry about the text format in Outline view. Format your text later.

- ✔ Word uses the Heading 1 through Heading 9 styles for your outline's topics. Main topics are formatted in Heading 1, subtopics in Heading 2, and so on.

- ✔ Use the Body or Normal style to make notes or add text to the outline. See the section "Adding a text topic," later in this chapter.

- ✔ An outline isn't a special type of document. It's just another Word document, presented with Outline view active.

Typing topics in the outline

Outlines are composed of topics and subtopics. *Topics* are your main ideas; *subtopics* describe the details. Subtopics can contain their own subtopics going down to several levels of detail. The amount of detail you use depends on how organized you want to be.

To create a topic, type the text. Word automatically formats the topic using a specific Heading style based on the topic level, as shown in Figure 25-2.

Figure 25-2:
Topics in
an outline.

⊕ Things I'm Proud Of
⊕ Things I Regret
   ⊖ Being captured by pirates
   ⊖ Going bankrupt
   ⊖ Two civil wars
   ⊖ Not conquering the world until I was 54

Keep your main topic levels short and descriptive. Deeper topics can go into more detail. Press the Enter key when you're done typing one topic and want to start another.

✔ Use the Enter key to split a topic. For example, to split the topic Pots and Pans, delete the word *and,* and then with the insertion pointer placed between the two words, press the Enter key.

✔ To join two topics, press the End key to send the insertion pointer to the end of the first topic. Then press the Delete key. (This method works just like joining two paragraphs in a regular document.)

✔ Don't worry about organizing your outline when you first create it. In Word's Outline view, you can rearrange topics as your ideas solidify. My advice is to start writing things down now and concentrate on organization later.

Rearranging topics

As you organize an outline, things change. In Outline view, you can reset a topic's priority, moving it up or down in the list. You can also promote and demote topics, moving subtopics to main topics and vice-versa.

To help your topics flow in a logical progression, change their order up or down as follows:

✔ Click the Move Up button (or press Alt+Shift+↑) to move a topic up a line.

✔ Click the Move Down button (or press Alt+Shift+↓) to move a topic down a line.

You can also drag a topic up or down: Point the mouse pointer at the circle to the topic's left. When the mouse is positioned just right, the mouse pointer changes to a four-way arrow (see the margin). I recommend using this trick only when you're moving topics a short distance; dragging beyond the current screen can prove unwieldy.

If you need to move a topic and all its subtopics, first collapse the topic. When the topic is expanded (open), only that line is moved. See the later section, "Expanding and collapsing topics."

Demoting and promoting topics

Outline organization also includes demoting topics that are really subtopics and promoting subtopics to a higher level. Making such adjustments is a natural part of working in Outline view.

To demote a topic into a subtopic, place the insertion pointer in the topic's text. Then on the Outlining tab, in the Outline Tools group, click the Demote button, shown in the margin.

To promote a subtopic, place the insertion pointer in the topic's text and click the Promote command button, shown in the margin.

You can continue creating subtopics by typing them and then pressing the Enter key at the end of each subtopic. Word keeps giving you subtopics, one for each press of the Enter key.

- ✔ The keyboard shortcut to demote a topic is Alt+Shift+→.

- ✔ The keyboard shortcut to promote a topic is Alt+Shift+←.

- ✔ To instantly make any topic a main-level topic, click the Promote to Heading 1 button.

- ✔ You can use the mouse to promote or demote topics: Drag the topic's circle left or right. I admit that this move can be tricky, which is why I use the keyboard shortcuts or buttons on the Ribbon to promote or demote topics.

- ✔ You don't really *create* subtopics in Word as much as you *demote* higher-level topics.

- ✔ Promoting or demoting a topic changes the text format. For example, demoting a top-level topic changes the style from Heading 1 to Heading 2. The subtopic also appears indented on the screen. (Refer to Figures 25-1 and 25-2.)

- ✔ The Level item in the Outlining tab's Outline Tools group changes to reflect the current topic level. You can also use this item's drop-down list to promote or demote the topic to any specific level in the outline

- ✔ Unlike main topics, you can get wordy with your subtopics. After all, the idea here is to expand on the main topic.

- ✔ According to Those Who Know Such Things, there must be at least two subtopics for them to qualify as subtopics. When you have only one subtopic, either you have a second main topic or you've created a text topic. See the later section, "Adding a text topic," for information.

Expanding and collapsing topics

A detailed outline is wonderful, the perfect tool to help you write that novel, organize a meeting, or set your priorities. To help you pull back from the detail and see the Big Picture, you can collapse all or part of an outline. Even when you're organizing, sometimes it helps to collapse a topic to help keep it in perspective.

Any topic with subtopics shows a plus sign in its circle. To collapse the topic and temporarily hide its subtopics, you have several choices:

✔ Click the Collapse button on the Outlining toolbar (shown in the margin).

✔ Press the Alt+Shift+_ (underline) keyboard shortcut.

✔ Double-click the plus sign to the topic's left.

When a topic is collapsed, it features a fuzzy underline, in addition to a plus sign in the icon to the topic's left. To expand a collapsed topic, you have several choices:

✔ Click the Expand button on the Outlining toolbar (shown in the margin).

✔ Press Alt+Shift++ (plus sign).

✔ Click the topic's plus sign.

The fastest way to display an outline at a specific topic level is to choose that level from the Show Level drop-down list. To find that command, look on the Outlining toolbar, in the Outline Tools group.

For example, to show only Level 1 and Level 2 topics, choose Level 2 from the Show Level button's menu. Levels 3 and higher topics remain collapsed.

To see the entire outline, choose Show All Levels from the Show Level menu.

When some of your subtopics get wordy, place a check mark by the Show First Line Only option. (Look on the Outlining tab in the Outline Tools group for this setting.) When active, Word displays only the first topic line of text in any topic.

The joy of collapsible headers

You may have seen a side effect of Word's Outline view when using the Heading styles in your document: A tiny triangle button appears next to a Heading-style paragraph when a document is shown in Print Layout view. Click that button to expand or collapse the heading and all its contents — including any subheadings. Using this trick is a great way to collapse parts of a document without having to switch to Outline view.

Adding a text topic

Outline view doesn't prevent you from actually writing text. When the mood hits you, write! Rather than write prose as a topic, use the Demote to Body Text command. Here's how:

1. **Press the Enter key to start a new topic.**

2. **On the Outlining tab, in the Outline Tools group, click the Demote to Body Text button (shown in the margin).**

   The keyboard shortcut is Ctrl+Shift+N, which is also the keyboard shortcut for the Normal style.

These steps change the text style to Body Text. That way, you can write text for your speech, some instructions in a list, or a chunk of dialogue from your novel, and not have it appear as a topic or subtopic.

Printing an outline

Printing an outline works just like printing any other document in Word but with one big difference: Only visible topics are printed.

Outline manipulation shortcut keys

I prefer using Word's shortcut keys whenever possible. Especially when working an outline, when I'm typing more than mousing, it helps to know these outline manipulate shortcut keys:

Key Combo	What It Does
Alt+Shift+→	Demotes a topic
Alt+Shift+←	Promotes a topic
Alt+Shift+↑	Moves a topic up one line
Alt+Shift+↓	Moves a topic down one line
Ctrl+Shift+N	Demotes a topic to body text
Alt+Shift+1	Displays only top topics
Alt+Shift+2	Displays first- and second-level topics
Alt+Shift+n	Displays all topics up to level n, such as Alt+Shift+4 for the fourth level
Alt+Shift+A	Displays all topics
Alt+Shift++ (plus sign)	Displays all subtopics in the current topic
Alt+Shift+_ (underline)	Hides all subtopics in the current topic

To control visible topics, use the Show Level menu, as discussed earlier in the "Expanding and collapsing topics" section. For example, to print the entire outline, choose All Levels from the Show Level menu and then print.

To print only the first two levels of your outline, choose Level 2 from the Show Level drop-down list and then print.

- ✔ Word uses the Heading styles when it prints the outline, although it does not indent topics.
- ✔ See Chapter 9 for more information on printing documents in Word.

Large Documents

The first novel I wrote (and never published, of course) was several hundred pages long. It was saved as a single document. Although Word documents can be *any* length, putting everything into one document that way is impractical. Editing, copying and pasting, searching and replacing, and all other word-processing operations become less efficient the larger the document.

A better solution for long documents is to keep each chapter, or large chunk, as its own file. You can then take advantage of Word's Master Document feature to put everything together when it comes time to print or publish.

- ✔ The *master document* stitches together all individual documents, or subdocuments, even continuing page numbers, headers, footers, and other ongoing elements. The end result is a large document that you can print or publish.
- ✔ What qualifies as a large document? Anything over 100 pages qualifies, as far as I'm concerned.

- ✔ When writing a novel, create each chapter as its own document. Keep all those chapter documents in their own folder. Further, use document filenames to help with organization. For example, I name chapters by using numbers: The first chapter is 01, the second is 02, and so on.
- ✔ This book is comprised of several dozen individual Word documents — one for each chapter, each part introduction, the front matter, the index, and so on.

Creating a master document

Word's Master Document feature helps you collect and coordinate individual documents — called *subdocuments* — and cobble them into one large document. When you have a master document, you can assign continuous page numbers to your work, apply headers and footers throughout the entire project, and take advantage of Word's Table of Contents, Index, and other list-generating features.

To create a big, whopping document from many smaller documents — to create a master document — obey these steps:

1. **Start a new, blank document in Word.**

   Press Ctrl+N to quickly summon a new, blank document.

2. **Save the document.**

   Yeah, I know — you haven't yet written anything. Don't worry: By saving now, you get ahead of the game and avoid some weird error messages.

3. **Switch to Outline view.**

   Click the View tab, and then click the Outline button.

4. **On the Outlining tab in the Master Document group, click the Show Document button.**

   The Master Document group is instantly repopulated with more buttons. One of these is the Insert button, used to build the master document.

5. **Click the Insert button.**

6. **Use the Insert Subdocument dialog box to hunt down the first document to insert in the master document.**

   The documents must be inserted in order. I hope you used a clever document-naming scheme, as recommended in the preceding section.

7. **Click the Open button to stick the document in the master document.**

   The document appears in the window, but it's ugly because Outline view is active. Don't worry: It won't be ugly when it is printed!

   If you're asked a question about conflicting styles, click the Yes to All button. It keeps all subdocument styles consistent with the master document. (Although it's best when all documents use the same document template.)

   Word sets itself up for you to insert the next document:

8. **Repeat Steps 5 through 7 to build the master document.**

9. **Save the master document when you've finished inserting all subdocuments.**

At this point, the master document is created. It's what you'll use to print or save the entire, larger document.

You can still edit and work on the individual documents. Any changes you make are reflected in the master document. In fact, the only time you really need to work in the master document is when you choose to edit the headers and footers, create a table of contents, or work on other items that affect the entire document.

✔ When you're ready, you can publish the master document just as you publish any individual document. See Chapter 9 for information on publishing a document.

✔ Use the Collapse Subdocuments button to hide all subdocument text. For example, if you need to create a table of contents or work on the master document's headers and footers, collapsing the subdocuments makes the process easier.

✔ See Chapter 21 for more information on creating a table of contents and an index for your document.

Splitting a document

Splitting a document isn't a part of creating a master document, but it might be the way you start. If you mistakenly wrote your novel as one long document, I recommend that you split it into smaller documents. A simple shortcut doesn't exist; instead you have to cut and paste to create smaller documents out of a huge one.

Here's how to split a document:

1. Select half the document — the portion you want to split into a new document.

Or if you're splitting a document into several pieces, select the first chunk that you want to plop into a new document. For example, split the document at the chapter breaks or a main heading break.

2. Cut the selected block.

Press Ctrl+X to cut the block.

3. Summon a new, blank document.

Ctrl+N does the trick. Or, if you're using a template (and you should be), start a new document with that template. See Chapter 16.

4. Paste the document portion.

Press Ctrl+V to paste. If the text doesn't paste in with the proper formatting, click the Home tab, and in the Clipboard group, click the Paste Options button. Choose the command button Keep Source Formatting (shown in the margin).

5. Save the new document.

Continue splitting the larger document by repeating these steps. After you've finished splitting the larger document, you can safely delete it.

Dan's Writing Tips

Nothing beats advice from someone who has been there and done that. As a professional writer, I'm excited to pass along my tips, tricks, and suggestions to any budding scrivener. That's why I wrote this section.

Choosing the best word

When two words share the same meaning, they're said to be *synonyms* — for example, *big* and *large*. Synonyms are helpful in that they allow you to find better, more descriptive words and, especially, to avoid using the same tired old words over and over. Obviously, knowing synonyms is a handy skill for any writer.

To find a word's synonym, right-click the word in your document. From the pop-up menu, choose the Synonyms submenu to see a list of words that have a similar meaning. Choose a word from the menu and it replaces the word in your document.

- ✔ To see more word alternatives, right-click a word and choose Synonyms ⇨ Thesaurus. The Thesaurus pane appears, listing multitudinous alternative words.

- ✔ To use a word from the Thesaurus pane, right-click the word and choose the Insert command. The word is placed in your document at the toothpick cursor's location.

- ✔ *Antonyms,* or words that mean the opposite of the selected word, might also appear on the Synonyms submenu.

- ✔ For more research on a specific word, right-click and choose the Smart Lookup command. The Insights pane appears, which lists sources from online references to help you determine whether or not you're using the best word.

Counting every word

You pay the butcher by the pound. The dairyman is paid by the gallon. Salespeople keep a percentage of their sales. Writers? They're paid by the word.

If you're lucky enough to be paid for your writing, you know that word count is king. Magazine editors demand articles based on word length. "I need 350 hilarious words on tech-support phone calls," an editor once told me. And novel writers typically boast about how many words are in their latest efforts. "My next book is 350,000 words," they say in stuffy, nasal voices. How do they know how many words they wrote?

The best way to see how many words dwell in your document is to view the status bar. The word count appears by the *Words* label, and the count is updated as you type.

If you don't see the word count at the bottom of the window, right-click the status bar and choose Word Count.

ABC 123 To obtain more than a word count, click the Review tab. In the Proofing group, click the Word Count button (shown in the margin). The detailed Word Count dialog box appears, listing all sorts of word-counting trivia.

Also see Chapter 23 for information on inserting a Word Count field in your document.

Writing for writers

Here's a smattering of tips for any writer using Word:

- ✔ You'll notice that, thanks to AutoFormat, Word fixes ellipses for you. When you type three periods in a row, Word inserts the ellipsis character (. . .). Don't correct it! Word is being proper. When you don't use the ellipsis character, be sure to separate the three periods with spaces.

- ✔ You can format paragraphs by separating them with a space or by indenting the first line of each paragraph. Use one or the other, not both.

- ✔ Keep the proper heading formats: Heading 1, Heading 2, and so on. Or create your own heading styles that properly use the Outline Level format. That way, you can easily create a table of contents as well as use other Word features that display headings in your documents.

- ✔ Use Outline view to collect your thoughts. Keep working on the outline and organizing your thoughts. When you find yourself writing text-level topics, you're ready to write.

- ✔ Use the soft return (Shift+Enter) to split text into single lines. I use the soft return to break up titles and write return addresses, and I use it at other times when text must appear one line at a time.

- ✔ Word is configured to select text one word at a time. This option isn't always best for writers, where it sometimes pays to select text by character, not by word. To fix that setting, from the File tab menu, choose Options. In the Options dialog box, click the Advanced item. Remove the check mark by the When Selecting, Automatically Select Entire Word item. Click OK.

Chapter 26

Let's Work This Out

Writing isn't a team sport, but it can be. Eventually, writers encounter collaboration, welcome or not. Often it comes in the form of an editor, but occasionally others chime in. To assist in that task, Word gives you some work-it-out-together tools. They help you share ideas, point out issues that need attention, and even see who has done exactly what to your precious text.

Comments on Your Text

You can write a note to yourself, or those reading your document can jot a note. They can do so right in the text, which is *très gauche*, coloring the text in another font, or using ALL CAPS, or surrounding it with triple curly brackets or some other such nonsense.

The better way to insert comments in a document is to use Word's Comment feature, found on the Review tab.

Adding a comment

To adroitly thrust a comment into your document, follow these steps:

1. Select the chunk of text on which you want to comment.

Be specific. Although you may be tempted to select the entire document, only the first few words of a longer chunk are necessary.

2. Click the Review tab.

3. In the Comments group, click the New Comment button.

The New Comment button is shown in the margin. Click it to see a Comments box to the right of the current page, similar to the one shown in Figure 26-1. The side of the page where the comment appears is called the *markup area.*

4. Type your comment.

Jot down your thoughts. I'm not sure how long a comment can be, although you probably don't want to write more than a few lines. If you desire, you can apply text formats to the comment.

5. Press the Esc key when you've finished typing the comment.

Or you can click in the document's text.

To comment on a comment, click the Add Comment button, shown in Figure 26-1. Type your reply to the earlier comment in the box. Click in the text when you're done.

Original comment   Add Comment

Figure 26-1: Comments on a text passage.

Comment on the comment

Displaying or hiding comments

Add a comment to your document and the markup area appears on the right side of the page. The markup area appears whenever a document features comments, but its appearance is controlled by settings on the Review tab.

To hide the markup area, click the Review tab. In the Tracking group, click the Display for Review button, shown in the margin. The four available options set how comments, as well as other document revisions (covered elsewhere in this chapter), are displayed:

> **Simple Markup:** Chose this item to display the markup area and view comments and revisions.

> **All Markup:** Choose this item to display the markup area. Any comments or revisions are shown, along with lines referencing their locations in the text.

> **No Markup:** Choose this item to hide the markup area. Comments don't appear, and any revisions are hidden in the text.

> **Original:** Choose this item to hide the markup area as well as any revisions made to the document. With regards to comments, this item is identical to No Markup.

The markup area appears best when viewing the document in Print Layout view. Web Layout view (not my favorite) also shows the markup area on the right side of the window.

If you choose Draft view, the comments appear as bracketed initials highlighted with a specific background color. For example, my comments look like [DG1], where *DG* are my initials and the 1 represents comment one. Position the mouse pointer at that text to view the comment in a pop-up bubble.

 When Word is in Read Mode view, comments appear as cartoon bubbles to the right of the text. Click a bubble, similar to what's shown in the margin, to view the comment.

> ✔ See Chapter 1 for more information on Word's different document views.

> ✔ To view all comments, no matter which document view is chosen, summon the Reviewing pane: Click the Review tab, and in the Tracking group, click the Reviewing Pane button. Choose either the horizontal or vertical display to summon the Reviewing pane and peruse comments as well as text revisions.

> ✔ See the later section, "Tracking changes as they're made," for information on revisions.

Reviewing comments one at a time

Rather than randomly scroll through your document to hunt down a comment, use the Next Comment and Previous Comment buttons. These buttons are found on the Review tab, in the Comments group.

Click the Next Comment button to jump to the next comment in the document.

Click the Previous Comment button to jump to the previous comment in the document.

Clicking either the Next Comment or Previous Comment button activates All Markup view, as covered in the preceding section.

Printing comments (or not)

I'll bet you were surprised! You went to print your document and, lo, there on the page along with all your wonderful formatted text were those silly comments. That's probably not what you intended.

To control whether a document's comments appear when printed, follow these steps:

1. **Press Ctrl+P.**

   The Print screen appears.

2. **Click the Print All Pages button.**

   A menu pops up, which I call the "print what" menu.

   At the bottom of the menu, you see a set of options, the first of which is Print Markup. This setting controls whether comments, as well as other text markup covered in this chapter, print with the rest of the document.

3. **Choose the Print Markup command.**

   When this command has a check mark by it, the comments print. When no check mark appears, you're directing Word not to print comments (and other types of text markup).

   Use the Print Preview window to confirm whether comments will print.

4. **Make any other settings in the Print window as needed.**

5. **Click the big Print button to print the document.**

The change made by completing these steps isn't permanent. You must follow these steps every time you print the document or else the comments print as well.

See Chapter 9 for more information on printing documents in Word.

Deleting comments

To delete a comment, work these steps:

1. **Click the Review tab.**

2. **Click the Next Comment button to locate the offending comment.**

   Or you can click the Previous Comment button, depending on where the insertion pointer blinks inside the document.

   Upon success, the comment is highlighted in the markup area.

3. **In the Comments area, choose Delete ⇨ Delete.**

   The Delete button is shown in the margin. It's one of those menu button icon things that you must click to access the commands.

4. **Repeat Steps 2 and 3 to remove additional comments.**

   Or just keep repeating Step 2 until you find a comment worthy of obliteration.

To delete all comments from a document in one single act of massive retaliation, use the Delete Comment button's menu: Choose Delete ⇨ Delete All Comments in Document.

The Yellow Highlighter

Word comes with a digital highlighter pen that lets you mark up and colorize the text in your document without damaging the computer's monitor. To highlight text, abide by these steps:

1. **Click the Home tab.**

2. **In the Font group, click the Text Highlight button.**

   The mouse pointer changes to a — well, I don't know what it is, but the point is that Word is now in Highlighting mode.

3. **Drag the mouse over the text you want to highlight.**

   The text becomes highlighted — just as if you used a highlighter on regular paper but far neater.

4. **Click the Text Highlight button again to return the mouse to normal operation.**

   Or press the Esc key to exit Highlighting mode.

The highlight doesn't necessarily need to be yellow. Click the menu button to the right of the Text Highlight button, and choose a different highlighter color from the palette displayed.

To remove highlighting from your text, highlight it again in the same color. If that doesn't work, choose None as the highlight color and then drag the mouse over any color of highlighted text to remove the highlight.

- ✔ To highlight multiple chunks of text, double-click the Text Highlight button. The mouse pointer stays in highlighting mode until you click the Text Highlight button again or press the Esc key.

- ✔ To highlight a block of text, mark the block and then click the Highlight button that appears on the mini toolbar.

- ✔ Highlighting isn't the background color. See Chapter 10 for information on setting the text background color.

- ✔ The highlighted text prints, so be careful with it. If you don't have a color printer, highlighted text prints in black or gray on hard copy.

Look What They've Done to My Text, Ma

I enjoy feedback. All good writers do. Still, I'd like to know what's been done to my text, not only to see the effect but sometimes to learn something. Word's revision-tracking tools make such a review possible.

Comparing two versions of a document

You have the original copy of your document — the stuff you wrote. You also have the copy that Brianne, the vixen from the legal department, has worked over. Your job is to compare them to see exactly what's been changed from the original. Here's what to do:

1. **Click the Review tab.**

2. **In the Compare group, choose Compare ⇨ Compare.**

   The Compare Documents dialog box shows up.

3. **Choose the original document from the Original Document drop-down list.**

   The list shows recently opened or saved documents. Choose one, or use the Browse item to summon the Open dialog box and hunt down the document.

4. **Choose the edited document from the Revised Document drop-down list.**

   Choose the document from the list, or use the Browse item to locate the changed, altered, or mangled document.

5. **Click OK.**

Word compares the two documents. The changes are displayed in a quadruple-split window, as shown in Figure 26-2. This presentation is actually a third document titled Compare Result.

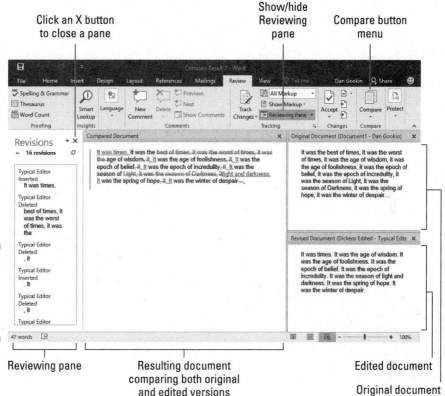

Figure 26-2:
The shameful changes show up here.

Click an X button to close a pane

Show/hide Reviewing pane

Compare button menu

Reviewing pane

Resulting document comparing both original and edited versions

Edited document

Original document

Look it over! Peruse the changes made to your pristine prose by the barbarian interlopers: Scrolling is synchronized between all three documents: original, edited, and compared. Click a change in the Reviewing pane (shown on the left in Figure 26-2) to quickly see which part of your document was folded, spindled, or mutilated.

✔ Changed text is highlighted in two ways: Added text is underlined. Removed text is shown in strikethrough style.

✔ You can confirm or reject the changes in the Compare Result document just as you would when tracking changes manually. See the upcoming section, "Reviewing changes."

Tracking changes as they're made

 To be a kind and gentle collaborator, activate Word's Tracking feature *before* you being making changes to someone else's text: Click the Review tab, and in the Tracking group, click the Track Changes button, shown in the margin. From that point on, any changes made to the document are color-coded based on who is making the changes and what level of markup is displayed:

- ✔ For Simple Markup, a color-coded bar appears to the left of a paragraph, indicating that some change was made.

- ✔ For All Markup, new text appears in a specific color, depending on who made the changes. Added text appears with a color-coded underline and deleted text appears with color-coded strikethrough. These text highlights are called *revision marks*.

- ✔ For No Markup, the changes are tracked but not displayed in the document. This is a great setting to choose for the least amount of distraction. (The revision marks can be seen by choosing All Markup instead of No Markup.)

Refer to the earlier section, "Displaying or hiding comments," for information on the Simple Markup, All Markup, and No Markup settings.

Word continues to track changes and edits in your document until you turn off Track Changes. To do so, click the Track Changes button again.

 Although the Track Changes button appears highlighted while the feature is active, a better way to check — and use — this feature is to activate the Track Settings option on the status bar. To set this option, right-click the status bar and choose Track Changes. As a bonus, you can click this item on the status bar to activate or deactivate revision marks in your document.

Reviewing changes

After your poor, limp document is returned to you, the best way to review the damage inflicted is to use the commands on the Review tab, located in the Changes group. These commands are illustrated in Figure 26-3; depending on the window size, you may or may not see text explaining what each one does.

To review changes throughout your document, click the Next or Previous buttons. Click a button to hop from one change in the text to the next change.

Accept a revision

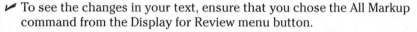

Figure 26-3:
Buttons for
reviewing
changes.

Reject a revision
Previous revision
Next revision

Accept
Changes

Click the Accept button if you can tolerate the change. To reject a change, click the Reject button. After clicking either button, you instantly see the next change in the document, until all the changes are dealt with.

> ✔ The Accept and Reject buttons are actually menus. They sport commands that accept or reject all the changes in your document in one fell swoop. The only thing missing is the "swoop!" sound when you use those commands.
>
> ✔ You can view a summary of changes by summoning the Revisions pane: On the Review tab, in the Tracking group, click the Reviewing Pane button. The Revisions pane doesn't show the changes in context, but it lists each one. Click an item in the Revisions pane to hop to each change in your document.
>
> ✔ To see the changes in your text, ensure that you chose the All Markup command from the Display for Review menu button.
>
> ✔ When you goof while approving or rejecting a change, press Ctrl+Z to undo.
>
> ✔ You can also right-click any revision mark to accept or reject it.

Collaborate on the Internet

Most document changes are made sequentially: You write something, save, and then someone else works on the document. If that chaos isn't enough for you, Word allows you to invite people to edit a document while you're working on it. This collaboration feature is called Sharing, probably because a better name wasn't available or Microsoft was pressed for time.

To make document sharing work, save your document to the cloud, or Internet storage. Specifically, the document must be saved to Microsoft's One Drive storage. See Chapter 8 for more information.

Sharing a document

After saving your document to OneDrive online storage, follow these steps to make it available for collaboration:

1. **Click the Share button.**

   This button is found above the Ribbon, near the top-right part of the document's window.

   Upon success, the Share pane appears.

2. **Fill in information about your collaborator(s).**

   Type in the Invite People box the email address of the person or people with whom you want to share the document. If you use Outlook as your computer's address book, click the Address icon to the right of the Invite People box to automatically add people.

3. **Choose whether or not the collaborators can edit.**

   Choose Can View from the menu and the people you invite can read the document. Choose Can Edit and they can make changes.

4. **Type a message in the Include a Message box.**

5. **Click the Share button.**

   The invites are sent.

Eventually, the recipients receive the email invite. To access the shared document, they click the link in the email address. Their web browser program opens and displays the document. If they want to edit the document, they click the link Edit in Browser button. At that point, their web browser displays the document as it appears in Word, complete with a customized version of the Ribbon. Hack away.

Checking updates

To determine whether someone has edited your shared document, or even if he's editing it right now, open the shared document and click the Share button found near the upper-right corner of the document window. The Share pane lists all collaborators and whether or not they're currently editing.

If any collaborators have changed the document, save your copy to view the updates: Click the Save icon on the Quick Access toolbar, or press Ctrl+S. Any changed content appears in the document with a colored overlay, similar to how revision marks are displayed, as covered earlier in this chapter.

To check to see whether updates are pending, click the File tab, and on the Info screen look for and click the button titled Document Updates Available.

Chapter 27

Mail Merge Mania

. . . .

. . . .

Here's a little quiz: What do these things have in common? Rocket science. Quantum mechanics. Brain surgery. Levitation. The answer: They're all a lot easier to accomplish than attempting mail merge in Word.

I'm not saying that mastering mail merge is impossible. True, it's an ancient word-processing tradition — something that just about everyone toys with at one time or another. Yet the way Word handles mail merge has been consistently frustrating. That's why I wrote this chapter.

About Mail Merge

The term *mail merge* is given to the process of opening a single document, stirring in a list of names and other information, and then combining *(merging)* everything. The result is a sheaf of personalized documents. Sounds useful, right? Peruse this section before attempting the process on your own.

Mail merge document types

In addition to a form letter, the main document in a mail merge can be an email message, an envelope, a set of labels, or anything else that can be mass-produced. Here are the official Word mail merge document types:

Letter: The traditional mail merge document is a letter, a document in Word.

Email messages: Word can produce customized email messages, which are sent electronically rather than printed.

Envelopes: You can use mail merge to create a batch of customized envelopes, each printed with its own address.

Labels: Word lets you print sheets of labels, each of which is customized with specific information from the mail merge. See Chapter 28 for specifics.

Directory: A directory is a list of information, such as a catalog or an address book.

Understanding Word's mail merge jargon

Although you may have your own delightful, descriptive terms for the steps required and pieces necessary to complete a mail merge, Word's terms are different. Before taking the mail merge plunge, I recommend that you review the terms Word uses:

Main document: This document is just like any other document in Word, complete with formatting, layout, and all the fancy stuff that goes into a document. The document also contains various fill-in-the-blank items, which is what makes it the main document.

Recipient list: This list contains the information that creates the customized documents. It's a type of *database*, with rows and columns of information used to fill in the form letters.

Field: Each of these fill-in-the-blanks items inside the main document is a placeholder that will be filled in by information from the recipient list. Fields are what make the mail merge possible.

Getting these three elements to work together is the essence of mail merge. All the commands necessary are located on the Mailings tab. In fact, the command groups are organized left-to-right in the order you use them. The remainder of this chapter describes the details.

✔ The key to mail merging is the recipient list. If you plan to create a mail merge as part of your regular routine, build a recipient list that you can use again and again.

✔ A mail merge document can have as many fields as it needs. In fact, any item you want to change can be a field: the greeting, a banal pleasantry, gossip, whatever.

✔ Fields are also known as *merge fields*.

✔ You can use information from the Outlook program, also a part of Microsoft Office, as a recipient list for a mail merge in Word. This trick works best, however, when you're in a computer environment that features Microsoft Exchange Server. Otherwise, making Outlook and Word cooperate can be a frustrating endeavor.

Reviewing the mail merge process

The typical mail merge involves five steps. These steps are presented in more detail throughout this chapter:

I. Build the main document.

Choose the document type, usually a letter, although other document types are listed in the nearby sidebar, "Mail merge document types." As you create the document, you decide which fields are needed. That way, you can build a recipient list.

II. Create the recipient list — the data for the mail merge.

The recipient list is a table, consisting of rows and columns. Each column is a field, a fill-in-the-blanks part of the document. Each row is like a record in a database, representing a person who receives his own, custom copy of the document.

III. Insert fields into the main document.

The fields are placeholders for information that is eventually supplied from the recipient list.

IV. Preview the merge results.

You don't just merge; first you must preview how the documents will look. That way, you can clean up any formatting, check for errors, and do other corrections.

V. Merge the information from the recipient list into the main document.

The final mail merge process creates the customized documents. They can then be saved, printed, emailed, or dealt with however you like.

The rest of this chapter covers the specifics.

Using the Mail Merge Wizard

If all this mail merge malarkey is just too intense for you, consider an alternative: Word offers the Mail Merge Wizard, which guides you through the entire ordeal one step at a time.

To run the wizard, click the Mailings tab, and choose Start Mail Merge ➪ Step-by-Step Mail Merge Wizard. You see the Mail Merge pane on the right side of the document's window. Answer the questions, choose options, and click the Next link to proceed.

The rest of this chapter assumes that you're crazy enough to do mail merge the macho way.

I. The Main Document

Mail merge begins with a document, or what I call the *main document.* It's the prototype for all the individualized documents you eventually create, so it contains only common elements.

The following sections discuss different types of main documents. Read the section that relates to the type of mail merge you're attempting, and then proceed with the section, "II. The Recipient List."

Creating a mail merge form letter

The most common thing to mail merge is the standard, annoying form letter. Here's how you start that journey:

1. **Start a new, blank document.**

   Press Ctrl+N.

2. **Click the Mailings tab.**

3. **In the Start Mail Merge group, choose Start Mail Merge ➪ Letters.**

4. **Type the letter.**

   You're typing only the common parts of the letter, the text that doesn't change for each copy you print.

5. Type the fields you need in ALL CAPS.

This step is my idea, not Word's. For text that changes for each letter, type in ALL CAPS. For example, FIRST NAME or HAT SIZE. Use short, descriptive terms. Figure 27-1 shows an example.

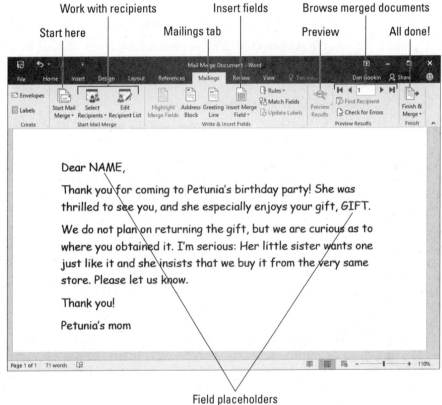

Work with recipients   Insert fields   Browse merged documents

Start here   Mailings tab   Preview   All done!

Dear NAME,

Thank you for coming to Petunia's birthday party! She was thrilled to see you, and she especially enjoys your gift, GIFT.

We do not plan on returning the gift, but we are curious as to where you obtained it. I'm serious: Her little sister wants one just like it and she insists that we buy it from the very same store. Please let us know.

Thank you!

Petunia's mom

Figure 27-1: A mail-merge main document.

Field placeholders

6. Save the main document.

If you already saved the document as you were writing it, give yourself a cookie.

After you create your letter, the next step is to create or use a recipient list. Continue with the section "II. The Recipient List," a little later in this chapter.

Creating mail merge email messages

Word lets you spew out custom email messages by using the E-Mail option for mail merge. This option works only when you configure the Microsoft Outlook program on your computer. After that's done, you start the main document for your email merge by obeying these steps:

1. **Press Ctrl+N to create a fresh document.**

2. **On the Mailings tab, choose Start Mail Merge ⇨ E-Mail Messages.**

   Word changes to Web Layout view, used for creating Internet documents in Word.

3. **Create your mail message.**

4. **If you anticipate inserting fields in the message, type them in ALL CAPS.**

   Normally, an email mail merge doesn't have fields in the document. Instead, email addresses are used to send out multiple copies of the message. Even so, you can insert fields just as you would for a form letter. See Step 5 in the preceding section for details.

5. **Save your document.**

The primary field you use when merging an email document is the recipient's email address. You can't email-merge without it. Continue your mail merge adventure in the later section, "II. The Recipient List."

Creating mail merge envelopes

To create a stack of mail merge envelopes, which is far classier than using peel-and-stick mailing labels, abide by these steps:

1. **Start a new document.**

2. **On the Mailings tab, choose Start Mail Merge ⇨ Envelopes.**

   The Envelope Options dialog box appears. You can set the envelope size and font options, if necessary.

3. **Click OK.**

   Word's window changes to reflect a typical envelope, a size specified in the Envelope Options dialog box (Step 2).

4. Type the return address.

Normally, an envelope mail merge doesn't use different return addresses for each envelope. So type the return address where the insertion pointer is blinking in the upper-left corner of the envelope.

Press Shift+Enter to place a soft return at the end of a line in the return address. The soft return keeps the lines in the return address tightly together.

5. Save the envelope.

That's pretty much it for a mail merge envelope. Word has placed a text box at the center, lower portion of the envelope. That's where fields for the recipient's name are inserted. You could type text in that box, but it's not really necessary.

Your next task is to use the recipient list to gather the information for your mailing. Keep reading in the next section.

II. The Recipient List

To make mail merge work, you need a list of items to merge, rows and columns as in a database. This information, called the recipient list, contains the items used to create the individual documents, email messages, envelopes, and so on.

Your options including building a new, custom recipient list, as covered in the next section. Once created, you can use a recipient list again. You can also pull in information from the Outlook program.

Building a new recipient list

Unless you already have recipient lists built and saved, you need to make one from scratch. This process involves setting up the list by adding fields you want and discarding fields you don't need. Once that chore is over, you fill in the data.

Because creating the recipient list can be involved, I've divided the task into four subsections.

Create the new recipient list

Before you can create a new recipient list, you must have created and saved the main document. Specific steps are provided in the earlier section,

"I. The Main Document." Creating the recipient list works the same no matter which mail merge document type you created.

1. **Click the Mailings tab.**

2. **In the Start Mail Merge group, choose Select Recipients⇨Type a New List.**

   You see the New Address List dialog box.

Add any new fields you need

The New Address List dialog box comes pre-stocked with fields. If you can use some, great! Otherwise, you must add fields not already present.

Follow these steps in the New Address List dialog box:

1. **Click the Add button.**

   The teeny Add Field dialog box pops into view.

2. **Type the field name and click the OK button.**

   Follow these rules for naming fields:

   - Name the field to reflect the kind of information in it; for example, Snake Bite Location.

   - No two fields can have the same name.

   - Field names can contain spaces but cannot start with a space.

   - Field names can be quite long, though shorter is best.

   - The following characters are forbidden in a field name: . ! ` [ ].

3. **Repeat Steps 1 and 2 for each new field you need in the main document.**

   The list of fields should match with the list of ALL CAPS text in the main document (if you chose to create them). Don't worry if it doesn't — you can add fields later, though it takes more time.

4. **Click OK.**

   You now see customized fields as column headings in the New Address List dialog box.

Remove any fields you don't need

Removing unnecessary fields is optional, but I include it out of spite: The New Address List dialog box comes with a basic assortment of fields. If you don't need them, remove them. Or you can skip ahead to the next subsection, "Add recipient data."

To remove extra fields from the New Address list dialog box, heed these steps:

1. **Click the Customize Columns button.**

   The Customize Address List dialog box appears, displaying fields that Word assumes you need. Such foolishness cannot be tolerated.

2. **Click to select a field that you *do not* need.**

   When you're merging an email message, you need the Email_Address field, whether it appears in the message body or not Word uses this field so that it knows where to send the message. Don't delete the field!

3. **Click the Delete button.**

4. **Click Yes in the confirmation dialog box.**

   The keyboard shortcut for the Yes button is the Y key.

5. **Repeat Steps 2 through 4 for each field you don't need.**

   Be careful not to remove any fields you added!

When you're done, the New Address List dialog box should contain only those fields you need.

Rather than delete all fields, you can rename some fields to match what you need: Select a field and click the Rename button. For example, I renamed First Name to First; Last Name to Last; and so on.

Add recipient data

After customizing the fields, your final job is to fill in the recipient list. You need to input *records,* one for each document you plan to create:

1. **Type the first record's data.**

   Type the information that's appropriate to each field shown in the New Address List dialog box: name, title, evil nickname, planet of origin, and so on.

2. **Press Tab to enter the next field.**

   After filling in the last field, you'll probably want to add another record:

3. **To add a new record, press the Tab key after typing in the last field.**

   When you press the Tab key in the last field in a record, a new record is automatically created and added on the next line. Keep filling in data!

4. **Review your work when you're done.**

   Figure 27-2 shows a completed recipient list.

   You can edit any field in any record by selecting it

Records   Fields   Click to sort the list

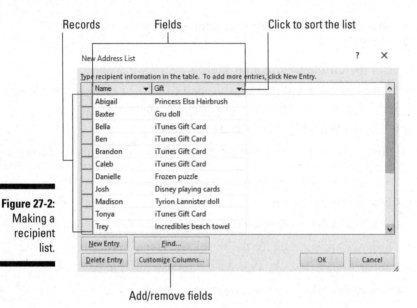

Figure 27-2:
Making a
recipient
list.

Add/remove fields

If you accidentally add a blank record at the end of the list, click to select it and then click the Delete Entry button. You do this because blank records are still processed in a mail merge, which can result in wasted paper.

5. Click OK.

The Save Address List dialog box pops up, allowing you to save the recipient list.

The recipient lists dwell in the folder named My Data Sources, found in the Documents or My Documents folder. Word automatically chooses (or creates) this folder.

6. Type a name for the address list.

Descriptive names are best. After all, you might use the same recipient list again.

7. Click the Save button.

You return to the document.

The next step in your mail merge agony is to stir the fields from the recipient list into the main document. Refer to the section "III. Fold in the Fields," later in this chapter.

Making a recipient list document

Here's a secret: You can create a document in Word and use it as a data source for a mail merge. The document contains a single element: a table. The table must have a header row, formatted in bold text, which identifies all the fields. Every row after that becomes a record in the recipient list database.

Using a table as a recipient list provides an easy way to import information into Word and use it for a mail merge. For example, you can copy information from the Internet or a PDF file and then paste that information into Word. Edit the information into a typical Word table, add a table heading row, and save the thing — and then you have a recipient list.

Follow the steps outlined in the nearby section, "Using an already created recipient list," to use the table document as your recipient list. Also see Chapter 19 for more information on tables in Word.

Using an already created recipient list

To use an existing recipient list for your mail merge, follow these steps after creating the main document:

1. **From the Mailings tab, choose Select Recipients ⇨ Use an Existing List.**

   The Select Data Source dialog box appears. It works like the Open dialog box, though it's designed to display recipient lists that Word can use or that you previously created and saved.

   Look for recipient lists in the My Documents folder, My Data Sources subfolder.

2. **Choose an existing recipient list from the displayed files.**

   I hope you used a descriptive name when you first saved the recipient list, which I recommend in the preceding section.

3. **Click the Open button.**

That's it: The recipient list is now associated with the main document.

Refer to the later section, "III. Fold in the Fields," for information on inserting fields into your document, which is the next step in the mail merge nightmare.

You can tell when a recipient list is associated with the main document because the Insert Merge Field button is available. Look on the Mailings tab in the Write & Insert Fields group for that button.

Grabbing a recipient list from Outlook

Assuming that you use Microsoft Outlook, and further that you have access to Exchange Server, you can follow these steps to create a recipient list:

1. **On the Mailings tab, in the Start Mail Merge group, choose Select Recipients ➪ Choose from Outlook Contacts.**

2. **If necessary, select your profile from the Choose Profile dialog box.**

3. **Click OK.**

4. **In the Select Contacts dialog box, choose a contact folder.**

   Contact folders are created in Outlook, not in Word.

5. **Click OK.**

6. **Use the Mail Merge Recipients dialog box to filter the recipient list.**

   If the list isn't too long, remove the check marks by the names of the individuals you don't want in the list. You can also click the Filter link in the dialog box to do more advanced filtering, which I'm loathe to describe right now.

7. **Click OK when you're done culling the recipient list.**

The next step in the painful experience known as Word mail merge is to insert fields into the master document. Keep reading in the later section, "III. Fold in the Fields."

Editing a recipient list

Although you can't add or remove fields from a recipient list, you can add or remove records. To do so, follow these steps:

1. **On the Mailing tab, in the Start Mail Merge group, click the Edit Recipient List button.**

   The button isn't available unless you're working on a main document and it has been associated with a recipient list.

2. **Select the data source.**

   In the lower-left corner of the Mail Merge Recipients dialog box, click the data source filename.

3. Click the Edit button.

You can now use the Data Form dialog box to edit each record in the recipient list or to add or remove fields and perform other chaos:

- Click the Delete button to remove the current record.
- Click the Add New button to create a new record.

4. Click the Close button when you're done editing.

5. Click the OK button to dismiss the Mail Merge Recipients dialog box.

If you need to add fields, you must edit the recipient list directly. The files are saved in the Microsoft Access file format, so if you don't have Access or software that can read that format, you're out of luck — unless you created your own recipients list as a table in Word document. In that case, you *can* edit the fields by adding new columns to the table.

III. Fold in the Fields

To make a mail merge work, the main document must be peppered with fields. The fields are placeholders, into which data from the recipient list is pulled and placed. Before this process takes place, ensure that you've created the main document and assigned a recipient list, as described earlier in this chapter.

If you've followed my advice in the section, "I. The Main Document," you can easily add fields by replacing the ALL CAPS text with the proper fields. Here's how it works:

1. Position the mouse pointer where you want the field to appear in the main document.

If you followed my advice from the earlier section, "Creating a mail merge form letter," select a placeholder, such as FIRST NAME.

2. On the Mailings tab, click the Insert Merge Field button.

3. Choose the field to add to the main document.

For example, choose the First Name field to stick it into the document.

After the field is inserted, you see its name hugged by angle brackets, such as <<First Name>>.

4. Repeat Steps 1 through 3 to add fields to the document.

When adding fields to an address, press Shift+Enter to end each line.

5. Save the main document.

Always save! Save! Save! Save!

The next step in your journey is to preview the results and fix any mistakes. Keep reading and continue with the next section.

- ✔ When the Insert Merge Field button isn't available, a recipient list isn't associated with the document. See the earlier section, "II. The Recipient List."

- ✔ To delete an unwanted field, select it with the mouse and press the Delete key.

IV. Preview the Merged Documents

Rather than just plow ahead with the merge, take advantage of the buttons in the Mailing tab's Preview Results group. That way, you can peruse the merged documents without wasting a lot of paper.

To preview, click the Mailings tab, and in the Preview Results group, click the Preview Results command button. The fields in the main document vanish! They're replaced by information from the first record in the recipient list. What you see on the screen is how the first customized mail-merge document appears. I hope everything looks spiffy.

Use the left and right triangles in the Preview Results group to page through each document. As you page, look for these problems:

- ✔ Formatting mistakes, such as text that obviously looks pasted in or not part of the surrounding text

- ✔ Punctuation errors and missing commas or periods

- ✔ Missing spaces between or around fields

- ✔ Double fields or unwanted fields, which happen when you believe that you've deleted a field but haven't

- ✔ Awkward text layouts, strange line breaks, or margins caused by missing or long fields

To fix any boo-boos, leave Preview mode: Click the Preview Results button again. Edit the main document to correct any mistakes. Then repeat the preview process.

Once everything looks up to part, you're ready to perform the merge, covered in the next section.

V. Mail Merge Ho!

The final step in the mail merge nightmare is to create personalized documents. The gizmo that handles this task is the Finish & Merge command button, the sole item in the Finish group on the Mailings tab. This section describes how to use that button to complete the mail merge.

Merging to a new set of documents

When you want to save merged documents and print them, follow these steps:

1. **Choose Finish & Merge ⇨ Edit Individual Documents.**

   The Merge to New Document dialog box appears.

2. **Ensure that the All option is selected.**

3. **Click OK.**

   Word creates a new document — a huge one that contains all merged documents, one after the other. Each document copy is separated by a Next Page section break. (See Chapter 14 for more information on section breaks.)

4. **Save the document.**

At this point, you can print the document, close it and edit it later, or do anything else you like.

Merging to the printer

The most common destination for merged documents is the printer. Here's how it works:

1. **Choose Finish & Merge ⇨ Print Documents.**

   A dialog box appears, from which you can choose records to print.

2. **Choose All from the Merge to Printer dialog box to print the entire document.**

   Or specify which records to print.

3. **Click OK.**

   The traditional Print dialog box appears.

4. **Click the OK button to print your documents.**

5. **Save and close the main document.**

See Chapter 9 for more information on printing documents in Word.

When merging and printing envelopes, use the printer's envelope slot or other special feeding mechanism. You may have to monitor the printer to insert the envelopes.

Merging to email

To send out multiple email messages, abide by these steps:

1. **Choose Finish & Merge ⇨ Send Email Messages.**

   The Merge to E-mail dialog box appears.

2. **Choose the e-mail address field from the To drop-down list.**

   Your document's recipient list must include an email address field, whether the field is used in the document or not. If not, go back and edit the recipient list to include the address.

3. **Type a message subject line.**

4. **Fill in any other fields in the Merge to E-mail dialog box.**

5. **Click OK.**

   It looks like nothing has happened, but the messages have been placed in the Outlook outbox.

6. **Open Outlook.**

   After you open Outlook, the queued messages are sent, or they sit ready to be sent when you give the command. (Whether the messages are sent right away depends on how you configured Outlook.)

Yes, this trick works only with Outlook, not with any other email programs.

Unsolicited email is considered spam. Sending spam may violate the terms of your Internet service provider's agreement and they can terminate your account. Send mass email only to people who have cheerfully agreed to receive such things from you.

Chapter 28

Labels and Envelopes

● ●

In This Chapter

▶ Printing a sheet of identical labels

▶ Merging an address list onto mail labels

▶ Printing a single envelope

● ●

Stretching the notion of what a word processor is capable of doing, Word features commands that let you print labels and envelopes. After all, a sheet of labels or an envelope is simply a different type of paper. Rather than conjure a hack to perform the task, Word offers ready-made label- and envelope-printing commands.

Labels Everywhere

Word's label powers include printing sheets of identical labels or creating individual labels for a mass mailing. This process works because the labels are, at their core, merely cells in a table. So to create a batch of labels in Word, you use special commands to muster a specially formatted table, and then print that document on a sheet of sticky labels.

✔ Label printer paper can be found wherever office supplies are sold. Avery is considered the top brand. Other brands use the Avery numbering scheme to describe different types of labels (size, rows, and columns).

✔ Buy label paper that's compatible with your printer. Laser printers need special laser printer labels. Some inkjet printers require special, high-quality paper to soak up the ink.

Printing sheets of identical labels

It might seem impractical to print a sheet of identical labels, yet I use such a sheet for my return address. This peel-and-stick trick comes in handy for other types of labels as well. Word deftly handles the chore. Just follow these steps:

1. Click the Mailings tab.

2. In the Create group, click the Labels button.

The Envelopes and Labels dialog box appears, with the Labels tab ready for action, as shown in Figure 28-1.

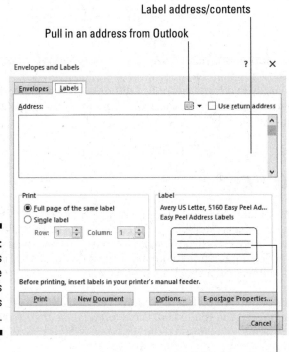

Label address/contents

Pull in an address from Outlook

Figure 28-1:
The Labels
side of the
Envelopes
and Labels
dialog box.

Click here to choose a label format

3. In the Address box, type the text you want printed on the label.

Press the Enter key at the end of each line.

You can apply some simple formatting at this stage: Ctrl+B for bold, Ctrl+I for italic, or Ctrl+U for underline, for example. If you right-click in the Address box, you can choose Font or Paragraph from the pop-up menu to further format the label.

4. **Click the Full Page of the Same Label radio button.**

5. **To choose a new label type, click in the Label area.**

   Use the Label Options dialog box to choose a label vendor, such as Avery, and then the proper stock number. For example, Avery US Letter 5160 (shown in Figure 28-1) is the standard address sticky label most folks use.

6. **Click the New Document button.**

   By placing the labels in a new document, you can further edit them, if you like.

   Save the document so that you can print the same batch of labels again.

7. **Print the labels.**

   Ensure that the sheet of label paper is loaded into your printer, proper side up. Use the Ctrl+P command to print the labels as you do for any document. See Chapter 9 for details on printing in Word.

On my PC I have a folder full of label documents I print from time to time. For example, one document holds my return address, one is for the IRS, and another has my lawyer's address. They all come in quite handy.

Printing an address list

To print a sheet of different labels, such as an address list, you encroach upon the terrifying territory of mail merge. That topic is covered in Chapter 27, so refer to that chapter for specific information. This section deals specifically with printing different labels.

Before getting started, you must have available a recipient list file. Refer to Chapter 27 for information on creating a recipient list. If you're fortunate enough to use the Outlook program as your digital address book, you can use it instead.

To print a list of names on a sheet of labels, follow these steps:

1. **Start a new document in Word.**

2. **Click the Mailings tab.**

   All commands and buttons mentioned in the remaining steps are found on the Mailings tab.

3. **Click the Start Mail Merge button, and from the menu, choose Labels.**

   The Label Options dialog box appears.

4. **Choose the label vendor and product number representing the sheet of labels on which you're printing.**

   For example, to print on a sheet of standard Avery address labels, use Avery catalog number 5160.

5. **Click OK.**

   Word builds a table in your document, one with cells perfectly aligned to match the labels on the sheet you selected. (The gridlines may be hidden, but the table is still there.)

   Do not edit or format the table! It's perfect.

6. **Click the Select Recipients button and choose Use an Existing List.**

   If you don't have such a list, you must build one. Refer to Chapter 27.

7. **Use the Select Data Source dialog box to choose the list.**

8. **Click OK.**

   The document is updated with all cells filled in except the first. The remaining cells feature the field titled <<Next Record>>. Your job is to create the first record, which sets the pattern for all the labels.

   The mouse pointer should be blinking in the first cell. If not, click that cell.

9. **Click the Insert Merge Field button.**

10. **Choose a field to place into the document.**

    For example, choose the First Name field to set the placeholder for the label's first name.

11. **Repeat Steps 9 and 10 to continue adding fields.**

    You can type text as well: Type a space to separate the First Name and Last Name fields. Press Shift+Enter to start a new line. Type a comma to separate the city and state.

    When you're finished adding fields, the document should look similar to what's shown in Figure 28-2.

12. **In the Write & Insert Fields group, click the Update Labels button.**

    Word populates the remaining cells in the table with the same fields and text placed into the first cell.

    If you made a mistake, press Ctrl+Z to undo. Fix the first cell. Repeat Step 12.

13. **Ensure that the proper label sheet is in the printer.**

    And that you have enough of them.

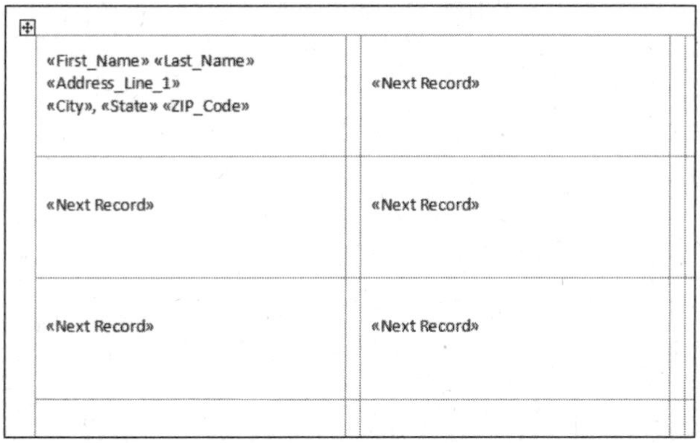
«First_Name» «Last_Name»
«Address_Line_1»
«City», «State» «ZIP_Code»
«Next Record»
«Next Record»
«Next Record»
«Next Record»
«Next Record»

Figure 28-2: The first label dictates how other labels are formatted.

14. **Click the Finish & Merge button and choose Print Documents.**
15. **Ensure that the All radio button is chosen in the Merge to Printer dialog box.**
16. **Click the OK button.**

    The traditional Print dialog box appears. Check that you have enough of the proper label paper in the printer, and that the labels are correctly oriented.
17. **Click the OK button in the Print dialog box.**

    The address labels print.

I recommend saving the document when you're done. That way, you can more easily preform the merge again or use the same document over to print a fresh batch of labels.

Instant Envelope

Suddenly you need an envelope! Don't revert to the last century and use your fist to scribble text on that envelope. Join the digital realm and let Word do the task for you. Obey these steps:

1. **Click the Mailings tab.**
2. **Click the Envelopes button.**

    The Envelopes and Labels dialog box appears with the Envelopes tab forward, as shown in Figure 28-3.

Type address here

Pull in an address from Outlook

Figure 28-3:
The Enve-
lopes side
of the
Envelopes
and Labels
dialog box.

Your address here

3. Type the recipient's address in the Delivery Address box.

Press Enter to separate the lines in the address. Word stacks each line atop the other, so don't fret over weird line spacing on the envelope.

If you use Outlook as your computer's address book, click the Address Book button to fetch the delivery address info.

4. Ensure that an envelope is queued and ready to print.

Most printers prompt you to manually enter envelopes. A guide on the printer's paper feed mechanism describes how to orient and insert the envelope.

5. Click the Print button.

You might have to press the printer's OK or Ready button to print, although some printers may instantly gobble up the envelope.

If you think you'll want to print the envelope again, save it: Before Step 5, click the Add to Document button. Word inserts a new first page into your document, which is the formatted letter. (The page size is specific to the type of envelope.) Once that's done, you can save the document so that you can reuse the envelope.

The Add to Document button's official purpose is to add an envelope to a letter. If you haven't written a letter in Word, you don't need the second (blank) page. To delete it, click on that page and press the Backspace key. The page is removed, leaving only the envelope.

✔ The return address is supplied by Word. If the field is blank, type your address. Word asks if you want to save the return address when the Envelopes and Letters dialog box closes. Click Yes.

✔ If the delivery address is already typed in your document, select it. When you summon the Envelopes and Labels dialog box, that selected text is automatically supplied as the delivery address.

✔ If you have trouble remembering which way the envelope feeds into your printer, draw a picture of the proper way and tape it to the top of your printer for reference.

✔ In the US, Size 10 is the common envelope paper size.

✔ To change the envelope size, click the envelope icon in the Preview area of the Envelopes and Labels dialog box. (Refer to Figure 28-3.) Use the Envelope Options dialog box to choose the proper envelope size.

✔ The Envelopes button merely creates a special Word document (or a single page). The paper size is set to an envelope. A text box is placed in the center of the page, into which you type the delivery address. The return address is text typed at the start of the page. You can use various Word commands to create such a page, but the Envelopes command saves you that trouble.

Chapter 29

A More Custom Word

I'm not one to customize things. Despite available options, I survive with the stock Windows desktop and background. I don't modify my phone's appearance. And I've only ever put only one bumper sticker on my car. Still, I'm all in favor of having the ability to modify things if I so choose. Customization seems to be a part of everything, and Word is no exception.

A Better Status Bar

Lurking at the bottom of the Word window is an extremely useful gizmo, the status bar. Chapter 1 introduces the status bar but only hints at its potential. Now it's time to reveal all: Right-clicking the status bar produces the helpful Customize Status Bar menu, shown in Figure 29-1.

The Customize Status Bar menu does two things: First, it controls what you see on the status bar (informational tidbits as well as certain controls). Second, it lets you turn on or off certain Word features.

From Figure 29-1, as well as on your screen, you can see the current status for many optional settings. A check mark indicates that an item is either visible or appears when necessary. To add an item, choose it. To remove a check marked item, choose it.

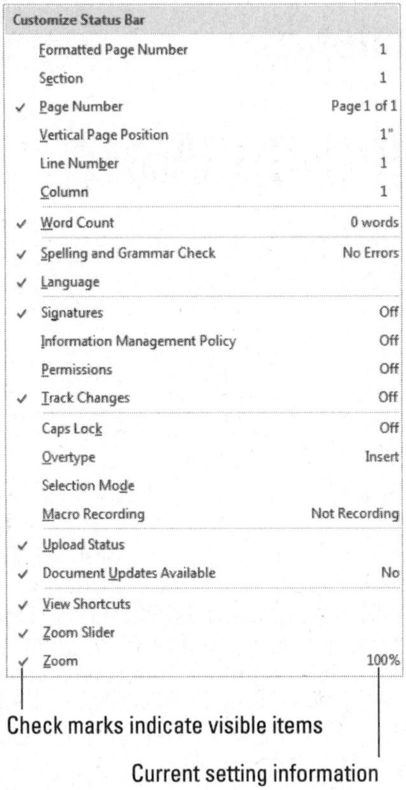

Customize Status Bar	
Formatted Page Number	1
Section	1
✓ Page Number	Page 1 of 1
Vertical Page Position	1"
Line Number	1
Column	1
✓ Word Count	0 words
✓ Spelling and Grammar Check	No Errors
✓ Language	
✓ Signatures	Off
Information Management Policy	Off
Permissions	Off
✓ Track Changes	Off
Caps Lock	Off
Overtype	Insert
Selection Mode	
Macro Recording	Not Recording
✓ Upload Status	
✓ Document Updates Available	No
✓ View Shortcuts	
✓ Zoom Slider	
✓ Zoom	100%

Figure 29-1:
The Custom-
ize Status
Bar menu.

Check marks indicate visible items

Current setting information

Here are my thoughts:

- Choosing an item from the menu doesn't cause the menu to disappear, which is handy. To make the menu go away, click the mouse elsewhere in the Word window.

- The topmost items on the menu display information about your document. To have that information displayed on the status bar, chose one or more of those items.

- The Selection Mode option directs Word to display the text *Extend Selection* on the status bar when you press the F8 key to select text. See Chapter 6 for more information on selecting text.

- The Overtype item places the Insert/Overtype button on the status bar. You can click this button to easily switch between Insert and Overtype modes. However, most Word users prefer to use Insert mode all the time.

- The last three items on the menu control whether the View buttons or Zoom shortcuts appear on the status bar.

The Quick Access Toolbar

Back in the old days, you could seriously mess with how the Word window looked. You could add toolbars, remove toolbars, modify toolbars, create your own toolbars, and generally use the word *toolbars* over and over again until it lost its meaning. Today, Word isn't quite as flexible as it once was, but you're still allowed to customize a toolbar.

The Quick Access toolbar is illustrated in Figure 29-2. It's found at the top-left corner of the window.

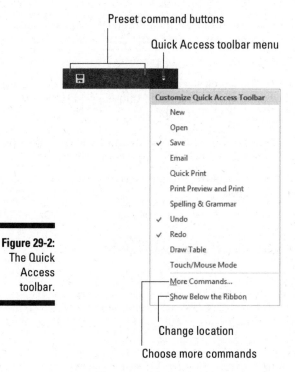

Preset command buttons

Quick Access toolbar menu

Change location

Choose more commands

Figure 29-2: The Quick Access toolbar.

Click a wee icon on the Quick Access toolbar to activate a feature. You can customize the toolbar by removing icons you don't use and adding icons you need.

TIP

✔ When the Quick Access toolbar grows too many custom buttons and begins to crowd into the document's title, place it below the Ribbon: Choose the command Show Below the Ribbon from the toolbar menu (refer to Figure 29-2). To move the Quick Access toolbar back atop the Ribbon, choose the command Show Above the Ribbon.

✔ Word is configured to show three buttons on the Quick Access toolbar: Save, Undo, and Redo. If you have a touchscreen PC, a fourth button appears, Touch/Mouse Mode.

Adding buttons to the Quick Access toolbar

When you enjoy using a Word command, and find yourself using it so much that the mouse is wearing a track in the program window, consider adding the command to the Quick Access toolbar.

Common commands are kept on the toolbar's menu. Refer to Figure 29-2 for the lot. To add one of those common commands, such as the Quick Print command, choose it from the menu.

To add any Word command to the Quick Access toolbar, locate its command button on the Ribbon. Right-click the command and choose Add to Quick Access toolbar from the shortcut menu that pops up.

✔ Word remembers the Quick Action toolbar's commands. They show up again the next time you start Word, in every document window.

✔ Some commands place buttons on the toolbar, and others place drop-down menus or text boxes.

Editing the Quick Access toolbar

To keep the Quick Access toolbar from getting out of hand, you can make adjustments beyond adding commands already on the menu. To do so, choose More Commands from the Quick Access toolbar's menu. You see the Word Options dialog box with the Quick Access Toolbar area shown, as illustrated in Figure 29-3.

Use the list on the left to choose a new command to add to the Quick Access toolbar.

The list on the right shows items currently on the toolbar. You can use that list to rearrange or remove Quick Access toolbar items.

Category list   Add/remove commands   Move selected command
                                                     up or down

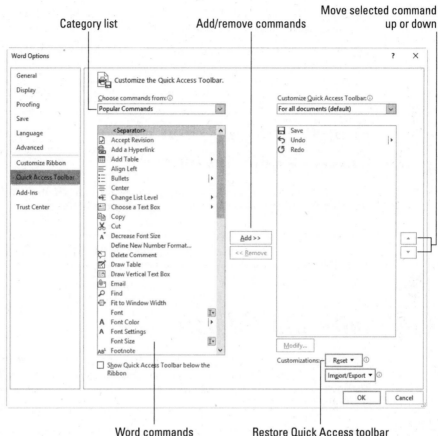

Figure 29-3:
Adjusting
the Quick
Access
toolbar.

Word commands   Restore Quick Access toolbar

Click the OK button when you're finished editing.

✔ Choose the All Commands item from the Choose Commands From
   menu (refer to Figure 29-3) to view every possible command in Word.
   Sometimes, a missing command that you think could be elsewhere ends
   up being available in the All Commands list — for example, the popular
   Save All command or the Tabs command, which quickly displays the
   Tabs dialog box.

✔ When your command list grows long, consider organizing it. Group similar commands by using the `<Separator>` item, which will appear as a
   vertical bar on the Quick Access toolbar.

- ✔ Yes, some commands lack specific graphics on their buttons; they show up as green dots on the toolbar.
- ✔ To return the Quick Access toolbar to the way Word originally had it, choose Reset ➪ Reset Only Quick Access toolbar from the Word Options window (refer to the bottom right in Figure 29-3).

Removing items from the Quick Access toolbar

To remove a command from the Quick Access toolbar, right-click its command button and choose Remove from Quick Access toolbar.

Likewise, you can choose a command with a check mark from the Customize Quick Access Toolbar menu. Or you can use the Word Options dialog box, as described in the preceding section, to remove items.

Customize the Ribbon

Word doesn't let you alter the basic tabs and groups on the Ribbon, which is probably a good thing for the sake of consistency. What Word will let you do, however, is create your own tab on the Ribbon or a new group on an existing tab.

Although this type of customization is popular and can be fun, I consider it an advanced topic. The task is not difficult to perform, but it can potentially mess things up. Proceed with caution.

Here's how that operation works:

1. **Click the File tab.**
2. **Choose Options.**
3. **In the Word Options window, choose Customize Ribbon.**

   The Word Options window changes its appearance. Tabs on the Ribbon are listed on the right, and Word commands are shown on the left. The Ribbon is your oyster.

To add a new group to an existing tab, click the tab on the right side of the window, and then click the New Group button. Click the Rename button to assign the group a name other than *New Group* and to add a symbol (if Word lets you).

To add commands to a custom group, click to select the group you created. Locate the command on the left side of the window, and then click the Add button to stick it into the new group.

If you want to go whole hog and add your own tab to the Ribbon, click the New Tab button. The new tab is created along with a new group; right-click both items to rename them. Then add commands to the custom tab's custom group as described earlier.

In Figure 29-4, you see the Dan Tab that I added to the Ribbon, along with two groups, A commands and Z commands.

Figure 29-4: A custom tab and groups on the Ribbon.

The changes you make to the Ribbon hold for every Word document you open. They aren't tied to a specific template.

- ✔ The tabs and groups on the Ribbon are shown on the right side of the Word Options window, using a hierarchical menu system: Click [+] to expand a tab or group; click [−] to collapse it.

- ✔ Use the Up and Down arrows to the right side of the Tabs list (in the Word Options dialog box) to shuffle the tabs, groups, and commands. You can rearrange the Ribbon any way you like, but keep in mind that in this book I assume that you haven't messed with anything.

- ✔ If you'd rather not see your custom tab or group, summon the Word Options dialog box (follow the steps in this section) and remove the check mark by your new tab or group. That action doesn't delete the item; it just prevents it from showing up.

- ✔ To restore the Ribbon to normal, click the Reset button found in the lower-right corner of the Customize window. Choose the command Reset All Customizations.

Part VI
The Part of Tens

Enjoy an additional Part of Tens chapter online at: www.dummies.com/extras/word2016.

In this part . . .

- ✔ Obey the ten commandments of Word.
- ✔ Discover some handy and useful tricks.
- ✔ Investigate some highly unusual Word features.
- ✔ Deactivate things that really bug you.

Chapter 30

The Ten Commandments of Word

I admit that I look nothing like Charlton Heston. Though I'm only guessing, I probably look nothing like Moses, either. Still, I feel compelled to return from Mount Sinai with some basic codes for word processing. I call them my Ten Commandments of Word.

Thou Shalt Remember to Save Thy Work

Save! Save! Save! Always save your stuff. Whenever your mind wanders, have your fingers dart over to the Ctrl+S keyboard shortcut. Savest thy work.

Thou Shalt Not Use Spaces Unnecessarily

Generally speaking, you should never find more than one space anywhere in a Word document. The appearance of two or more spaces in a row is a desperate cry for a tab. Use single spaces to separate words and sentences. Use tabs to indent or to align text on a tab stop. To organize information into neat rows and columns, use a table.

- ✔ Refer to Chapter 12 on setting tabs.
- ✔ Refer to Chapter 19 for creating tables.

Thou Shalt Not Abuse the Enter Key

Word wraps text. As you type and your text approaches the right margin, the words automatically advance to the next line. Therefore, there's no need to press the Enter key, unless you want to start a new paragraph. An exception is a one-line paragraph, in which case pressing the Enter key at the end of the line is okay.

If you're pressing the Enter key to add more "air" after a paragraph, you really need to choose another paragraph format. Refer to Chapter 11 for information on the Space After format.

When you don't want to start a new paragraph but you need to start a new line, such as when typing a return address, press Shift+Enter, the *soft* return command.

Thou Shalt Not Neglect Keyboard Shortcuts

When you type text in a word processor, you're fingers are over the keyboard. As such, it pays to use keyboard shortcuts instead of pausing to grab the mouse.

Word is rife with handy and memorable keyboard shortcuts. For example, stab the Ctrl+S key combo to quickly save a document. Press Ctrl+P to print or Ctrl+O to open a document. You don't have to know all the keyboard commands, but remembering a few helps.

> ✔ Also see Chapter 31 for information on keyboard accelerators to speed up access to the Ribbon.
>
> ✔ Refer to this book's online Cheat Sheet for a full-on list of keyboard shortcuts mentioned in this book. You can find the Cheat Sheet here:
>
> `www.dummies.com/cheatsheet/word2016`

Thou Shalt Not Manually Number Thy Pages

Word has an automatic page-numbering command. Refer to Chapter 13 for details on how to use it.

Thou Shalt Not Force a New Page

When you need to start text at the top of a new page, you use the *manual page-break* command. Its keyboard shortcut is Ctrl+Enter. That's the best and most proper way to start a new page. Also see Chapter 13.

The worst way to start a new page is to brazenly press the Enter key a couple of dozen times. Although the result may look okay, this strategy doesn't guarantee anything; as you continue to edit your document, the page break moves back and forth and ends up looking butt-ugly.

Thou Shalt Not Forget Thy Undo Command

Undo any unwanted change to your document by pressing Ctrl+Z, the Undo command. A shortcut is also found roosting on the Quick Access toolbar.

Honor Thy Printer

Before you print anything, verify that the printer is on, healthy, stocked with ink and paper, and ready to print before you direct Word to print something.

Using the Print command a second time when it fails the first doesn't fix the problem. Instead, Word continues trying to print the document, despite whatever issues are preventing the printer from working.

Thou Shalt Have Multiple Document Windows Before Thee

In Word, as in most Windows applications, you can work on more than one document at a time. In fact, you can have as many document windows open as you can stand. Word even lets you view a single document in multiple windows. Refer to Chapter 24 to see how to do these things.

✔ You don't have to close one document to open and view another document.

✔ You don't have to quit Word to run another program, either. In Windows, you can run multiple programs at a time. You shouldn't quit Word when you plan to start it again in just a little while.

Neglecteth Not Windows

Word is a program. Windows is an operating system. Word is designed for productivity; it's word-processing software. Windows is designed to control a computer and to drive human beings crazy. Word and Windows are two different things.

Word creates document files. Windows manages those files. If you need to rename a file, copy the file to a thumb drive, move the file to another folder, or recover the file from the Recycle Bin, you use Windows, not Word. They work together.

Verily I tell ye, know both Word and Windows and he shalt be truly rewarded.

Chapter 31

Ten Cool Tricks

*W*hen it comes down to it, just about everything Word does can be considered a cool trick. I still marvel at how word-wrap works and how you can change margins after a document is written and all the text instantly jiggles into place. Everything in this book can be considered a cool trick, but when it came down to the wire, I found ten cool tricks barely (or not) mentioned anywhere else and then listed them here.

Automatic Save with AutoRecover

Someday you will sing the praises of Word's AutoRecover feature. What it does is periodically save your document, even when you neglect to do so. That way, in the event of a computer crash, Word recovers your document from a safety copy that it has secretly made for you. That's very kind of Word, don't you think?

Ensure that AutoRecover is active. Heed these directions:

1. **Click the File tab.**

2. **On the File screen, choose Options.**

   The Word Options dialog box appears.

3. **Choose Save.**

4. **On the right side of the dialog box, ensure that a check mark appears by the item Save AutoRecover Information Every 10 Minutes.**

   You can change the time, although 10 minutes seems good.

5. **Click OK to close the window.**

   Whew! You're safe.

Most of the time, you never notice AutoRecover. On that rare, frightening occasion when the computer crashes, go ahead and start Word. If any unsaved documents can be recovered, you'll see them listed in the Document Recovery pane. To recover a document, point the mouse pointer at its name. Use the menu button that appears to open and recover the document.

The best way to avoid accidentally losing your stuff is to *save now* and *save often!*

Accelerate the Ribbon

Word has always been a mouse-based program, even when it ran in text mode on old DOS PCs. Still, the keyboard remains a fast and effective way to access commands, especially given that in a word processor you're fingers are hovering over the keyboard most of the time.

If you're willing to learn, eschew the mouse and instead use some keyboard accelerators to access commands on the Ribbon.

The secret is to use the Alt key: Tap Alt and you see letters in boxes appear on the Ribbon, like tiny square freckles. Within each box are one or two letters, which are the accelerator keys. Tap a letter or the two letters in sequence to "click" a specific part of the Ribbon.

For example, to change the page orientation to landscape mode, you press Alt, P, O to display the Orientation menu. Press the down-arrow key to choose Landscape. Press Enter to choose that menu item.

- ✔ If you accidentally tap the Alt key, press it again to exit accelerator mode.

- ✔ You can also press the F10 key to access the Ribbon accelerators.

Ancient Word Keyboard Shortcuts

While on the topic of keyboard shortcuts, Word once relied upon keyboard commands before the Ribbon rode into town, and even before the first "Word for Windows" version appeared decades ago. These ancient Word keyboard shortcuts used the function keys to carry out their duties, and they still work in Word today.

F4. The F4 key is the Repeat key, exactly the same as Ctrl+Y, the Repeat key.

Shift+F4. Another repeat key, but this one is the Repeat Find command. It works whether or not the Find dialog box (or Navigation pane) is visible.

Shift+F5. This key combo is the Go Back command, which returns to the spot you last edited. See Chapter 3 for details.

Shift+F8. The Shrink Selection key is the opposite of the Selection key, F8. I cover F8 in detail in Chapter 6. The Shift+F8 key is the opposite: When the entire document is selected, press Shift+F8 to select only the current paragraph. Press Shift+F8 again to select only the current sentence. Press it again to select only the current word. Press Shift+F8 one more time to unselect the word.

F12. Tap this key to quickly summon the Save As dialog box. I use this key a lot because it's quicker than wading through the Backstage to summon the Save As dialog box.

Ctrl+F12. This key does for the Open dialog box what F12 does for the Save As dialog box. It's not redundant to the Ctrl+O command, which conjures the Backstage. Ctrl+F12 always brings up the familiar, friendly Open dialog box.

Build Your Own Fractions

Word's AutoCorrect feature can build common fractions for you. Actually, it doesn't build them as much as it pulls them from a set of existing fraction characters. Sadly, Word has only a few of these fraction characters. When you need your own specific fraction, such as 3/64, you can create it this way:

1. **Press Ctrl+Shift+= (the equal sign).**

   This keyboard is the shortcut for the superscript command.

2. **Type the *numerator* — the top part of the fraction.**

   For example, type **3** for 3/64.

3. **Press Ctrl+Shift+= again to turn off superscripting.**

4. **Type the slash character (/).**

5. **Press Ctrl+= to turn on subscripting.**

6. **Type the *denominator* — the bottom part of the fraction.**

    For example, type **64** for ³⁄₆₄.

7. **Press Ctrl+= to turn off subscripting.**

There's your fraction.

Electronic Bookmarks

They sure do make those LCD monitors tough! Try as you might, you can't dog-ear the corner of your document. When you have to find your place in a document, you can write text like WORK HERE or you can take advantage of Word's Bookmark command.

To set a bookmark in your document, follow these steps:

1. **Place the insertion pointer where you want to insert the bookmark.**

2. **Click the Insert tab.**

3. **In the Links group, click the Bookmark button.**

    The Bookmarks dialog box appears.

4. **Type a name for the bookmark in the Bookmark dialog box.**

    Try to keep the bookmark name to one word, letters only.

5. **Click the Add button.**

    The bookmark is created — but it's invisible. You don't see any sign of it in your document.

To visit bookmarks in a document, use the Go To command: Press Ctrl+G. You see the Find and Replace dialog box, Go To tab forward. Choose Bookmark from the Go To What list. Select the bookmark name from the list on the right side of the dialog box. Click the Go To button to visit that bookmark's location. Click the Close button to dismiss the dialog box.

Lock Your Document

When you really, *really* don't want anyone messing with your document, you can lock the document. Several levels of protection are available, but you start the journey by following these steps:

1. **Click the File tab.**

2. **Choose Info.**

3. **Click the Protect Document button.**

   Of the several choices, I recommend these options:

   Mark as Final: The document is flagged as *final,* which means that further editing is disabled. Still, you can easily override it by clicking the Edit Anyway button that appears.

   Encrypt with Password: The document is encrypted and a password is applied. To open the document in Word, you must enter the password. You cannot remove a password after it's applied.

   Restrict Editing: You can limit whether a user can edit a document or whether all changes are tracked or restrict that person to make only comments.

4. **Choose an option and answer the questions in the dialog boxes that appear.**

5. **Click OK.**

   The document protection you've chosen is applied.

 Locking your document is a serious decision! I cannot help, nor can anyone else, if you forget a password or are otherwise unable to remove the restrictions you've applied to your document.

The Drop Cap

A *drop cap* is the first letter of a report, an article, a chapter, or a story that appears in a larger and more interesting font than the other characters. Figure 31-1 shows an example.

To add a drop cap to your document, follow these steps:

1. **Select the first character of the first word at the start of your text.**

   For example, select the *O* in *Once upon a time,* as shown in Figure 31-1.

Figure 31-1:
A drop cap.

O nce upon a time

2. **Click the Insert tab.**

3. **In the Text group, click the Drop Cap button.**

4. **Choose a drop cap style.**

    And there's your drop cap.

It helps if the drop cap's paragraph is left justified and not indented with a tab or any of the tricky formatting operations discussed in Part III.

You can undo a drop cap by repeating the steps in this section, but choose None in Step 4.

Map Your Document

The Navigation pane can not only find text in your document but also help you see the big picture. Follow these steps:

1. **Click the View tab.**

2. **In the Show group, click to put a check mark by the Navigation Pane item.**

    You see a document summary listed by heading style, as shown in Figure 31-2.

Click a heading inside the map to instantly jump to that part of your document.

To close the Navigation pane, click its X close button.

The Navigation pane replaces a popular but now gone Word feature called the Document Map.

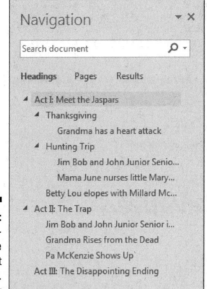

Figure 31-2:
The Naviga-
tion pane
document
map.

Sort Your Text

Sorting is one of Word's better tricks, although it's surprising how few people know about it. You can use the Sort command to arrange text alphabetically or numerically. You can sort paragraphs, table rows and columns, and more.

Save your document before sorting. It's just a good idea.

Sorting isn't difficult. First, arrange whatever needs to be sorted into several rows of text, such as:

```
Lemon
Banana cream
Apple
Cherry
Rhubarb
Tortilla
```

After you know what you're going to sort, follow these steps:

1. **Select the lines of text (or parts of a table) as a block.**

2. **Click the Home tab.**

3. **In the Paragraph group, click the Sort button.**

   The Sort Text dialog box appears. It's most useful when sorting multi-column items, which is where the Then By parts of the dialog box are most useful.

4. **Choose Ascending or Descending to sort your text A-to-Z or Z-to-A, respectively.**

5. **Click the OK button.**

As if by magic, the selected text is sorted.

Map Ctrl+F to the Advanced Find Command

If you're like me, and you demand that the Ctrl+F keyboard shortcut bring up the traditional Find and Replace dialog box and not that silly Navigation pane, you can correct Word's heinous mistake. Follow these steps to reassign the Ctrl+F keyboard shortcut:

1. **Click the File tab.**

2. **Choose Options to bring up the Word Options dialog box.**

3. **Choose the Customize Ribbon item.**

   The Customize Ribbon item is found on the left side of the dialog box.

4. **Click the Customize button, found at the bottom of the dialog box.**

   The Customize Keyboard dialog box appears.

5. **From the list of Categories, choose Home Tab.**

6. **From the list of Commands, choose EditFind.**

7. **Click the mouse in the Press New Shortcut Key text box.**

8. **Press the Ctrl+F key combination on the computer's keyboard.**

   You may notice that Ctr+F is already assigned to the NavPaneSearch command. That assignment is about to change.

9. **Click the Assign button.**

10. **Click OK.**

Go ahead: Press Ctrl+F. You see the Find and Replace dialog box with the Find tab upfront. Congratulations!

The Navigation pane can still be accessed as described earlier in the section, "Map Your Document."

Chapter 32

Ten Bizarre Things

*I*f Word were only about word processing, this book would end at Chapter 17. Fully half the book talks about things I consider to be along the lines of desktop publishing or even graphics, tasks that can be done far better by using other software. Beyond those capabilities exist things I consider even more strange and unusual. Welcome to the *Twilight Zone*, Word edition.

Equations

Here's a feature that everyone demands, as long as everyone graduated from college with a degree in astrophysics or quantum mechanics. It's Word's Equation tools, which you need whenever you're desperate to stick a polynomial equation in your document and don't want to endure the tedium of building the thing yourself.

You can pluck a premade equation from the Insert tab's Equation button menu, as long as the equation you need appears there. Otherwise, just click the button by itself (not the menu triangle) and two things happen: An equation *content control* is inserted in your document at the insertion pointer's location, and the Equation Tools Design tab appears on the Ribbon. Creating equations was never easier! Well, creating them is easy, but knowing what they mean is a different story altogether.

No, Word won't solve the equation.

Video in Your Document

For some reason, the video-in-a-document feature was showcased in an older release of Word. I can see why! So many people were demanding it.

Not really.

Obviously, the Online Video feature isn't intended for anything you plan to print. No it's an electronic publishing thing, which is why the topic dwells in this chapter listing Bizarre Things.

To insert a video, click the Insert tab's Online Video button. Search for a video by using Microsoft Bing (of course) or YouTube or by pasting a video link. Eventually, after little toil, the video appears as a large graphical object in your document. You can play it right there on the screen. Apparently, people have been demanding such a word-processing feature since the Electric Pencil program debuted back in 1976.

 Videos are best viewed when a Word document is presented in Read mode — which in itself is yet another bizarre thing. To enter Read mode, click the Read Mode button on the status bar (shown in the margin) or click the Read Mode button on the View tab.

Hidden Text

What's the point of writing when you can't see it? I don't have a clue as to why, but Word does let you apply the hidden format to random bits of text in your document. The text doesn't show up as blank lines either, it just doesn't show up.

To apply the hidden text format, select the text and press Ctrl+Shift+H. The same keyboard shortcut deactivates this format. The following text is hidden:

To show hidden text, click the Show/Hide command button (in the Paragraph group on the Home tab) as described in Chapter 2, in the section about dealing with spots and clutter in the text. The hidden text shows up in the document with a dotted underline.

The Developer Tab

Word's advanced, cryptic features lie on a tab that's normally hidden from view: the Developer tab. To display the Developer tab, obey these steps:

1. **Click the File tab.**
2. **Choose the Options command to display the Word Options dialog box.**
3. **Choose the Customize Ribbon item on the left side of the dialog box.**
4. **Under the Customize Ribbon list on the right side of the dialog box, place a check mark by the Developer item.**
5. **Click OK.**

The Developer tab is aptly named; it's best suited for people who either use Word to develop applications, special documents, and online forms or are hellbent on customizing Word by using macros. Scary stuff.

Hyphenation

Hyphenation is an automatic feature that splits a long word at the end of a line to make the text fit better on the page. Most people leave this feature turned off because hyphenated words tend to slow down the pace at which people read. However, if you want to hyphenate a document, click the Page Layout tab and then the Page Setup group, and choose Hyphenation ⇨ Automatic.

Hyphenation works best with paragraph formatting set to full justification.

Document Properties

When your company (or government agency) grows too big, there's a need for too much information. Word happily obliges by providing you with a sheet full of fill-in-the-blanks goodness to tell you all about your document and divulge whatever information you care to know about who worked on what and for how long. These tidbits are the *document properties*.

To eagerly fill in any document's properties, click the File tab and choose the Info item. Document properties are listed on the far-right side of the window. Some information cannot be changed, but when you click the lighter-colored text, you can type your own stuff.

Cross-References

The References tab sports a bunch of features that I don't touch on in this book, not the least of which is the Cross-Reference button in the Captions group. The Cross-Reference command allows you to insert instructions such as *Refer to Chapter 99, Section Z* in your document. This feature works because you absorbed excess energy from the universe during a freak lightning storm and now have an IQ that would make Mr. Spock envious. Anyway, the Cross-Reference dialog box, summoned by the Cross-Reference command, is the place where cross-referencing happens. Page 653 has more information about this feature.

Collect and Paste

I hope the word-processing concept of copy and paste is simple for you. What's not simple is taking it to the next level by using Word's Collect and Paste feature.

Collect and Paste allows you to copy multiple chunks of text and paste them in any order or all at once. The secret is to click the dialog box launcher in the lower-right corner of the Clipboard group on the Home tab, right next to the word Clipboard. The Clipboard pane appears on the screen.

With the Clipboard pane visible, you can use the Copy command multiple times in a row to collect text. To paste the text, simply click the mouse on that chunk of text in the Clipboard pane. Or you can use the Paste All button to paste into your document every item you collected.

Even more bizarre: You can actually select multiple separate chunks of text in your document. To do so, select the first chunk, and then, holding down the Ctrl key, drag over additional text. As long as the Ctrl key is held down, you can drag to select multiple chunks of text in different locations. The various selected chunks work as a block, which you can cut, copy, delete, or to which you can apply formatting.

Click-and-Type

A feature introduced in Word 2002, and one that I don't believe anyone ever uses, is *click-and-type*. In a blank document, you can use it to click the mouse pointer anywhere on the page and type information at that spot. *Bam!*

I fail to see any value in click-and-type, especially when it's easier just to learn basic formatting. But click-and-type may bother you when you see any of its specialized mouse pointers displayed; thus:

That's click-and-type in action, with the mouse pointer trying to indicate the paragraph format to be applied when you click the mouse.

See Chapter 33 for information on disabling this feature.

Word and the Internet

Microsoft went kind of kooky in the 1990s when Bill Gates suddenly realized that his company was behind the curve on the Internet. In response, many Microsoft programs, including Word, suddenly started to bud various Internet features, whether the features were relevant to the software's original intent or not. For example, Word has — even to this day — the capability to create web pages or post to a blog.

Word is an excellent word processor. Word is a lousy web-page editor. Though you can write a blog post, the steps involved to configure that process are complex and rarely meet with success. (And, yes, I tried and tried to get it to work.) Therefore, I cover none of that stuff in this book.

This book is about *word processing*. If you want software for email, making web pages, using an Internet fax, creating a blog, or using the Internet to find pictures of famous celebrities in compromising poses, you must look elsewhere.

Chapter 33

Ten Automatic Features Worthy of Deactivation

· ·

· ·

*Y*ou really don't have to put up with it. You know what I'm referring to: those annoying things that Word does. Those features you might dislike but tolerate simply because no one has told you how to turn them off. Until now.

Bye-Bye Start Screen

I prefer to see a blank page when I start Word, not a screen full of options. That screen, the Word Start screen, can easily be disabled. Follow these blessed steps:

1. Click the File tab.

2. Choose Options.

The Word Options dialog box appears.

3. **Choose the General category.**

4. **Remove the check mark by the item Show the Start Screen When This Application Starts.**

5. **Click OK.**

After completing these steps, Word starts with a blank document, or whichever document you've opened.

Restore the Traditional Open and Save Dialog Boxes

When you use the Ctrl+O or Ctrl+S commands, you're thrust into the Open or Save As screens, respectively. These screens are referred to as the Backstage, and I find them one more annoying step in a process that eventually ends up at the traditional Open and Save dialog boxes.

To dismiss the Backstage, follow these steps:

1. **Click the File tab and choose Options to bring up the Word Options dialog box.**

2. **Choose the Save category.**

3. **Place a check by the item Don't Show the Backstage When Opening or Saving Files.**

4. **Click OK.**

One advantage of the Backstage is that it does show recent files. It also lets you pin popular files so that they're easy to find. See Chapter 8.

Turn Off the Mini Toolbar

When you use the mouse to select text, Word displays the mini toolbar, which looks like Figure 33-1. You may find its assortment of commands useful, or you may just want to set the thing on fire. If the latter, you can disable the mini toolbar by following these steps:

1. **Click the File tab and choose Options.**

2. **Choose General.**

3. Remove the check mark by the item Show Mini Toolbar on Selection.

4. Click OK.

If you would rather not eternally banish the mini toolbar, note that it hides itself whenever you move the mouse pointer beyond the selected chunk of text.

Text-selection mini toolbar   Right-click mini toolbar

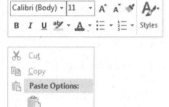

Figure 33-1:
The mini
toolbar.

Select Text by Letter

When you're selecting more than a single word, the mouse tends to grab text a full word at a time. If you want Word to select text by characters rather than by words (which is what I prefer), follow these steps:

1. **Click the File tab and choose Options to display the Word Options dialog box.**

2. **Choose Advanced.**

3. **Under the Editing Options heading, remove the check mark by the item labeled When Selecting Automatically Select Entire Word.**

4. **Click OK.**

You can still select text a word at a time: Double-click to select a word, but keep the mouse button down. As you drag, text is selected one word at a time.

Disable Click-and-Type

Click-and-Type is that feature where you can click anywhere in a document and start typing. The feature is evident by lines around the insertion pointer, as covered in Chapter 32. To mercifully disable this feature, follow these steps:

1. **Click the File tab menu and choose Options.**

   The Word Options dialog box appears.

2. **Choose Advanced.**

3. **Under the Editing Options header, remove the check mark by Enable Click and Type.**

4. **Click the OK button.**

Seriously: Who uses this feature? Send me an email if you do.

Paste Plain Text Only

When you copy and paste text from one part of a document to another, the format is retained. Similarly, the format is kept when you paste text copied or cut from another document. If you like, you can direct Word to paste only plain text or attempt to paste formatted text. Heed these directions:

1. **Click the File tab and choose Options.**

2. **In the Word Options dialog box, choose Advanced.**

   The four pasting options are listed under the Cut, Copy, and Paste heading. The options tell you how text is pasted based on its source.

3. **Change the paste settings according to how you prefer text to be pasted.**

   In most cases, keeping the source formatting is what you want. I prefer to choose the option Keep Text Only because it doesn't mess up my document's formatting.

4. **Click OK.**

You can use the Paste Special command at any time to override your decision: Click the Home tab and, in the Clipboard group, click the Paste button to choose whether or not to keep the formats. See Chapter 6 for details.

Disable AutoFormat Features (×4)

The final four items in the list of ten items worthy of deactivation fall under the domain of the AutoCorrect dialog box. Specifically, the overeager AutoFormat feature, which aggressively interrupts your writing with jarring suggestions you probably don't want to see.

Start your disabling binge by summoning the AutoCorrect dialog box. Follow these steps:

1. **Click the File tab and choose Options.**
2. **In the Word Options dialog box, click the Proofing category.**
3. **Click the AutoCorrect Options button.**

    The AutoCorrect dialog box shows up.
4. **Click the AutoFormat as You Type tab.**

    You've arrived.

Here are four annoying features you can disable:

Automatic Bulleted Lists: This feature assumes that whenever you start a paragraph with an asterisk (*) you really want a bulleted list, so it changes the format.

Automatic Numbered Lists: This feature works like Automatic Bullet Lists, but does the same annoying thing for any paragraph you start numbering.

Border Lines: Type three dashes in a row and you see this feature activated. Use the Borders paragraph format instead. See Chapter 18.

Format Beginning of List Item Like the One Before It: This feature assumes that just because the first word of the preceding paragraph is in bold or italics that you desire all other paragraphs to start that way as well.

Deselect each of these items. Oh, and while you're at it, look for other things to disable in the AutoCorrect dialog box. Some of those features may bother you more than they bother me.

Index

• *G* •

Multiple option, Line spacing drop-down list, 121
Multiple Pages drop-down list, Page Setup dialog box, 148

• N •

naming documents, 81, 82, 184, 272–274
navigating documents, 29–35
  Go To command, 34–35
  keyboard shortcuts, 34
  moving insertion pointer, 31–33
  scrolling, 29–31
Navigation pane, 340–341
New Address List dialog box, mail merge, 304–305
Next Comment button, Review tab, 289–290
Next revision button, Review tab, 295
No Formatting button, Find and Replace dialog box, 50, 51
No Markup display option, Review tab, 289, 294
nonbreaking spaces, 255–256
nonprinting characters, 25–26
Normal setting, Page Setup dialog box, 148
Normal style, 171, 181
Normal template, 144, 184–185
numbered lists, 197, 234–235
numbering pages
  adding automatic page number, 148–149
  adding number to headers and footers, 165–166
  removing page numbers, 151
  Roman numerals, 150–151
  starting with different page number, 149–150
numeric keypad, keyboard, 20

• O •

odd headers and footers, 167
Odd Page section break, 160
1 o'clock mouse pointer, 21
OneDrive cloud storage, 78, 81, 99, 296
Online Video feature, 344
Open dialog box, 273
Open screen, documents, 84
opening documents
  multiple documents, 267–268
  one document within another, 86
  with Open command, 84–86
ordinals, 196
orientation
  keyboard shortcuts, 336
  landscape, 144–145, 227–228
  portrait, 144–145
  of text in text boxes, 259
Original display option, Review tab, 289
Outline view
  overview, 14–15, 276–277
  printing outline, 281
  topics, 277–281
Outlining tab, Ribbon, 276–281
Outlook program
  forming recipient list from, 308
  send document via, 98–99
Outside Borders command, Borders menu, 206
Overtype item, Customize Status Bar menu, 322

• P •

page borders, 209–210. *See also* borders
page breaks
  Continuous section break, 160
  hard, 152, 153
  manual, 42–43, 333
  Odd Page section break, 160
  overview, 24–25

Page Down key, 33–34
page formatting
  adding watermark, 154–155
  background, 153–155
  color, 153–154
  cover page, 162–163
  headers and footers, 163–169
  inserting blank page, 152–153
  margins, 145–146
  numbering, 148–151
  orientation, 144–145
  Page Setup dialog box, 146–147
  printing colored page, 154
  sections, 157–161
  setting page size, 143–144
  starting text on new page, 152
Page Number Format dialog box, 150
Page Setup dialog box
  Book Fold setting, 148
  Layout tab, 145–147
  Margins tab, 146–147
  Mirror Margins setting, 148
  Multiple Pages drop-down list, 148
  Normal setting, 148
  Paper tab, 147
  2 Pages per Sheet setting, 148
Page Up key, 33–34
pages. *See also* page formatting
  colored, 154
  cover page, 162–163
  deleting, 40
  margins, 145–148
Paper tab, Page Setup dialog box, 147
Paragraph dialog box, 117
paragraph formatting
  alignment, 118–119
  commands, 116–118, 126
  indentation, 122–125
  justification, 118–119
  line spacing, 120–121
  overview, 115–116
  space between, 121–122
Paragraph style, 172

About the Author

Dan Gookin has been writing about technology for over 25 years. He combines his love of writing with his gizmo fascination to create books that are informative, entertaining, and not boring. Having written over 130 titles with 12 million copies in print translated into over 30 languages, Dan can attest that his method of crafting computer tomes seems to work.

Perhaps his most famous title is the original *DOS For Dummies,* published in 1991. It became the world's fastest-selling computer book, at one time moving more copies per week than the *New York Times* number-one bestseller (though, as a reference, it could not be listed on the *Times'* Best Sellers list). That book spawned the entire line of *For Dummies* books, which remains a publishing phenomenon to this day.

Dan's most popular titles include *PCs For Dummies, Laptops For Dummies,* and *Android Phones For Dummies.* He also maintains the vast and helpful website www.wambooli.com.

Dan holds a degree in Communications/Visual Arts from the University of California, San Diego. He lives in the Pacific Northwest, where he enjoys spending time with his sons playing video games indoors while they enjoy the gentle woods of Idaho.

Publisher's Acknowledgments

Acquisitions Editor: Katie Mohr

Project Editor: Susan Pink

Copy Editor: Susan Pink

Editorial Assistant: Claire Brock

Sr. Editorial Assistant: Cherie Case

Project Coordinator: Kumar Chellapan

Cover Image: balein/Shutterstock